HANDBOOK OF CUSTOMER SATISFACTION AND LOYALTY MEASUREMENT

T0371729

HANDBOOK OF CUSTOMER SATISFACTION AND LOYALTY MEASUREMENT

Third Edition

Nigel Hill and Jim Alexander

Routledge
Taylor & Francis Group

LONDON AND NEW YORK

First published in paperback 2024

First published 2006 by Gower Publishing

Published 2016 by Routledge
4 Park Square, Milton Park, Abingdon, Oxon OX14 4RN

and by Routledge
605 Third Avenue, New York, NY 10158

Routledge is an imprint of the Taylor & Francis Group, an informa business

Publisher's Note
The publisher has gone to great lengths to ensure the quality of this reprint but points out that some imperfections in the original copies may be apparent.

British Library Cataloguing in Publication Data
Hill, Nigel
    Handbook of customer satisfaction and loyalty measurement
    – 3rd ed.
    1. Consumer satisfaction – Evaluation 2. Customer relations
    3. Marketing research
    I. Title II. Alexander, Jim III. Handbook of customer
    satisfaction measurement
    658.8'12

Library of Congress Control Number: 2006928088

ISBN: 978-0-566-08744-8 (hbk)
ISBN: 978-1-03-283868-7 (pbk)
ISBN: 978-1-315-23927-9 (ebk)

DOI: 10.4324/9781315239279

CONTENTS

LIST OF FIGURES

LIST OF TABLES

PREFACE

A grocery store in Connecticut, USA, holds the world record for the highest sales per square foot. Stew Leonard's has built its success on the maxim that 'if you take good care of the customer, customers will take good care of you'. Founder, Stew Leonard, calculates the lifetime value of one of his customers is $50,000 based on an average weekly spend of $100 and a 10-year lifetime. He encourages his staff to treat customers not as a $100 customer but as a $50,000 asset. If they see a customer with a frown on his or her face they should see $50,000 walking away from the store.

Stew Leonard's success is based on building that customer lifetime value by keeping existing customers satisfied. Perfect in theory, but how do you do it? If a Stew Leonard customer has a furrowed brow, what has caused it? From the vast choice of improvements that Stew Leonard's could make to its total product, what would be the one improvement that would contribute most to putting a smile back on that customer's face? Would it be a wider choice of fresh fish, would it be more free-range eggs, would it be a children's play area, or shorter waiting times at the checkout, lower prices, or perhaps a friendlier approach from the shop assistants?

Let's assume we know the answer in this one instance because we have done the sensible thing and asked the frowning customer and we have discovered that the cause of his or her dissatisfaction was the restricted range of freshly-baked bread. If we invest management effort, time and money in overcoming that weakness and improving the range of freshly-baked bread will we see a return on that investment? Is our frowning customer one of many who are disappointed with the fresh bread or is he or she an exception? Could we increase the overall satisfaction (and lifetime value) of our customer base to a greater degree by offering a delivery service or by adding more cream cakes to the range?

Without formally measuring customer satisfaction we'll never know. We'll base crucial management decisions on 'gut feel', investing in freshly-baked bread when the main problem perceived by customers as a whole is the congested car park.

This book explains how to measure your customers' satisfaction and how to use that information to improve business performance in those areas which will contribute most to increasing customer satisfaction. In short, it will help you to increase your profits through 'doing best what matters most to customers'.

In writing this book we are grateful to many people. First and foremost to the many clients who demonstrate that high levels of customer satisfaction can be achieved provided reliable information is regularly gathered *and acted upon*.

Our thanks also go to the staff of Gower, who have been more than helpful to us whilst writing this book. Jonathan Norman has provided guidance and encouragement in the right measure at the right times, and Nikki Dines has been instrumental in helping us turn a weighty manuscript into the finished article you have before you.

Last but not least our thanks go to Ruth Colleton at The Leadership Factor who produced the diagrams and provided invaluable help with the amendments and organisational challenges of producing this third edition.

Needless to say, any opinions or errors are all our own. We hope you enjoy the book.

NIGEL HILL AND JIM ALEXANDER

The Leadership Factor
Huddersfield, UK

1 INTRODUCTION

In recent times organisations of all types and sizes have increasingly come to understand the importance of customer satisfaction. It is widely understood that it is far less costly to keep existing customers than it is to win new ones, and it is becoming accepted that there is a strong link between customer satisfaction, customer retention and profitability. For many organisations in the public sector customer satisfaction will itself be the measure of success.

Customer satisfaction has therefore become the key operational goal for many organisations. They have invested heavily in improving performance in areas that make a strong contribution to customer satisfaction, such as quality and customer service. Loyalty schemes have proliferated in the retail sector and are now moving into the business sector. Companies are investing in 'database marketing', 'relationship management', and 'customer planning', to get closer to their customers. Organisations in the public sector have developed customer charters to demonstrate their commitment to customer service, and just about every 'mission statement' includes a reference to satisfying or, increasingly, delighting customers.

But what is the result of all this effort and investment? How do we know if we are succeeding in satisfying, let alone delighting, our customers? The truth of the matter is that many organisations don't. It is a widely accepted adage in the quality world that 'if you can't measure it, you can't manage it'. This principle applies equally to customer satisfaction as it does to thousands of products coming off a production line. However, most companies measure (and consequently manage) the manufacturing process far more thoroughly than they do customer satisfaction. Indeed, many companies and organisations still do not measure customer satisfaction at all – and many who claim to be measuring it do so in an inadequate way.

A poorly conceived and administered survey will produce data that is not sufficiently reliable for management decision making. Most companies would not adopt an amateurish approach to SPC (statistical process control) on the production line but many do exactly that where customer satisfaction measurement is concerned. This is strange in view of the massive investments they are often making to improve customer satisfaction!

This book explains how to carry out professional customer surveys which will accurately measure your customers' satisfaction and provide reliable data on which you can base important management decisions and monitor improvements in performance.

Before previewing how these issues will be tackled, it will be useful to agree a definition of customer satisfaction. Our own definition is:

Customer satisfaction is a measure of how your organisation's total product performs in relation to a set of customer requirements.

Of course, the customer's view of your organisation's performance will be a perception. Customer satisfaction is in the customer's mind and may or may not conform with the reality of the situation. We know that people form attitudes quickly but change them only slowly. How many years did it take Jaguar to overcome the reputation for poor quality that it developed whilst owned by British Leyland? Under John Egan, Jaguar had massively improved its quality long before customers widely perceived its cars as reliable and free of problems. So customers may be wrong about your quality or your service, but it is on these unreliable perceptions that millions of purchase decisions are made every day.

Customer satisfaction measurement is therefore about measuring how customers perceive your performance as a supplier.

This explains why you cannot rely solely on internally generated information as a guide to your success in satisfying customers. Your quality assurance department may be faithfully reporting zero defects and your warehouse manager 100 per cent on-time despatch, but customers' perceptions may not have kept pace with your improvements in performance. Research studies demonstrate that internal performance measures usually overstate customer satisfaction levels. It also explains why for many organisations customer surveys indicate that they have a communications task to improve customers' perceptions of performance rather than a need to improve performance itself.

This book covers the whole process of customer satisfaction measurement, from designing a survey to drawing conclusions and determining action after the survey. It is not a book on how to implement that action. There are plenty of other texts covering topics such as customer service, quality, change management and the like.

The book starts by examining some of the concepts underlying customer satisfaction, such as 'performance gaps', 'lifetime customer values', 'customer retention' and 'customer loyalty'. Chapter 2 concludes that a successful customer retention strategy will be based on 'doing best what matters most to customers' and that this can be guided only by customer satisfaction measurement.

Chapter 3 examines customer loyalty and Chapter 4 integrates loyalty and satisfaction through the value–profit chain concept.

Chapter 5 points out that many customer surveys carried out by organisations cannot possibly enable them to judge if they are 'doing best what matters most to customers', because their surveys only ask about satisfaction with the supplier's performance and not about what matters to the customer. To be of any value a customer satisfaction measurement exercise must provide information on customers' priorities as well as the supplier's performance.

Chapters 6 and 7 are concerned with designing a customer survey. To be accurate it must be based on a detailed understanding of the customer–supplier relationship and customers' buying behaviour. This usually necessitates 'exploratory research' which will ensure that the survey covers the factors which actually make the greatest contribution to customer satisfaction rather than the issues which the supplier thinks are most important.

Chapters 8 to 11 are about implementing a customer survey in a professional manner in order to produce reliable data for decision making purposes. The first, and usually most important aspect that will distinguish a professional from an amateur survey is the sampling. Accurate sampling is essential in order to demonstrate that the survey is based on a representative group of customers. If the sample is not truly representative the survey results will be meaningless because you will never know whether they represent the views and satisfaction levels of customers in general. Chapter 9 examines different survey types, including personal interviews, telephone surveys and self-completion questionnaires and considers how to maximize response rates for postal surveys. Chapter 10 explains how to design a questionnaire and Chapter 11 provides guidance on interviewing.

Having conducted a customer survey you will need to analyse it and report the results. These issues are discussed in Chapter 12, which also looks at how to effectively display and communicate the results to other staff within the organisation.

The PR aspects of customer satisfaction measurement are further developed in Chapter 13 which suggests ways of approaching customers before the survey in order to ensure their willing participation, and explains how to provide feedback to customers after the survey, demonstrating that the exercise has been worthwhile. The internal market is equally important, and the chapter suggests ways of involving fellow staff and driving home the implications of the survey results.

Chapters 14 and 15 return to loyalty and the value–profit chain concept, showing how you can use satisfaction and loyalty measures to forecast and manage the future performance of your organisation.

The final chapter suggests how organisations can build on customer satisfaction measurement in order to improve performance in those areas highlighted by the survey. To gain maximum value from customer satisfaction measurement, organisations should use the results to determine 'priorities for improvement' (PFIs) which will enable them to focus their resources in improving areas which will make the greatest contribution to increasing customer satisfaction. The chapter also considers the benefits of carrying out customer satisfaction measurement in a professional manner, as endorsed by Tom Peters in his book *A Passion for Excellence*, when he wrote the following about best practice in top US companies.

> *Customer satisfaction is measured frequently. Sampling is extensive. Surveys are quantitative as well as qualitative (i.e. delivery times and feelings count equally); the measures are taken very, very seriously. They are reviewed unfailingly by top management. The development of such measures is taken as seriously as the development of budgetary measures or product reliability measures. Evaluation of people in all functions at all levels is significantly affected by the satisfaction measures.*

At the end of the book you will find a number of appendices which provide additional information. Appendix 1 provides examples of questionnaires for customer satisfaction measurement. Appendix 2 examines SERVQUAL, a standard approach to measuring customer satisfaction in service industries developed by several American academics. Appendix 3 provides a detailed glossary of terms which you will find helpful if you are unfamiliar with some of the technical terms used in customer satisfaction measurement. Finally, you will find contact information for relevant organisations such as focus group studios and suppliers of specialist software as well as suggested further reading.

2 WHY MEASURE CUSTOMER SATISFACTION?

AIMS

By the end of this chapter you will:

- Appreciate the consequences of excessive rates of customer decay.
- Be able to analyse the causes of customer decay.
- Contrast the cost of customer decay and the value of customer retention.
- Appreciate the fundamental role played by customer satisfaction measurement in any aim to improve the customer service provided by your organisation.

Customer Decay

The average business loses between 10 and 30 per cent of its customers each year; but they often don't know which customers they have lost, when they were lost, why they were lost, or how much sales revenue and profit this customer decay has cost them.

Far from worrying about customers they are losing, most companies have traditionally placed more emphasis on winning new customers. Companies can become like a bucket with a hole in the bottom: their customers drain away but the company managers, instead of concentrating (like Henry in the song) on fixing the hole, devote resources to pouring more and more new customers into the top (Figure 2.1).

Service Gaps

Dissatisfaction is clearly the fundamental reason for customer decay, but what causes customer dissatisfaction? A considerable amount of research has been undertaken in this area in recent years and the outcome is the theory of 'satisfaction gaps'. The overall gap which results in

The average company loses
10-30% of its customers each year

But few know

Which?   When?   Why?

OR

How much is lost in sales revenue?

Figure 2.1   Customer decay

a dissatisfied customer is the gap between expectations and experience, but the root cause of that dissatisfaction can usually be traced back to one of five earlier gaps (promotional, understanding, procedural, behavioural and perception – see Figure 2.2).

GAP 1: THE PROMOTIONAL GAP

The origin of the problem can often be traced back to the company's marketing communications. In their eagerness to win customers by selling the benefits of their product or service companies can very easily create expectations in the minds of customers that will be difficult to fulfil. A few years ago an American airline ran a TV advertisement featuring a passenger asleep with his shoes off. A stewardess quietly removed the shoes, polished them and returned them without

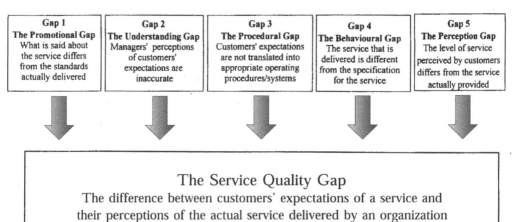

Gap 1 **The Promotional Gap** What is said about the service differs from the standards actually delivered	Gap 2 **The Understanding Gap** Managers' perceptions of customers' expectations are inaccurate	Gap 3 **The Procedural Gap** Customers' expectations are not translated into appropriate operating procedures/systems	Gap 4 **The Behavioural Gap** The service that is delivered is different from the specification for the service	Gap 5 **The Perception Gap** The level of service perceived by customers differs from the service actually provided

The Service Quality Gap
The difference between customers' expectations of a service and their perceptions of the actual service delivered by an organization

Figure 2.2   Service gaps

a word. The ad was seen as a sick joke by regular passengers (who did not recognize this level of service) and created false expectations, leading to disappointment for new passengers. This may be an extreme case, but every day in many small ways it is easy to generate such unrealistic hopes. A common example is the sales person promising a delivery date to secure an order without first making absolutely certain that the date can be met.

GAP 2: THE UNDERSTANDING GAP

The next possible problem area is that the managers of the organisation do not have an accurate understanding of customers' needs and priorities. If they don't really know what's important to customers it is extremely unlikely that the organisation will 'do best what matters most to customers' however much emphasis it places on quality and service. Many organisations seeking to measure customer satisfaction perpetuate this problem by failing to include in the survey a section which clarifies what is important to the customer. See the section on the 'Internal Survey' at the end of Chapter 12 for how to highlight understanding gaps.

GAP 3: THE PROCEDURAL GAP

Assuming that the organisation does have a full understanding of what matters most to customers it will still fail to deliver customer satisfaction if it has not translated customers' expectations into appropriate operating procedures and systems. For example, a hotel may be fully aware that customers become very irritated if they have to spend more than five minutes checking out, but if the manager does not set sufficient staffing levels during the busy 8.00–9.00 a.m. period many customers will inevitably wait longer and leave dissatisfied.

GAP 4: THE BEHAVIOURAL GAP

Sometimes organisations have clear procedures which are well matched to customers' needs and priorities but do not achieve a consistently high level of customer satisfaction because staff are insufficiently trained or disciplined to follow the procedures to the letter at all times. As you will see in Chapter 5 a well-designed customer satisfaction survey will highlight the main gaps between customers' expectations and your organisation's performance. It is then a straightforward task to identify whether your procedures adequately cover those aspects of service delivery. If they do you will need to take steps to monitor staff behaviour to ascertain whether the procedures are being consistently followed.

GAP 5: THE PERCEPTION GAP

It is possible that gaps 1–4 do not exist but your customer survey still shows an unacceptable level of dissatisfaction. This is because customers' perception of the performance of your organisation may differ from reality. A customer who was upset by offhand, unhelpful service some time in the past will form an attitude that your organisation is uncaring and it may take some considerable time and much experience of good personal service before that perception is modified. It was Tom Peters back in 1985 in *A Passion for Excellence* who first pointed out that the customers' perception is reality. Customers may be behind the times, they may be slow to change their attitudes, they may label your organisation as unhelpful, uncaring when, in reality, it now offers the most wonderful level of customer service imaginable. But that is what customers think. It is those perceptions, however inaccurate, on which they are basing their purchase decisions. This book will explain how to determine whether low customer satisfaction ratings are caused by poor performance on the part of your organisation or a mistaken perception on the part of your customers. If it is the latter we will outline steps that you can take to modify customers' perceptions.

As shown in Figure 2.2, any of the five gaps can result in the overall Service Quality Gap which leaves your customers dissatisfied. No organisation intends to provide poor service and gaps usually arise because of differences in perception between what the business thought it was providing and what customers believe they have received. Only regular customer satisfaction measurement will enable you to identify and close the gaps.

The Cost of Customer Decay

Research has now demonstrated conclusively that it is far more costly to win one new customer than it is to keep an existing customer. A relatively simple task is to work out how much it costs to win each new customer (Table 2.1).

For example, let us assume that in the UK a company has a cost per appointment or sales lead of £2 500. To this must be added a cost per sales call of perhaps £1 000 and possibly nine visits for each new customer won. The average number of visits per sale will be a factor of the average number of visits required to convert a new customer and the conversion ratio. If you have to make an average of three calls to a new prospect before making your first sale and you convert only one in three of the new prospects you visit, your average number of visits per sale is nine. (For some companies the average number of visits per sale will be far higher than nine.) The

Table 2.1   The cost of new customers

Cost of new customers (hypothetical example)	
Cost per appointment (promotion, lead generation, telesales)	£2 500
Cost per sales call	£1 000
Visits per sale	9
Selling cost per new customer	£9 000
Total cost per new customer	£11 500
Breakeven sales per new customer @ 40% GP	£28 750

selling and promotional cost will give you a total cost per new customer – that is, the gross profit you need to earn to make any money out of that new account.

So, taking the figures in Table 2.1, if your gross margin is 40 per cent your break-even sale per new customer will be £28 750; if it's 20 per cent it will be £57 500.

All this may well underestimate the real cost of customer acquisition because it ignores the cost of salaries and other overheads in sales and promotional support.

A more accurate, if more complicated, method is to isolate sales and marketing costs including salaries and other overheads. Split your selling costs between servicing existing customers and winning new customers. Take the proportion of selling costs, add 100 per cent of promotional costs and divide this figure by the number of new customers your company won in the past year, giving a true average acquisition cost for each new customer.

If you carry out this exercise thoroughly, including all relevant costs, you may find the cost of winning each new customer is disconcertingly high.

The Value of Customer Retention

Just as winning new customers is very costly, keeping existing customers is very profitable. In recent years more and more organisations have realized this fact, resulting in a proliferation of 'loyalty schemes'.

The best loyalty scheme is, of course, customer satisfaction. This is achieved by 'doing best what matters most to customers', with tokens, bonus points and other loyalty schemes making only a marginal difference. The fundamental justification for measuring customer satisfaction is to provide the information which enables managers to make the right decisions to maximize customer satisfaction and therefore improve customer retention.

Examining the concept of lifetime customer values will enable us to see how improved customer retention feeds through into increased profitability. The lifetime value of a customer is a function of the customer's average spend with the business, multiplied by the length of time the business will retain the customer. Thus, if the average supermarket customer spends around £100 per week, or £5 000 per annum, and remains loyal for ten years, the lifetime value to the business is £50 000. The power of the concept is demonstrated by what can be achieved through very small increases in customer retention. Indeed, with a very small incremental improvement in customer loyalty, turnover can be increased quite dramatically and with relatively little associated cost. Thus, much of the gross profit from that additional turnover would find its way onto the bottom line.

Without accurate customer satisfaction measurement, management is most unlikely to make the right decisions to consistently achieve the required incremental improvements in customer retention. Success will always rely, as we have already said, on 'doing best what matters most to customers'.

Motivation and Commitment

If sustainable improvements in customer service are to be made the whole organisation needs to be motivated and committed from top to bottom. However, all the evidence points to the fact that whilst senior management claim to be committed to improving customer service that message is not percolating through the ranks. A survey by Colin Coulson-Thomas for Bain & Company asked chief executive officers, managers and employees what was important for their organisation. Figure 2.3 shows that 92 per cent of chief executive officers, 77 per cent of managers but only 8 per cent of employees believed that improving customer service is a top priority for their company. Either chief executives are not telling their staff that improving customer service is a top priority or, if they are, the staff don't believe them. Interestingly, employees thought the most important priority was 'hitting targets' (stated by 90 per cent).

Carrying out a thorough customer satisfaction measurement exercise, communicating the results internally (as outlined in Chapter 12) and then updating the survey and monitoring progress (as suggested in Chapter 16) will do more than anything to demonstrate the importance of customer satisfaction to all employees. There is considerable evidence that measurement in itself motivates staff to work for improved results. This is partly because it demonstrates management commitment and partly because human beings are naturally

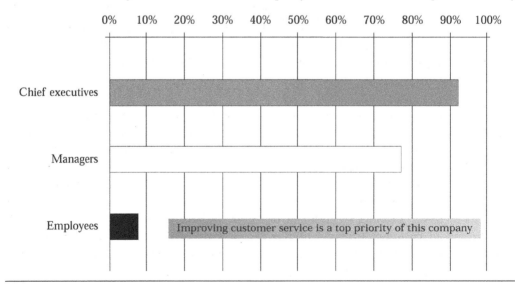

Figure 2.3   The perceived importance of customer service

competitive, enjoying the challenge of aiming at targets and the satisfaction of hitting or exceeding them. It is also because the survey and appropriate follow-up serve to demonstrate that senior management is serious about the importance of improving customer satisfaction. Where staff believe it is important to management they will take it seriously; but, if they form any suspicion that management is only paying lip-service to the concept they will become totally cynical.

Profits

The most powerful reason for doing anything in business is that it will increase profitability. Measuring customer satisfaction, and acting appropriately on the results, will increase profitability. The surest route to success for most organisations (in both the private and public sector) is to 'do best what matters most to customers'. Customer retention rates will improve and customers will pay more for a product or service which precisely matches their needs. The well-documented PIMS (Profit Impact of Marketing Strategies) studies have found that companies rated highly for customer service charge 9 per cent more on average than those rated poorly. Moreover, PIMS has also found that a 50 per cent decrease in the rate of customer decay leads to a 25–85 per cent increase in profit. These concepts are expanded in the next two chapters.

Conclusions

- Too many organisations are like buckets leaking customers through a hole in the bottom. Worse still, they tend to allocate more resources to pouring new customers into the top of the bucket than to plugging the leak in the bottom.
- Customer decay is caused by dissatisfaction and its causes can be traced to a gap between customers' expectations and their experience, which in turn is fed by five more precise service gaps. Only through a well-designed customer satisfaction measurement exercise can these gaps be identified and tackled.
- A high rate of customer decay is extremely costly but improving the rate of customer retention becomes extremely profitable over a period of time.
- Research suggests that many organisations have failed to communicate to their staff the importance of improving customer service. The required level of staff motivation will be generated only by measuring customer satisfaction which provides the basis for demonstrating the commitment of senior management and using targets and rewards to motivate staff.
- There is a growing body of well-documented and highly respected research evidence that directly links improvements in customer satisfaction with increased profitability.

3 LOYALTY

AIMS
_____

By the end of this chapter you will:

- Understand the difference between customer retention and customer loyalty.
- Appreciate the true meaning of the word 'loyalty' and question its applicability to customer behaviour.
- Recognize different types and levels of customer 'loyalty'.
- Understand the key concept of customer commitment.
- Appreciate the link between the accurate design of a customer survey and its value, in terms of providing reliable satisfaction and loyalty information.
- Recognize that in the twenty-first century companies will have to be loyal to their customers rather than expect loyalty from them.

Since it is now widely recognized that it is much less costly and much more profitable to keep existing customers than to win new ones, customer retention has become an important goal for most organisations. In principle it's simple: you just have to keep your existing customers. But how? Many companies have adopted the idea of customer loyalty to spearhead their retention strategies, but it is very doubtful whether the loyalty concept is fully understood or effectively implemented by many who embrace it.

Loyalty is a historical word, rooted in feudal times when allegiance to the sovereign was fundamental to the success, perhaps even the survival, of the state. The Oxford Dictionary's definition of the word 'loyal' is:

> *True or faithful (to duty, love or obligation); steadfast in allegiance, devoted to the legitimate sovereign or government of one's country.*

On that basis, why should anybody be loyal to a commercial enterprise? What legitimacy does the enterprise possess? Why do its customers have any obligation to show allegiance to it?

Of course they don't, and the more the education, confidence and power of consumers have grown, the more they realize it. In fact, in the twenty-first century it is the other way round. It is the customer who is king and the supplier that needs to be *'true, faithful and steadfast in allegiance to meeting the legitimate needs of its customers'*.

It is the woeful misunderstanding of the loyalty concept amongst senior managers (and especially amongst the marketing profession – the very people who ought to know better) which has been responsible for the plethora of misguided strategies that have been introduced in the name of securing customer loyalty. Many involve cheap attempts to bribe the customer. How many leaders have secured the long-term loyalty of their citizens/followers/employees by such tactics? Whether you are president of a country or a company, loyalty has to be earned. Let's examine this through the eyes of the educated, confident and increasingly powerful customers. Why should they choose to continue to give their business to the same supplier? The answer is simple. That supplier has to meet their needs better than any of the alternative suppliers. Returning to our definition in Chapter 1, the total product (total value package) offered by the supplier has to meet or exceed the customer's requirements to result in customer satisfaction. To secure customer retention in a competitive market the supplier's total value package has to match customer's requirements better than anything offered by competitors.

Clearly, we need to clarify the whole concept of loyalty and how it applies to the relationship between a commercial enterprise and its customers. That is the purpose of the remainder of this chapter.

Types of Loyalty

There are many types of loyalty, many reasons why suppliers retain the business of their customers. As shown in Table 3.1, most bear little relation to the true meaning of the word loyalty, involving very little allegiance, devotion or duty. Monopoly loyalty is an extreme example, but does illustrate the point. Where customers have little or no choice, their 'loyalty' is far from devoted. It is often resentful. Our experience based on thousands of customer satisfaction surveys shows that customers with little or no choice often feel very dissatisfied. Other suppliers are notionally in a competitive situation. Their customers could use alternative suppliers – in theory. In some situations, however, the cost, difficulty or hassle factor involved in changing suppliers is so great that customers will do it only as a last resort. Again, our research shows that they will live with much lower than normal levels of satisfaction before they switch suppliers. But this reluctance to change suppliers cannot be describe as 'loyalty'. It certainly involves little allegiance, duty or devotion.

Incentivized loyalty has possibly been the most over-hyped marketing strategy in recent years. It may have some effect on customers who are not spending their own money, frequent

Table 3.1   Types of loyalty

	Example	Degree of allegiance
Monopoly loyalty	Rail commuters	Low
Cost of change loyalty	Financial software	Medium
Incentivised loyalty	Frequent business flyers	Low to medium
Habitual loyalty	Petrol stations	Low
Committed loyalty	Football club	High

business flyers being an obvious example, but the success of Southwest Airlines in the US and easyJet in the UK is already dispelling that myth. Most people in the UK hold the 'loyalty' cards of more than one competing supermarket, store group, airline or petrol station. They see the loyalty points as something they may as well take when it meets their wider needs to use that supplier. In 1999 UK supermarket Asda trialled a loyalty card, known as the Asda Club Card, but withdrew it when their research showed that customers preferred lower prices rather than points. Asda's market share has not suffered even though its main competitors have loyalty schemes.

Habitual loyalty may be the most common form of repeat business. As time becomes an increasingly scarce commodity for many customers, familiar routines that can be quickly accomplished with minimal thought become part of the lifestyle. The weekly food shop is conducted at the same supermarket because it is convenient and familiar. Petrol is bought at the filling station that is passed every day on the way to work. Colleagues meet in the same pub after work. Companies with high levels of customer retention may feel a misleading sense of security because allegiance to suppliers in these situations can be very low. If a new supermarket, pub or petrol station opens which is more convenient, bigger, more modern or more competitively priced, the original supplier may find that there was very little 'loyalty' under-pinning the previous levels of customer retention.

Contrast the 'allegiance, devotion and duty' of the previous four loyalty types with the loyal customers of a football club. All three words apply to their loyalty which is often rooted in their core values (they were brought up to *believe* that Manchester United are the greatest!), rather than in their attitudes. (See Chapter 6 for an examination of these concepts.) But a business is not a football club. It commands no emotional, irrational loyalty. It must continually earn its customer retention by delivering that total value package which meets its customers requirements at *every* customer encounter.

Loyalty Levels

Whatever the loyalty type and the customer-supplier relationship, there will be different degrees of customer loyalty and these are variously depicted in the literature as a ladder, a pyramid, a continuum. Figure 3.1 adopts the pyramid approach since this graphically represents the typical spread of customers through the various levels.

The degrees of customer loyalty can be defined a follows:

- *Suspects*   Includes all the buyers of the product/service category in the marketplace. Suspects are either unaware of your product offering or have no inclination to purchase it.
- *Prospects*   Potential customers who have some attraction towards your organisation but have not yet taken the step of doing business with you.
- *Customers*   One-off purchasers of your product (although the segment may include some repeat buyers) who have no real feelings of affinity towards your organisation.
- *Clients*   Repeat customers who have positive feelings of attachment towards your organisation but whose support is passive rather than active, apart from making purchases.
- *Advocates*   Clients who actively support your organisation by recommending it to others.
- *Partners*   The strongest form of customer–supplier relationship which is sustained because both parties see partnership as mutually beneficial.

It can be seen therefore that loyalty involves more than just making a purchase or even repeat purchases. Loyalty represents a positive level of commitment by the customer to the supplier and it is the degree of positive *commitment* which distinguishes truly loyal customers.

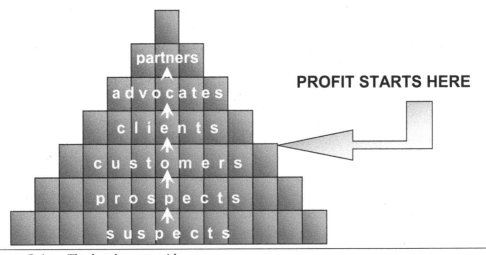

Figure 3.1   The loyalty pyramid

As we will see in Chapter 14, the degree of customer commitment can be used in customer satisfaction measurement to segment the customer base and identify those customer groupings that are most at risk of defection. Customer loyalty segments will often have different needs and priorities, they will certainly have different perceptions of the performance of your organisation and, consequently, you will probably need to define distinct strategies for different loyalty segments.

Commitment

The concept that businesses should focus on when seeking to maximize customer retention is not loyalty but commitment. Customer commitment will often be reflected in customers' behaviour. They may choose to recommend a favoured supplier. They might demonstrate commitment by travelling further than necessary or paying a higher price if they believe a supplier provides a superior total value package. Commitment might also be reflected in their attitudes. Committed customers will believe that their chosen supplier is the best in its field. Our research shows that many apparently 'loyal' customers rate their current supplier as the same as most other companies in the field, making them an easy target for competitors' advances.

Whilst it may be unreasonable for a commercial enterprise to expect its customers to be 'loyal', it is feasible to aim for customer commitment. Most organisations have some customers who are committed to them, but often it is too few. Our surveys show that in many cases no more

Committed customers stay longer

- Buy more often

- Buy more (range)

- Spend more (less price sensitive

- Recommend more

- Consider competitors less

- Feel committed

Figure 3.2 Customer commitment

than 10 per cent of the customer base is 'totally committed', even to some very well respected suppliers. (See Chapter 14 for how such measures are established.) However, the value of those totally committed customers is immense. As well as remaining with the supplier longer, committed customers buy more often and tend to buy a wider range of products from the supplier. Partly due to that, they spend more, but this also occurs because the most committed customers are less price sensitive than the least committed. According to PIMS (Profit Impact of Marketing Strategies) they are prepared to pay an average 9 per cent price premium. The most committed also recommend more and consider competitors less. Above all, they feel more committed. Whereas it may be unrealistic to expect devotion and duty, affinity, allegiance and commitment are attainable. But only with considerable effort. This brings us back to our assertion that the loyalty concept should be applied to the suppliers rather than the customers. Ultimately, the customers hold the aces. The suppliers have to earn the considerable rewards that a committed customer base provides. This has implications for organisations' entire philosophy and operations, but it is the implications for effective customer satisfaction and loyalty measurement that are the concern of this book.

The Implications for Customer Satisfaction and Loyalty Measurement

There is growing evidence that satisfaction with past transactions is the main determinant of customer commitment. It is therefore essential that your customer survey produces accurate measures of satisfaction and loyalty and, crucially, establishes the relationship between the two. This will be achieved only if your survey covers the right issues and, unfortunately, many don't.

In 1999, the UK consumer magazine *Which?* described the rail operators' customer satisfaction surveys as 'close to useless' because the questions they asked avoided many of their customers' main requirements. If you really want to know how satisfied your customers feel and whether you are likely to retain their business, the questions asked in your survey have to cover customers' main requirements[1]. Companies are tempted to include questions on areas where they've invested heavily or made improvements, but if these are of marginal importance to customers they will make little impact on how satisfied customers feel. *Which?* conducted a survey to identify rail passengers' main requirements and the top ten are shown in Figure 3.3. The worst culprit amongst the rail operators was GNER, whose survey covered only one item from customers' top ten. They did ask about the on-train catering, and about staff appearance. Both came close to the bottom of customers' priorities in the *Which?* survey.

---

1. 'Off the Rails' *Which?* Magazine, January 1999, p.8-11.

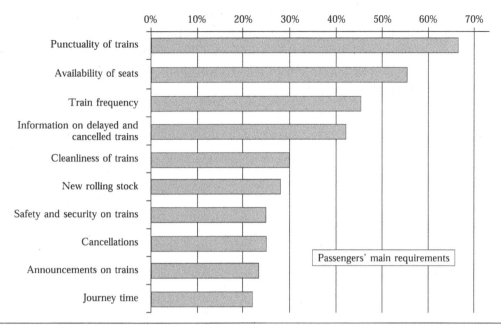

Figure 3.3   Rail passengers' main requirements

Based on our definition of customer satisfaction, organisations have no choice over what should be included on a customer satisfaction questionnaire. It should cover the total product – everything the organisation does that contributes to its meeting, or failing to meet, customers' requirements. Since the number of possible items fitting this description is usually too great for inclusion on a questionnaire, the items that are most important to customers are the ones that must be included. Chapter 5 explores survey objectives in more depth, and Chapter 7 explains how the correct list of topics for the questionnaire should be identified.

Conclusions

- Customer retention and customer loyalty are not the same thing. Customers may stay with a supplier through habit or inertia without feeling loyal to it.
- The concept of loyalty is rooted in the past, emphasizing characteristics such as allegiance, duty, obligation and devotion. It it totally unrealistic for most commercial enterprises to expect their customers to have such feelings towards them.
- It is true that there are different levels of customer 'loyalty', from suspects and prospects to advocates and partners. It is their degree of positive commitment to the supplier which characterizes the advocates and partners.
- Advocates and partners are immensely valuable to a business, but organisations have to work very hard to earn and keep that level of commitment.

- Winning and maintaining customer commitment is such a demanding task that organisations should stop thinking about customers' loyalty to them and start thinking in terms of their own loyalty to their customers. It is only through total 'devotion, duty and allegiance' to meeting customers' requirements that organisations will reap the full rewards of a committed customer base.

4 THE VALUE-PROFIT CHAIN

AIMS

By the end of this chapter you will:

- Understand how investment in customer satisfaction relates to increased profitability.
- See the value of the ownership experience and the customer value package.
- Understand the importance of employee satisfaction in creating customer commitment and profitability.

The Advantages of Satisfied Customers

DOES GOOD CUSTOMER SERVICE PAY?

That is the question many people put to us before embarking on a programme of research to measure and improve their company's ability to 'do best what matters most to customers'. The theory is fine! A customer who is well treated is more likely to bring more business your way, by repeat purchase, recommendation, putting a larger share of spend in your hands and so on. In addition loyal customers are less likely to seek the lowest prices and the cost of selling to them is much less than the cost of capturing new customers from the competition. Happy customers are the cheapest and most effective form of advertising you can get. Conversely, disappointed customers will not only take their business away but will probably tell several others about the experience too. Whilst it may take repeated positive encounters to create customer loyalty it usually only takes two negative ones to make an enemy for life. There are not many third chances. Consider your own experience and behaviour as a customer for a moment and you will recognize these facts, whether in your personal or business life.

As we pointed out in Chapter 2 the first sale is usually a very small part of the potential 'lifetime value' of the customer. If a family of four eating out in a pub spend £50 on their first visit they are unlikely to pay for the advertising that attracted them unless they visit very many more times. However, if they ate out once a fortnight for twenty years they would spend £26 000. If you wanted a good share of it you would need to look after them very well. When employees can be persuaded to think of customers having a value of £26 000 rather than just £50 they should take a much greater interest in their satisfaction.

It is also true in many cases that the initial sale is only a small part of the client–supplier relationship. When buying cars, household appliances, entertainment equipment, computers and so on the actual purchase is only the beginning of the customers' relationship with the product, but often it is the end of their relationship with the salesperson. If regular servicing is required or a fault occurs then a relationship with service personnel is needed. In three years of car ownership there will be several opportunities for the dealership's service department to demonstrate their customer handling skills and if they get it wrong it is likely that when (or if) the salesman seeks the next sale his extensive training will be to no avail. It is ownership experience which makes the second sale, not the salesman.

Successful organisations plan a customer handling strategy that respects the change in relationships as they develop. Sales people should be heavily involved before the sale and from time to time afterwards. Service people need to be properly trained and motivated to care for customers during their ownership experience.

The Link Between Satisfaction and Profit

The link between customer satisfaction and company success has historically been a matter of faith but there is now a growing body of evidence to support the case. For many companies profit can be traced back to customer satisfaction which, in turn is related to employee satisfaction. In essence, this chain of events is depicted in Figure 4.1.

It used to be thought that market share was the best determinant of profitability and this led to many mergers and takeovers in the hope that economies of scale would reduce cost and increase profit. Naturally this works to a degree but there are many exceptions, in which companies who do not have the largest market share are more profitable than those with a bigger share because they have discovered that customer loyalty is more profitable than market share.

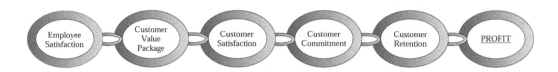

Figure 4.1 The value–profit chain

Keep Customers Longer and Make More Money

Studies have shown that a 5 per cent increase in customer loyalty can produce profit increases of 25 to 85 per cent across a range of industries. Retaining existing customers for longer usually has a much lower associated cost than winning new ones, so a large proportion of the additional gross profit goes straight to the bottom line (Figure 4.2).

Committed Customers Stay Longer

As we pointed out in Chapter 3, it is misguided to believe that customer retention will be achieved through 'loyalty'. This concept simply does not apply in its true sense to most businesses since there is no 'loyalty' in a commercial transaction. In commercial markets the onus is on the supplier to convince the customer that it is in the latter's best interests to remain a customer. It is self-interest, not loyalty that keeps customers 'loyal'. Commitment is therefore a better word to describe the feeling that produces the benefits of customer retention such as repeat purchase, recommendation and reduced price sensitiveness. As we explain later in the book, repeat purchase can be habitual, with very little commitment on the part of the customer and these apparently 'loyal' customers can be easy prey for competitors. Committed customers are much less vulnerable to competitors' advances because they are convinced that their existing supplier meets their long-term requirements better than any other. Commitment is therefore the best lead indicator of retention (see Figure 4.3) and in Chapter 14 we explain how to measure customer commitment.

Satisfied Customers Are More Committed

Businesses as diverse as banks, office equipment suppliers, telecommunications suppliers and car manufacturers have published figures showing a very strong relationship between customer satisfaction and commitment. The data in Table 4.1 was released by the British bank, Royal Bank of Scotland, but other companies have also published similar figures. They show a very

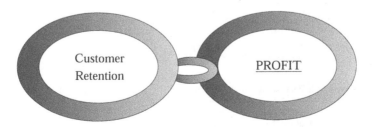

Figure 4.2   Customer retention is linked to profit

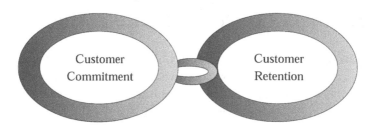

Figure 4.3   Commitment drives retention

steep relationship between customer satisfaction and intended loyalty, with customer retention guaranteed only at the highest levels of satisfaction.

The relationship between satisfaction and commitment is not fixed. It differs across markets and even between suppliers in the same marketplace. In Chapters 14 and 15 we explore the measuring and modelling implications of this phenomenon. Short-term marketing activity (price reductions, special incentives, etc.) can entice satisfied customers away for a while, but rarely totally satisfied customers, and there is growing evidence to show that, all things being equal, the more satisfied customers are, the more likely suppliers are to retain them.

To Satisfy Customers, Meet Their Needs

To satisfy customers you must meet their needs. You must 'do best what matters most to customers'. It sounds so obvious that it's not worth saying, but many suppliers don't do it. They make people queue for lengthy periods, they make them use filthy toilets, they break delivery and service promises and even, on occasions, are downright rude to customers. Our

Table 4.1   The link between satisfaction and commitment in a UK bank

Satisfaction – Loyalty links

Customer's stated level of satisfaction	Subsequent loyalty rate
Excellent/very satisfied	95%
Good/satisfied	65%
Average/neither satisfied nor dissatisfied	15%
Poor/quite dissatisfied	2%
Very poor/very dissatisfied	0%

company conducts hundreds of customer satisfaction surveys each year and we know that these things are still happening. We also know that a very definite relationship usually exists between dissatisfaction and disloyalty. Unhappy customers are unlikely to return, and will probably discourage others from becoming customers.

The customer value package is the combined set of benefits provided by the supplier to customers. In Chapter 2 we called it the total product. If your customer value package meets customers' needs they will be satisfied and are much more likely to be committed. Where you do not meet their requirements there will be 'satisfaction gaps' and if there are many of these customers will not be satisfied and commitment will be low. Figure 4.4 shows a company that is not 'doing best what matters most to customers'.

The customer value package must therefore form the basis of your customer satisfaction survey, and we will see in Chapter 7 how you should identify its component elements. As we indicated in Chapter 2 and demonstrate in much more detail in Chapter 12, improving the customer value package in the eyes of customers is often achieved by making significant improvements in a small number of its component elements. These are the priorities for improvement (PFIs), where customers' requirements are currently not being met. By following the advice on customer satisfaction measurement outlined in this book, it is possible to determine how much you need to increase customer satisfaction with the PFIs to produce a specific gain in overall customer satisfaction and loyalty, and this concept will be pursued in Chapter 15.

Employees Deliver the Customer Value Package

At this point it is worth considering the people involved in delivering the service. Recruitment policy for some companies places a higher priority on customer orientation than on specific skills or knowledge. The view is taken that it is quicker to train someone in a skill than it is to change their cultural attitude. In organisations which have adopted this customer-focused approach to business the result is often measurable, not just in customer satisfaction, but also in increased efficiency. Employees who are more motivated to achieve customer satisfaction tend to adopt a more flexible approach to their work, make fewer mistakes, and use more initiative.

The cost of replacing employees is usually measured in terms of recruitment and training cost but for most service jobs an even greater loss is connected with reduced productivity and decreased customer satisfaction. Customers place a high value on dealing with people they know and trust and who are knowledgeable and helpful. Customers will often be prepared to pay higher prices for a service they trust rather than make a small saving which involves the risk of service deterioration. From the customer viewpoint a trusted contact may be lost even if they move to another position in the same organisation, when the damage can be the

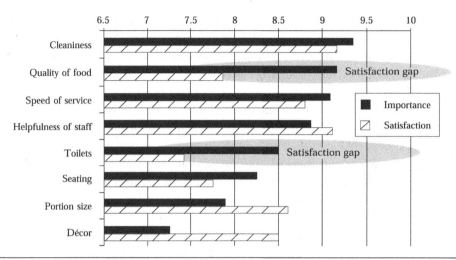

Figure 4.4   Satisfaction gaps

same as if they had left. Organized transfer of skills and knowledge to minimize customer disruption should be the target, since the alternative of restricting staff progress would cause other problems.

Employee satisfaction is often based on their ability to 'do a good job'. If they feel that the company, through its strategies, procedures or lack of efficiency is constraining their ability to deliver the customer value package, employee satisfaction will be reduced. Equally, if they feel that the customer value package is reduced by the other colleagues or departments they will be demotivated. An organisation's ability to satisfy its internal customers along the chain of events which produces the customer value package is fundamental to its success in maintaining a satisfied employee force and satisfied customers (Figure 4.5).

Internal quality is measured by the feelings that employees have towards their jobs, colleagues and employer. Employees' satisfaction is often affected by their ability and authority to achieve results for customers. It is company policy at Southwest Airlines (and many other customer-focused companies) to give employees the authority to do whatever they feel 'comfortable' doing to satisfy the customer, and only to ask higher authority if they feel 'uncomfortable'. Internal quality is also driven by the way colleagues treat each other. People need to identify their 'customers' within the organisation, understand their needs, seek improvements and implement them.

Conclusions

- Investment in customer satisfaction does bring improvements in profitability.
- Customers should be thought of in terms of their long-term value rather than as a one-off sale.

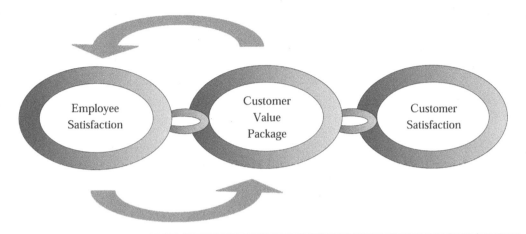

Figure 4.5   The customer value package is linked to employee satisfaction

- Marketing strategies and budgets need to place greater emphasis on the relationship customers have with the organisation and less on encouraging one-off sales.
- It is the ownership experience rather than the buying experience which plays the greatest part in the decision to repurchase.
- Profitability results from customer commitment, which results from satisfaction.
- Customer satisfaction is strongly linked to employee loyalty and motivation which is linked to employee satisfaction.
- Employee satisfaction is strongly affected by the organisation's philosophy on empowerment and the quality of internal customer service within the company.

5

SURVEY OBJECTIVES

Before considering the overall objectives of any customer satisfaction measurement exercise, first we must decide what we need to measure.

What Are You Measuring?

To decide what to measure, we must return to our original definition: 'Customer satisfaction is a measure of how an organisation's total product performs in relation to a set of customer expectations'.

Three questions arise at this point. Firstly, 'What is your "total product"?', secondly, 'Who should define it?', and thirdly, 'Are there any alternatives to this basis for your measure?'

THE CUSTOMER VALUE PACKAGE

This first question is easily answered. Your total product encompasses anything and everything contributing to how customers evaluate the total package of benefits provided versus the cost of acquiring them. We can call it the customer value package. In addition to your core product (what you sell), your organisation's image and your customer's satisfaction will be influenced by a wide range of additional factors. To illustrate this, let's consider the customer value package of a restaurant (Figure 5.1). The restaurant's core product is obviously the food, the main factor contributing to the success of the business. So, if the food is disappointing customer satisfaction and repeat business will be low and the restaurant will soon develop a poor reputation even with people who have never dined there. On the other hand, if the food is delicious, that benefit alone may secure enough repeat business and favourable word-of-mouth comment to ensure the success of the business regardless of the other aspects of the restaurant's total product.

However, few businesses will be at either extreme of this spectrum. More typically, customers' overall level of satisfaction and the consequent success of the business will be based on many additional factors – the quality of the food will not always be the most important one. Diners will certainly be influenced by the decor and the ambience of the restaurant, by the friendliness of the waiter or waitress and by the efficiency and quality of the service. Perhaps the chef will add value by talking to diners about the dishes offered. How they are presented and described on the menu, the quality of the menu's print and graphic design may also play a part. For some diners, the atmosphere and image the restaurant creates will be the deciding factor – they will choose the restaurant because it is 'the place to go'.

The customer value package is, then, a very diverse animal; so, if your customer satisfaction measurement is to be meaningful it should cover all of its components, as shown in Figure 5.2.

Figure 5.1   The customer value package

DEFINING THE CUSTOMER VALUE PACKAGE

This brings us to our second question: 'Who should define your total product?' The simple answer is your customers. The practice is more complex and will be explained fully in Chapter 7, but at this stage it is enough to establish the rule that customers must be instrumental in defining the components of your customer value package. After all, it is against your customers' expectations that you will be measuring its performance.

ALTERNATIVES TO THE CUSTOMER VALUE PACKAGE

Some organisations shy away from using the full customer value package as their basis for CSM, using three main alternatives. Some companies focus on service quality, as shown in Figure 5.3. Measuring service quality or service delivery is a perfectly valid exercise, but it must be taken for what it is – a measure of service, not a measure of satisfaction. The two must not be confused and may be far apart. A rail passenger who was unable to find a seat on a train which arrived very late is unlikely to be satisfied however good was the service provided by staff on the train and at the station.

One reason why some organisations are tempted to measure service quality rather than customer satisfaction is that service is controllable, whereas elements of the full customer value package may not be, as shown in Table 5.1.

Some people argue that you should measure only things you can control and that staff may be demotivated if dissatisfaction is caused by things they can't affect, such as the location of the supermarket or interest rates in financial services. And what about the ultimate non-controllable, the weather? We know from CSM studies that the weather and the snow conditions are key

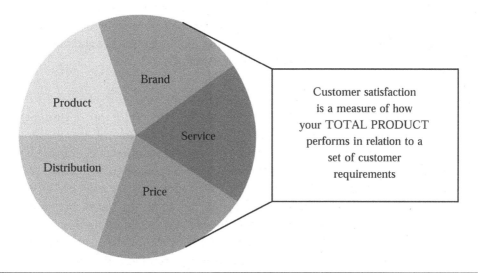

Figure 5.2   Customer satisfaction and the total product

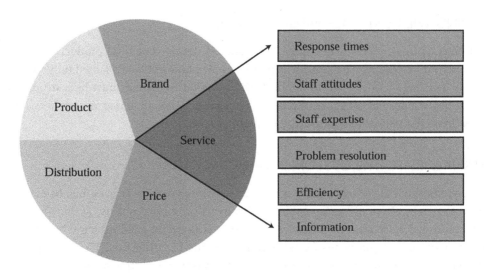

Figure 5.3   Measuring service quality

elements in the satisfaction of customers at ski resorts and of their intention to revisit. True, the staff cannot control the weather, but if the organisation is losing its customers due to dissatisfaction caused by the weather it needs to know. If it's aware of the problem it may be able to develop strategies which help to mitigate problems caused by poor weather conditions and improve its competitiveness against resorts where the weather tends to be more favourable. A complete understanding of customer satisfaction and loyalty will be produced only by a survey which includes non-controllables as well as controllables.

The third option which is advocated by some people is to focus on differentiators rather than givens. As shown in Table 5.2, givens are items such as safety on an aeroplane, which might be very important to customers but do not distinguish between competing suppliers because they are all perceived to have equal performance in that area. You must have good safety simply in order to operate an airline. It's a given not a differentiator.

Some people argue that since it is on the differentiators that competing suppliers' performance is likely to diverge more widely, it is a waste to include givens on a customer survey questionnaire. The survey should focus on differentiators since this will provide more useful information for management decision making. This argument is attractive in theory but flawed in practice. Items, such as many of those shown in Table 5.2, are often regarded as givens even when suppliers' performance is far from perfect. We know from the evidence of very many customer surveys that suppliers do not always perform well on the basics such as cleanliness or consistent quality. And if you're not performing well you really do need to know, because whilst superb toilets may not be a differentiator which will win new customers, filthy toilets will certainly cause customer decay. Moreover, customer perception will not always accord with reality. Even on fundamental givens such as airline safety, a past problem or disaster may have

Table 5.1   Controllables versus non-controllables

Controllables

- Staff appearance
- Staff helpfulness
- Speed of service

Non-controllables

- Convenience of location
- Adequate toilet facilities
- Interest rates
- Weather?????

Table 5.2   Givens or dfferentiators?

Givens	Differentiators
★ Safety	★ Efficient service
★ Cleanliness	★ Friendly staff
★ Location of store	★ Helpful staff
★ Adequate car parking	★ Problem resolution
★ On time delivery	★ Technical service
★ Consistent quality	★ Field sales support

resulted in a poor perception of an airline's safety performance. If such a mistaken perception exists you definitely need to know. Customer surveys should therefore cover givens as well as differentiators. As we will see in Chapter 12, statistical techniques can be used to highlight which customer requirements may be key differentiators.

Broad objectives

To be of maximum value, a customer satisfaction measurement exercise should identify the following objectives:

- customers' priorities;
- customers' tolerance band;
- your own performance;
- your performance relative to your customers' priorities;
- your performance relative to your competitors' performance;
- priorities for improvement.

Let's examine each of these in more detail.

CUSTOMERS' PRIORITIES

Succeeding in the marketplace is all about meeting customers' needs – giving customers what they want – but, as we shall see in Chapter 6, the customers' needs and expectations are not equal; some are far more important to the customer than others.

For example, if I travel by train it is *extremely important* to me that the train arrives on time, *very important* that I have a seat for the whole journey, *quite important* that light refreshments are available, and of *no importance* whether alcoholic drinks are available. If most of the other passengers on the train have similar priorities to mine, it is clearly more important for the service provider to invest resources in improving punctuality than in widening the range of choice in the buffet car.

Of course, customers' priorities can differ considerably – even in very similar markets. On long-haul flights, for example, the range and quality of food and drink may assume much greater importance than it would for short haul or for our train example.

Any customer survey must therefore identify the relative importance of each component aspect of customer satisfaction. Without that knowledge, taking the right management decisions to ensure that your organisation is 'doing best what matters most to customers' may prove difficult.

CUSTOMERS' TOLERANCE BAND

For each component aspect of customer satisfaction, customers will have a tolerance band. This may or may not relate directly to the importance of that customer need. Research into customers' tolerance should identify customers' ideal, expected and unacceptable levels of performance. Let's return to our train example. My most important priority is the punctual arrival of the train, and my second most important the availability of a seat for the whole journey. If questioned in more detail I would say that my ideal level of service is total punctuality but my expected level of service would be significantly inferior – perhaps one-third of trains arriving a few minutes late and a small proportion being subject to serious delays. I may consider 10 per cent lateness (12 minutes in a two-hour journey) an acceptable level of service, but 20 per cent (24 minutes late) an unacceptable level. Regarding seating, my ideal level of service would be a seat always available and my expected level of service a seat virtually always available, even if I have not reserved one. To have even a 10 per cent deviation from my ideal level of service on seat availability would be unacceptable since it would mean having to stand for the entire two hours in one journey out of ten, or standing for 12 minutes on most journeys.

So, the relative importance of customers' priorities does not tell us the full story. A customer's satisfaction with the performance of a supplier will be affected by that customer's expectations. For example, if I expect to queue in a supermarket at lunchtime but not in a bank, a five-minute wait in the supermarket will probably be acceptable but five minutes' queuing in the bank will not.

YOUR OWN PERFORMANCE

The main purpose of a customer survey is to measure the performance of an organisation, as perceived by its customers. But do not delude yourself into believing that you can learn anything from a very quick survey that only asks customers about the performance of your company, product or service.

The type of survey that asks customers to fill in a postcard or small leaflet with a few tick boxes falls into this trap. Often found at the point-of-sale, for example a hotel bedroom, it might ask about friendliness, promptness and efficiency in reception, about the quality of food, speed of service and ambience in the restaurant, providing tick boxes graded 'Excellent', 'Good', 'Fair' and 'Poor' for the guest to complete.

Now, if a guest ticks 'Good' for every level of performance, what does it tell the hotel management? Only that there are no problems. It does not reveal two vital determinants of the guest's future buying behaviour. Firstly, whatever the level of the hotel's performance, how does it compare with the guest's priorities and expectations? And, secondly, how does the hotel's performance compare with that of alternative hotels? The guest will probably take into account these two questions before making a repeat booking.

Rating your company's performance will be the key objective of most customer surveys, but the survey design must also identify your performance relative to customers' priorities and relative to competitors' performance.

YOUR PERFORMANCE RELATIVE TO YOUR CUSTOMERS' PRIORITIES

You are very unlikely to be best at everything and customers have a range of priorities when making any purchase – some things are more important to them than others. Therefore, your primary objective is to 'do best what matters most to customers' so a customer survey must identify your success in attaining this aim. To do so there are two fundamental factors which must be incorporated into your survey design.

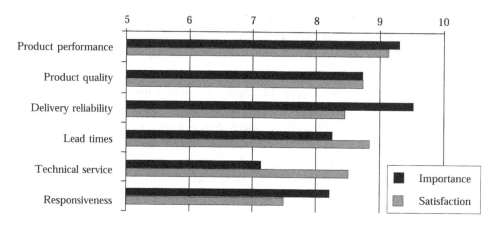

Figure 5.4 A company which is not 'doing best what matters most' to customers

Firstly, when designing the survey you must allow customers an opportunity to define what is important to them in choosing a supplier. By all means include some internally generated performance criteria and test how important they are to customers but, as a guiding principle, the components of your survey should be customer led. Secondly, having defined a set of performance criteria which influence customers' choice of supplier, your survey must devote two separate sections to those criteria: the first asking customers how important each criterion is and the second asking how they feel your organisation performs against each of the criteria listed. By using the same rating scales (see Chapter 10) you can compare your performance with what is important to your customers. This will enable you to see very clearly whether you really are 'doing best what matters most' to customers'.

The six criteria shown in Figure 5.4 illustrate a company not doing best what matters most to customers. Their top priority is reliable delivery (keeping delivery promises) which receives a very high score of 9.5 out of 10. Unfortunately, reliable delivery is not what the company does best, the customers scoring it 8.4 out of 10, it's the second poorest performance of the six criteria measured. It is obvious that the company is putting more resources into trying to provide a fast response with quick deliveries – at short notice if required. But squeezing in deliveries in this way is probably playing havoc with delivery scheduling, perhaps at the expense of the silent majority of customers who do not chase for their delivery. These customers have made their feelings clear in the survey: they would prefer longer delivery times if it means that delivery promises will be kept.

YOUR PERFORMANCE RELATIVE TO YOUR COMPETITORS' PERFORMANCE

Added value from customer satisfaction measurement can be derived if you are able to compare your customers' perception of your performance with that of your main competitors. Your company may feel really pleased with its ability to respond to service calls within 24 hours, but however much effort it has made to achieve this, customers will not rate it highly if they can obtain same-day service from your competitor.

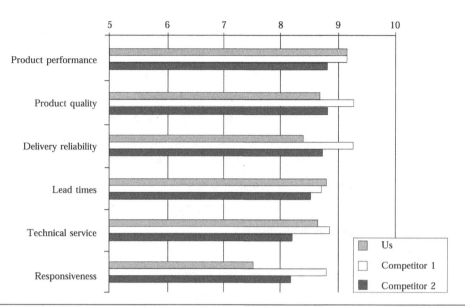

Figure 5.5   Comparisons against competitors

Customers' satisfaction with a supplier over a period of time will be affected by what they see other suppliers offering. Our local pub has a large grassy area with a swing and slide enabling children to play whilst adults drink at outside tables. For several years parents were quite satisfied with this arrangement. Recently, a couple of pubs in the same district have developed far more extensive play areas for children and provided indoor family rooms as well. As a result, parents' expectations have been raised and the original pub is rated far less highly as a venue for a family visit even though its performance in that respect has remained constant.

How our own performance compares with that of other suppliers is shown in Figure 5.5. For this exercise to be valid all suppliers must, of course, be measured against the same list of performance criteria using the same rating scale – in this case a mark out of 10.

PRIORITIES FOR IMPROVEMENT (PFIs)

The five objectives described so far are concerned with ensuring that a customer survey provides results which are sufficiently valid to form a reliable basis for management decision making. The sixth objective is about making these decisions and taking action.

If customer satisfaction measurement is to be of more than academic interest it must result in action, but what action? How can you really be sure that the measures you adopt to improve customers' satisfaction represent the best use of your limited time and resources? With a poorly designed survey it is likely you will make improvements in those areas where your performance ratings are lowest, but this may not be the right course of action. A well designed survey, meeting all the objectives listed in this chapter, may well identify completely different PFIs.

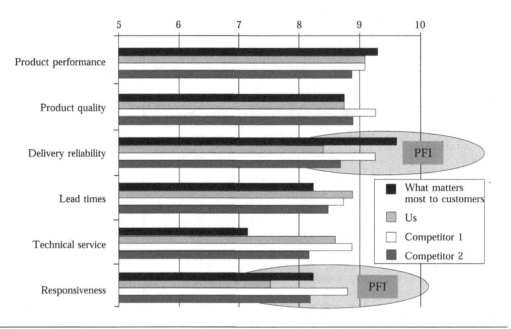

Figure 5.6   Priorities for improvement

To highlight PFIs let's examine Figure 5.6. This figure is an amalgamation of Figures 5.4 and 5.5 in this chapter. The lowest score for performance is 'Responsiveness', so it might appear to be the area where customers are least satisfied and therefore the first priority for improving our service. But a closer look reveals that the primary PFI is 'Reliable delivery': this is the area where the company falls most short of customers' expectations and where it is furthest behind the competition. Using this simple numerical rating scale and visual display of the results it is easy to see at a glance the main areas of both under-performance and over-performance. It is obvious that the company is putting too much resource into technical service and quick deliveries (neither of which are priorities for our customers) and not enough resource into keeping delivery promises. It is also obvious that Competitor 1 is the most successful supplier at 'doing best what matters most to customers' and will almost invariably have the highest market share as a result.

Customer perception or market standing survey?

A common dilemma faced by organisations about to measure customer satisfaction is whether to carry out a simple 'customer perception survey' involving only the company's existing customer base or whether to undertake a more complex 'market standing survey'. The latter requires a sample of all buyers in the marketplace to rate the performance of competing suppliers (Figure 5.7).

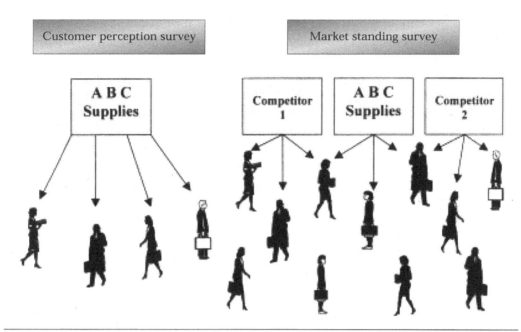

Figure 5.7   Customer perception or market standing survey

CUSTOMER PERCEPTION SURVEY

A customer perception survey is of most value to those organisations able to achieve their objectives by keeping their existing customer base satisfied.

For organisations in the public sector, where competitive forces are few and priorities less pressing, a customer perception survey will be suitable, as indeed it will be for many service businesses in the private sector. These latter businesses include professional service providers who rely for much of their income on repeat business from existing customers. Such customers will often have little knowledge of the performance of competing suppliers.

So, if our dentist or solicitor did happen to contemplate measuring their customers' satisfaction (to my knowledge, neither has contemplated it yet!) we would advise them to carry out a customer perception survey. Where customer satisfaction is measured at the point-of-sale or point of consumption (often the same for services), customer perception surveys are widely used, focusing on a customer's most recent transaction.

Certain types of manager within organisations are also likely to be more interested in a customer perception survey. Quality managers and customer service managers who are interested in monitoring their company's ability to provide good quality and good service can quite adequately check their own performance through a survey of existing customers. In fact, ISO 9000 assessment bodies are encouraging companies registered with them to undertake customer satisfaction surveys in order to demonstrate that their quality management systems really are working. A customer perception survey would be appropriate for this purpose.

As we have seen (Figure 5.4), PFIs too can be identified by comparing a company's performance with its customers' priorities, the data often being used as a basis for monitoring improvements over time. If effective action is taken on PFIs, you will be able to improve retention rates and to build account values.

A further advantage of customer perception surveys is that they are far easier to carry out reliably than market standing surveys and can sometimes be accomplished through a self-completion questionnaire. This is important for organisations whose resources do not stretch to commissioning an outside research agency to undertake a survey. So, if you are going for a DIY job, it really would have to be a customer perception survey.

You can use a customer perception survey to:

- measure customers' satisfaction with your total product;
- compare your own performance with customers' expectations;
- identify PFIs;
- provide data for monitoring improvements;
- improve customer retention rates;
- build average account values;
- keep ISO 9000 assessment bodies happy.

However, one disadvantage of a customer perception survey is that the company is directing its survey questions only at its own customers; those who have chosen that company as a supplier. As this choice presumably means they prefer its services to those obtainable elsewhere, there may be some difficulty in obtaining a truly representative view of how the company is seen by customers at large. That picture can be painted only by a market standing survey.

MARKET STANDING SURVEY

A market standing survey adds two extra dimensions to customer satisfaction measurement. Firstly, it involves questioning a representative sample of all the buyers/users of a product or service, thus providing a more objective view of how a company is perceived. Secondly, it will ask customers not just about their view of your company but also about how they perceive your competitors.

For some companies, a market standing survey will provide a wider picture of how they are performing in the marketplace. In fact, a good market standing survey will enable the production of a 'league table' for the industry depicting suppliers' overall competitive performance as defined by customers (see Chapter 12 for a worked example of such a league table). As well as producing an overall league table it is possible to look at individual components of customer satisfaction to compare the performance of competing suppliers and, using simple statistical techniques, examine variations in competitive performance in different segments, perhaps by size of company, by end-user industry, by location, or by DMU (decision making unit) member (see Chapter 6). These techniques provide valuable information for fine tuning marketing strategies on a segment-by-segment basis. A market standing survey is useful for comparing suppliers' images, but the ultimate objective will be to use the information to improve market share; as such, it tends to be of most interest to sales and marketing managers and to those with general management responsibilities. Use a market standing survey to:

- achieve all the objectives of a customer perception survey;
- rank suppliers' competitive performance;
- compare suppliers' performance against specific customer needs;
- evaluate suppliers' performance in different market segments;
- compare perceived images of different suppliers;
- improve market share.

The main disadvantage of a market standing survey is that it is more complex to design and requires time and a high standard of research skills to carry out. The most significant problem is compiling an accurate sampling frame of all the customers in the market. Most companies have records of their own customers, but few have comprehensive lists of all the customers of a product or service. Basing the results on an accurate sample will therefore be a very complex, time-consuming and, sometimes impossible task. (For more details of sampling see Chapter 8.) If your organisation does not possess these skills in-house it will have to commission an outside agency, thus adding further to costs.

It is useful at this point to consider the question of whether to use an outside agency and also to explore another issue which must be resolved before undertaking a market standing survey – whether to disclose the identity of the company for whom the survey is being undertaken.

In our opinion, a market standing survey can be adequately undertaken only through an external research agency.

USING AN OUTSIDE AGENCY

There are two reasons why a market standing survey is best administered by an independent research agency. Firstly, the use of independent, trained interviewers will provide a far more objective outcome. However objective they try to be, your own staff will never produce an equally objective outcome because they can never get away from the fact that this is an interview between seller and buyer which will inevitably distort the responses, especially in sensitive areas of questioning such as price. Secondly, many customers are reluctant to discuss with one supplier the performance of another supplier; most customers will be far more open and frank with an independent research agency once they are assured that any direct comments or performance ratings they express will not be passed on by the agency. As a result, an independent agency will almost invariably secure more information than your own staff would.

In using an external agency there is, of course, a significant financial cost to bear (although the hidden cost of using your own staff should not be forgotten). So, when budget restrictions simply cannot be stretched to afford the services of an outside agency, using your own staff is feasible, but only for a customer perception survey.

In these circumstances it is always tempting to use the company sales force to conduct the survey, on the grounds that they regularly visit customers. In practice, the sales force are least likely to produce an objective outcome since they are too familiar with their customers and unable to truly detach themselves from an existing selling relationship.

Therefore, if you are to administer your own survey it is advisable either to use a self-completion questionnaire (see Chapter 9) or, where personal or telephone interviews are to be adopted, staff who do not have much direct contact with customers in the normal course of their duties. Many companies carry out perfectly adequate customer perception surveys in this way.

The application of professional research techniques benefits most aspects of customer satisfaction measurement. This is apparent in focus groups (see Chapter 7), which should always be run by a skilled facilitator, sampling which must be very accurate (see Chapter 8), and questionnaire design and analysis which requires specialist expertise.

One option for organisations with limited budgets is that of using external support for parts of the exercise such as facilitating focus groups or conducting interviews. It is also possible to improve the skills of your own staff through specialist training courses and workshops on customer satisfaction measurement and to buy in consultancy advice for key areas such as analytical techniques and the identification of PFIs.

In Table 5.3 the advantages and disadvantages of using your own resources or those of an external agency are considered.

Some organisations use a mix of internally and externally administered surveys depending on the scale and the complexity of the task. For example, UK bank, First Direct, monitors its customers' satisfaction through quarterly tracking. In the first three quarters of the year a postal survey of existing customers is internally administered; in the fourth quarter, a market standing survey is conducted by an external agency. This serves to re-benchmark customers' priorities and, because the survey is validated by the external agency, results and customer comments can be used in First Direct's advertising and other promotional activities.

Table 5.3   Internal or external resources?

	Internal resources	External agency
Cost	The main reson for using internal resources, although this approach is far from free	Several thousand pounds usually required for a full customer satisfaction measurement study
Objectivity	Concern about the objectivity of the outcome is the main disadvantage of using internal resources	The most objective outcome, especially for a market standing survey
Research expertise	May not be adequate unless you employ a market research professional	Will be familiar with the latest research techniques
Focus groups	Unwise to run your own focus groups unless you have a skilled facilitator	Experienced in running and recruiting focus groups
Interviewing	Can use your own trained staff if basic training is provided	Have resources to complete interviews quickly if required
Analysis & reporting	Feasible in-house if you have suitable spreadsheet skills	Specialist software and skills for analysis and displaying results
Product knowledge	Plentiful in-house and may be essential for some highly complex products	Costly learning curve for complex products
Sampling	Feasible in-house if the advice given in Chapter 8 is closely followed	Many need an agency if external databases are to be used in consumer markets
Questionnaire design	Relevant specialist skills may not reside in-house	Will help to ensure validity of questionnaire to maximize response on self-completion questionnaires
Credibility	May lack credibility, especially with your own employees	Credibility of external research findings can help to drive internal change and can be used in marketing communication

DISCLOSURE

As there is only one supplier involved in a customer perception survey, respondents, of course, will know which organisation the survey is being undertaken for. This applies whether an organisation carries out its own survey or commissions an external agency. On the other hand, in undertaking a market standing survey there are advantages and disadvantages in disclosing to respondents the name of the supplier.

The main argument in favour of keeping the name of the supplier anonymous is to secure the most objective outcome. Indeed, when we first became involved in customer satisfaction measurement in the 1980s we were convinced that a meaningful market standing survey could be carried out only if the name of the commissioning supplier remained undisclosed. In the intervening years we have gained more experience of customer satisfaction measurement and our views have evolved.

There are two major disadvantages in refusing to disclose the name of the supplier. Firstly, as the volume of research undertaken in almost all markets continues to grow it is becoming gradually more difficult to secure the willing participation of respondents. The problem here is not the extra time and difficulty required to secure cooperation – that is a mere irritation. Much more serious is the damage to sampling accuracy which is caused by a significant number of refusals. As we shall see in Chapter 8, accurate sampling is one of the essential foundations of a meaningful customer satisfaction measurement exercise.

The second problem caused by withholding the identity of the supplier is the difficulty of repeating the survey whilst retaining supplier anonymity. This is especially true of many business-to-business markets which are close-knit communities in which it is very difficult to keep secrets. It would be virtually impossible to update annually a market standing survey in a close industrial market and to retain the anonymity of the sponsoring supplier. The only way to achieve this would be to develop a joint industry survey, perhaps under the auspices of a trade association – as happens with much market size and trend research. The drawback with this approach is, of course, that all your competitors end up with the same information which defeats one of the main objectives of a market standing survey – securing a competitive advantage.

Our view now is that a perfectly valid market standing survey can be undertaken with supplier disclosure, provided it is carried out by a third party. In our experience, most customers will be prepared to talk about their perceptions of different suppliers to an objective, professional interviewer who can assure respondents that their comments will remain totally confidential.

Project planning

As with any project, a customer satisfaction measurement study should include a formal brief outlining objectives and a plan as to how they will be achieved. The plan may involve

Table 5.4   CSM project plan

The **Leadership** Factor

Customer Satisfaction Measurement 2006

Objectives	1. To track customers' ongoing satisfaction with research services 2. To identify and quickly resolve any problems arising from specific issues 3. To re-benchmark customers' priorities 4. To identify customers' underlying perception of our performance 5. To determine and implement PFIs		
Tasks	**Key Points**	**Date**	**Action**
Exploratory research	Depth interview agenda. Twelve depth interviews (recruit and conduct)	March March	NH/GR
Exploratory findings	Circulate short executive summary	April	GR
Questionnaire design	Customer priorities; our performance; loyalty; customer comments	April	GR
Sampling	Stratified random sample of clients segmented by company size; account value; contact DMU role	April	NH
Appoint interviewer	Select and appoint appropriate third party to conduct interviews	April	NH
Customer invitations	Letter; survey objectives and description	April	JN
Survey	Telephone interviews	May	External agency
Internal survey	Self-completion questionnaire completed by own staff	May	GR
Analysis	SPSS	June	JW
Internal reporting	Report; presentation; workshop;	June	GR
Development of action	Actions to address PFIs	June	GR/JN/JW
Feedback to customers	Thank you and short report	June	GR
Internal review	Review of progress on implementing action on PFIs	Monthly	GR/JN/JW
Customer update	Progress report for clients on PFIs and other developments	December	GR
Tracking	Annual survey to update results and monitor progress	May 2007	GR

more than one method of collecting information on customer satisfaction. (See Chapter 9 for discussion of continuous versus periodic customer satisfaction measurement.) An example of such a plan, Table 5.4, was produced for our own company. (The plan's component parts are discussed in more detail in later chapters.)

Note the frequent involvement of customers in the exercise, both before and after the survey, with a further mid-term report on progress being sent to customers at the end of the year. This complies with one of the rules of customer satisfaction: 'Don't assume customers will notice your improvements – TELL THEM!'

Conclusions

- Involve customers in defining the component elements of customer satisfaction.
- To be of maximum value, a customer satisfaction measurement exercise should identify:
    - customers' priorities;
    - customers' expectations and tolerance band;
    - an organisation's performance as perceived by its customers;
    - an organisation's performance relative to its customers' priorities;
    - an organisation's performance relative to that of its competitors;
    - priorities for improvement (PFIs).
- A customer perception survey will involve only one supplier and will measure satisfaction of its own customer base. Its use is suitable for organisations in less competitive environments and is often carried out in-house using an organisation's own resources.
- A market standing survey, rather than a customer perception survey, is more meaningful for companies in competitive markets. It involves gathering perceptions from a representative sample of customers in the market about the performance and image of suppliers to that market. It is necessary to use an external agency – at least for the interviewing element of a market standing survey.
- A customer satisfaction measurement study requires careful planning and accurate scheduling if it is to be effectively carried out.

6 UNDERSTANDING CUSTOMER BEHAVIOUR

AIMS

By the end of this chapter you will:

- Understand the main differences between the buying behaviour of individuals and that of organisations.
- Realize the importance of developing a detailed understanding of buyer behaviour before attempting to measure customer satisfaction.
- Understand how variations in buyer behaviour will affect the way in which customer satisfaction should be measured.

As we have already seen in Chapter 2, a significant part of a customer's satisfaction with a product or service is determined before its consumption. It is before, and sometimes during, purchase that the customer forms expectations about the forthcoming benefits of the product or service, and thereafter its performance will always be judged against those expectations.

Anyone involved in measuring customer satisfaction must therefore have a detailed understanding of the ways in which customers make and evaluate their purchase decisions.

These decision-making processes will differ between consumer and organisational markets and according to the complexity of the decision. For customer satisfaction measurement to succeed, accurate information must also be acquired regarding the different people involved in a purchase decision. This so-called decision-making unit (DMU) can be quite large for some products and services in organisational markets and it is essential that the views of all DMU members are accommodated in a customer survey.

Individual Buying Behaviour

The steps an individual takes in making a buying decision may appear simple enough, but considerable activity (both mental and physical) may contribute to the process (see Figure 6.1).

Let's explore the process, examining each step in more detail.

FELT NEED

In our everyday life we constantly experience all kinds of needs: for warmth and food ('biogenic' needs), for the more sophisticated needs associated with job satisfaction and social status ('psychogenic' needs), and so on.

Before the purchase decision-making process can begin the consumer must first become aware of the existence of a need. This is sometimes called 'problem recognition'. Once the consumer has perceived this felt need, he or she will be motivated towards its satisfaction.

A need can be aroused through internal or external stimuli – hunger pangs may originate purely internally if a long time has elapsed since eating, or they may be triggered by external stimuli such as walking past a baker's shop.

A supplier of goods will aim to stimulate needs through means such as advertising: in the late 1970s people did not know that they needed video recorders until advertising pointed out their existence and benefits.

Once a person is aware of a need it becomes a 'drive', so called because he or she feels driven or urged to satisfy it. Companies and organisations must therefore understand what it is

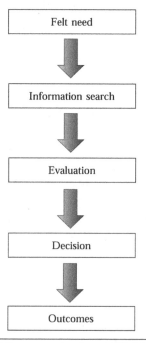

Figure 6.1   The buying decision process of an individual purchaser

that drives a consumer to choose their particular product or service rather than that of their competitors. Car purchase may, for example, satisfy a need for transportation, a need for status, or a need for excitement. Organisations use promotional and selling techniques to position their product or service in the market in such a way that it will appeal to potential customers.

INFORMATION SEARCH

Once aware of a need or problem, an individual will set about solving it. Sometimes a problem is solved immediately: hunger is felt and a biscuit may be eaten. Sometimes the problem is more complex and the individual has to seek out information to help him or her solve it (see Figure 6.2).

The first source of information most people turn to is memory. If you need a new exhaust for your car, your first thought will almost certainly be towards the solution of this problem the last time it arose. Who fitted the new exhaust? Was it all right? Was the service efficient? Was it reasonably priced? If your memory is favourable, that may be the end of it. You may skip the evaluation stage and make the decision to return to the same supplier as last time.

There is a major implication in this for customer satisfaction measurement. An individual's memory is often not a particularly reliable guide to what actually happened and subjective perceptions of events are usually not overburdened with the need to conform to reality. We often remember those things we choose to remember. In particular, we tend to remember bad, as opposed to good, experiences more vividly and for longer.

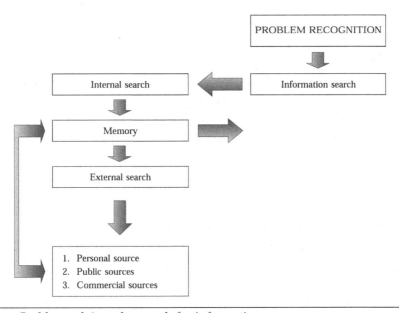

Figure 6.2   Problem solving: the search for information

But the individual customer will be quite happy with all this: his or her perception of events is reality and has to become reality for any supplier trying to sell goods or services to that individual. Often, however, the information search will be more lengthy. You may not be entirely satisfied that the information stored in your memory is enough to enable you to make the best decision regarding your car exhaust. If this is the case, you will turn to external sources of information: you might ask for prices from two or three different suppliers.

But what if you have never had to replace an exhaust before? One answer is to consult external sources of information. Let's consider three such sources. You might use personal sources of information: a friend, the next door neighbour, or a relative who has experience of this kind of purchase and could give you good advice. You might consult *Yellow Pages* or *Thomsons Directory*. For some products, buyers' guides are a good source of information, as is a consumer magazine such as *Which?* These sources will provide a good comparison of alternative products. Lastly, you might rely on commercial sources of information, which in this case would consist mainly of exhaust centres advertising in the local press. You could telephone several such centres and ask for details of their service, the kind of exhaust they fit, the duration of the guarantee offered, and the price.

A new exhaust is not a major purchase apart from the requirement for urgency which necessarily puts a time limit on the information search stage. Some products, however, represent a big step for buyers to take. In wanting to make the right decision they may spend a considerable time at the information search stage. They will not be actively seeking information the whole time but they will be in a stage of heightened attention. In other words, they will be alert to any information concerning that felt need whether it arises in advertisements, articles or casual conversation.

EVALUATION

By this time a number of alternative ways of meeting a felt need will have become evident. These alternatives must now be evaluated (see Figure 6.3) and this involves determining how well each option meets the felt need. This process may be very objective, with the advantages and disadvantages of each option weighed against other alternatives; some people might even compile a list to help in their evaluation.

However objective the individual intends to be, subjective factors always influence the evaluation process to a greater or lesser extent. Three sets of subjective factors usually have an influence at the evaluation stage: beliefs, attitudes, and intentions.

Beliefs

Beliefs are deeply entrenched views, often based on the core values of an individual's country, sub-group (for example, ethnic group), and social class.

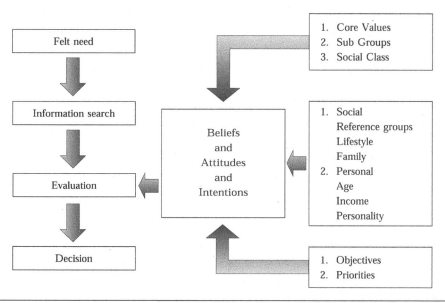

Figure 6.3   Evaluation of alternatives

Although beliefs are sometimes hard to articulate they nevertheless form the foundation for much decision-making behaviour. Beliefs are also, of course, social, political and religious, but for our purposes we will take a commercial example: an individual might believe that 'branded' products are of a higher quality than 'own label' products.

Attitudes

An individual's underlying beliefs help to form attitudes about specific events, places, products, services and such like.

These attitudes are liable to change more frequently than beliefs, being strongly influenced by family, social reference groups, lifestyle, age and income.

Again thinking in commercial terms, an individual's attitude towards particular brands of coffee might be influenced by that individual's spending power, the type of coffee favoured by his or her friends, and by the underlying belief mentioned above, that the quality of branded products is higher than that of own label products.

Therefore, the individual might hold the attitude that, for example, Gold Blend coffee provides better value for money than do cheaper own label alternatives.

Intentions

Individuals also have objectives, priorities, and aspirations that they are striving to attain, and these will often be reflected in their purchasing decisions, especially for conspicuous purchases such as cars or clothing. Thus one factor in an individual's choice of Gold Blend coffee might be wanting visitors to know that he or she uses good coffee.

Familiarity with all three components of the customer's evaluation process is necessary to understand customers' satisfaction. The process also illustrates the fact that customer satisfaction is rarely a simple relationship between supplier and customer. An individual's evaluation of a product or service will almost always be affected by others.

This has implications for exploratory research and for sampling – if you want to understand customers' perceptions, rather than just identify a few quick measures of satisfaction.

DECISION

Having weighed up the alternatives a decision is made. Even this decision may still be little more than an 'intention to purchase'. Unless the buyer is in the shop handing over cash for the item or on the telephone placing an order, the purchase decision is usually a stage which precedes the purchase by some time. Indeed, where expensive items are being considered, the decision in principle to buy and the choice of one of the alternatives could precede the actual purchase by a lengthy period, perhaps several months.

An additional factor at this stage is the level of risk the customer will associate with his or her purchase. The risk level is higher for expensive items where the buyer's product knowledge is poor and, consequently, difficulty arises in evaluating alternatives. Conspicuous purchases, which may affect the buyer's credibility in the eyes of others, also tend to be associated with a high level of risk. Some individuals of course are more prone to uncertainty than others, but virtually everyone will be uncertain about some purchases.

OUTCOMES

Of those decision makers who do carry out their intention to purchase, some will be totally satisfied with the product and others less so. Whatever the outcome, the buyer is likely to remember this level of satisfaction and, for all but the most trivial purchases, memory is likely to be influential in subsequent similar decision-making situations.

Some purchases, particularly important and expensive ones, tend to result in a great deal of subsequent reappraisal by buyers. Leon Festinger coined the phrase 'cognitive dissonance' to describe these second thoughts. Doubts can be experienced by consumers when they realize that some of their unchosen alternatives also have desirable attributes; their state of heightened attention is often increased after a purchase. Promotional material will be noticed, other competing products inspected and their owners possibly questioned. It is as though buyers are trying to convince themselves that they were smart enough to have made a good decision.

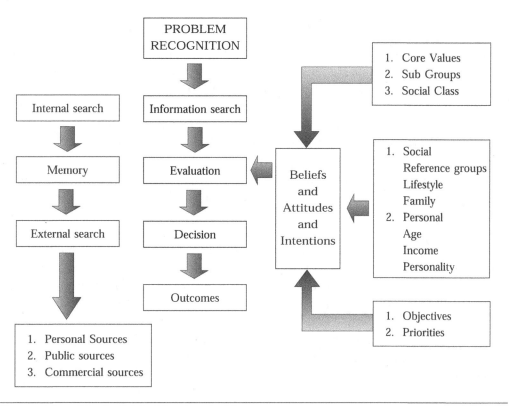

Figure 6.4   The individual buying decision process

In this situation it is wise for companies to do all they can to reinforce consumers' confidence in their choice. Some advertising for inherently high-risk purchases such as cars is aimed at recent purchasers by showing satisfied buyers with their new car. Supportive communications can also be sent through the post or reassuring telephone calls made. It is in these situations that post-transaction customer satisfaction measurement is most useful. The possibility of cognitive dissonance should always be borne in mind by those carrying out the measurement; it is particularly important to ensure swift action to resolve any customer dissatisfaction, however slight. An implication here is that post-transaction customer surveys should not be anonymous. (The complete individual buying process is shown in Figure 6.4).

Complexity of Purchase: Individual Buying

As was suggested earlier in this analysis of consumer buying behaviour, the process will not be the same for all purchases. Quite simply, some purchases are much more important than others and although we cannot put all buying categories neatly into boxes, we can attach labels to broad bands of purchases according to their complexity. Let's address some of them.

HIGH-INVOLVEMENT PURCHASES

The most difficult type of purchase facing the consumer is a high-involvement purchase. The key factor making a purchase high involvement is the level of risk perceived by the customer. The 'involvement' of the decision increases in line with the likelihood and the consequences of getting it wrong. A poor decision is obviously more likely if the consumer has little or no experience of the product category. This will reduce the buyer's confidence in his or her ability to evaluate alternatives, even though a very thorough information search may have been conducted. Other decisions are high involvement because of the severe consequences of getting it wrong. Consequences include personal disappointment, which would arise for example if a poor holiday decision is made – or even as a result of a relatively low cost decision, such as what film to see.

Other consequences may include a fall in the esteem of others (if an unfashionable item of clothing is purchased) or the cost, time and upset involved in a wrong decision and its aftermath (say, the operation of a complex technical product proving beyond an individual's ability).

The severity of the consequences of a poor decision will clearly increase in line with the duration of consumption – a house being the most obvious example – and older consumers are more likely to regard decisions as a lifetime purchase.

This is defined as a state of 'extensive problem solving' and it is clear that companies most able to help buyers with decision making will improve their chances of making a sale. Educating buyers about the product class makes it easier for them to learn more about a specific product's attributes and benefits; and, by reinforcing their own products' high standing within the relevant product class, a company contributes to reducing buyer uncertainty. This is also important at the post-purchase stage when the danger of cognitive dissonance will need to be countered.

LOW-INVOLVEMENT PURCHASES

Some purchases are so everyday that little or no conscious thought goes into buying decisions. Most habitual purchases come into this category: the commuter buying a newspaper on the way to the station or the smoker buying cigarettes. This simplest type of buyer behaviour is defined as 'routinized response'.

Virtually all the steps in the purchase decision-making process can be absent. Consumers may move from felt need to purchase with no thought given to the interim stages or the outcome unless something untoward has occurred – such as their normal newspaper being unavailable.

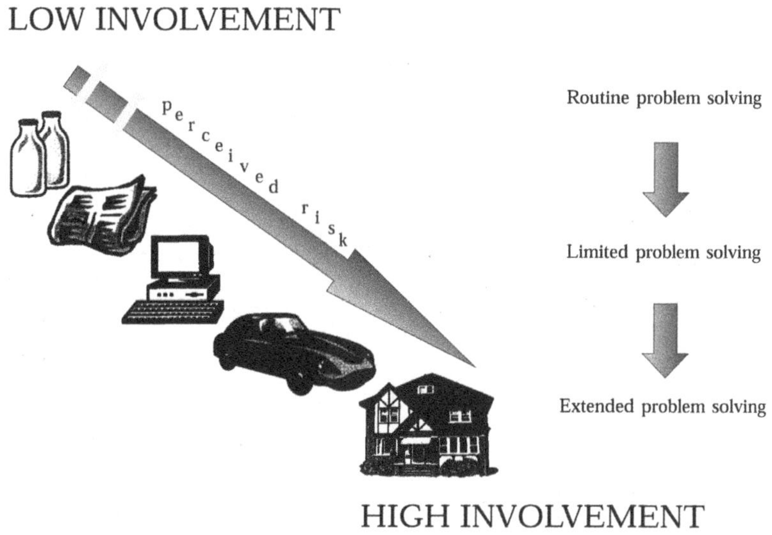

LOW INVOLVEMENT

Routine problem solving

Limited problem solving

Extended problem solving

HIGH INVOLVEMENT

Figure 6.5   Decision categories: individual buying

Most buyer behaviour does not fall into either of these extreme categories (see Figure 6.5). Most purchases are of more or less familiar products, but since buyers' knowledge is rarely complete and new or modified products are continuously being introduced, a certain amount of information gathering and evaluation does usually take place. This we can call 'limited problem solving': the buyer goes through most of the steps in the buying decision process but does so very quickly.

Organisational buying

There are several key areas of difference between the typical buying process of individuals and that of organisations. The first, and most apparent difference is the number of people involved in the buying process within organisations. Individual purchasers tend to consult or be influenced by other people when making some purchases but organisational purchases almost always include decision making by several people, and the people involved often have different priorities.

This type of committee decision may also occur in consumer markets: for example, a holiday choice when members of a family have different priorities. Most purchase decisions in consumer markets, however, do not involve this type of decision-making unit.

A second difference is the greater formality of the organisational buying process, driven by the need to keep everybody informed and to arrive at a decision which is broadly acceptable to the people involved.

Average DMU by size of organization	
Number of employees	Size of DMU
Below 200	3.43
201–400	4.85
401–1000	5.81
Over 1000	6.50

Figure 6.6   Average DMU size by organisation. The number of people influencing purchasing decisions

Thirdly, organisational decisions tend to be more rational than those made by consumers – and there is less room for impulsive or emotional purchases. The relative formality and rationality of organisational buying tend to make it easier to identify what is important to customers when undertaking a customer satisfaction measurement exercise.

The most obvious difference between individual and organisational buying is that the organisational buyer is not spending his or her own money. (There is a widely held view that purchase decisions made by small, owner-managed businesses bear more resemblance to individual rather than organisational buying.) Achieving value for the organisation is uppermost in the mind of the buyer. This increases the importance of customer satisfaction measurement since habit and loyalty will figure less prominently in the organisational buying process – the buyer will usually change supplier if he or she believes better value can be obtained for the organisation by doing so.

In the remainder of this chapter key aspects of the organisational buying process are examined and the implications of customer satisfaction measurement considered.

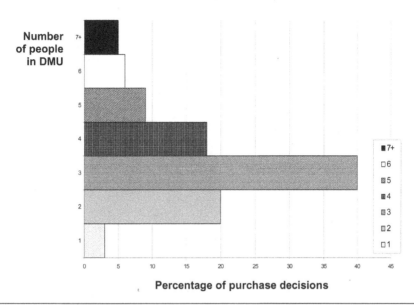

Figure 6.7   The number of people involved in the DMU

The DMU

However large a company or organisation, it is people who make enquiries, negotiate, place orders, and so on. So, we can assume that a number of individuals are involved in purchase decisions (Figure 6.6) and that they are collectively known as the decision-making unit (DMU).

Of course, the larger the organisation the more people tend to be involved in the DMU. It is most unusual for only one person to be making decisions in the buying process. What is certain is that several people are almost always involved (Figure 6.7). The DMU can be a formal committee but more usually is an informal group of people each with a different involvement in making a purchase. The exact make-up of a DMU cannot be predicted from one company to another. The roles people take vary but will, apart from in the smallest companies, generally include a buyer or purchasing manager in charge of all the administrative aspects of purchasing. Specialists are also likely to be involved. If equipment for the factory floor is to be bought, the production manager would be influential; if a new computer for the office is under consideration the IT manager would be important, and so on. These managers might also choose to include in decision making those members of their department who are going to use the equipment purchased. People from the finance department will be consulted when it comes to payment or, if the sum involved is a large one, they may have to give their approval. For important purchases senior management, even the whole board of directors, might be involved.

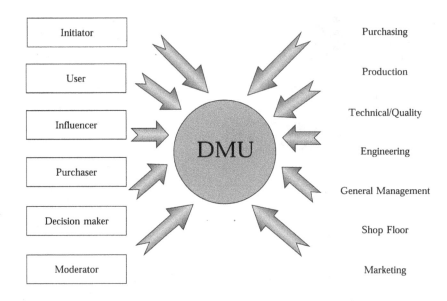

Figure 6.8   The decision-making unit

DMU PERSONNEL

Let's now look more closely at some of the people involved in the DMU and the responsibilities they carry (Figure 6.8).

Initiator

All purchases have to start somewhere. Although organisations may experience a state akin to felt need (for example, stocks of a regularly purchased material running low), research has shown that most important purchases arise as a result of a suggestion. The initiator of such a suggestion could be an employee who sees possibilities for improved efficiency, a senior manager, or even an individual from outside the organisation, such as a consultant or specifier.

User

Users are those individuals in the organisation who will be using the equipment, materials or services purchased. They can come from any level within the hierarchy and the extent of their involvement will depend partly on their seniority and partly on the prevailing attitude towards involving employees in the decision-making processes. Most often, users are relatively low in status and influence but they can have a critical effect at certain stages of some industrial purchases. For example, skilled workers in a plastic moulding factory may well insist that a new material is difficult to work or performs less well than existing materials. This may be enough to ensure that the material is not considered for purchase by more senior staff. In customer satisfaction measurement the user manager (the production manager in the plastic moulding case) is often seen as the representative of user departments, but exploratory research should always seek to identify the role of the real users as they may also need to be included in the survey.

Influencer

By supplying information for the evaluation of alternatives or modifying specifications, influencers affect the purchase decision. Technical staff, such as engineers, chemists or computer experts, are often cast in this role, exerting a significant influence on industrial purchase decisions through their specialist knowledge that more senior management may lack. They can stop a sale proceeding and can also be sufficiently powerful to sway decision makers to their preferred choice. For more expensive purchases, the finance department will exert a similar level of influence.

Purchaser

The purchaser is usually the individual with formal authority for selecting a supplier and implementing all the procedures that result in placing the order. In some instances, however, buyers may not even be influencers let alone decision makers, but will merely carry out the administrative functions involved in the purchase. Be aware of a purchasing manager's role and priorities when you design a customer satisfaction measurement survey – you must not make the mistake of assuming that the buyer is the most important person to target.

Decision makers

Those who are most influential in the making of the purchase decision can be identified as the decision makers. It may be one individual or an entire committee. Although most important purchasing decisions will involve senior management, in many organisations the identification of the final decision makers is often the most difficult task facing suppliers. Arguably, for customer satisfaction measurement purposes, it is wise to banish the notion of one particular decision maker since this role will vary between organisations. It is preferable to ensure that your survey sample covers a representative cross-section of the DMU (as outlined in Chapter 8).

Moderators

These are people in roles which moderate everyone else's behaviour without actually controlling it. Examples are quality managers and environmental managers. Such posts are becoming increasingly common in a wide variety of organisations and are almost invariably of relevance in customer satisfaction research. The DMU is a complex phenomenon which may vary in its composition from one organisation to another. The buying roles do however guide researchers towards the kind of people they should be including in a customer satisfaction measurement exercise in organisational markets. This theme will be developed when exploratory research is examined in the next chapter.

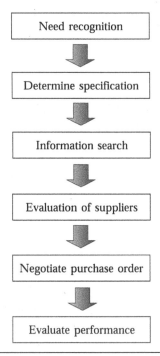

Figure 6.9   The organisational buying decision process

The Organisational Buying Decision Process

Most writers agree that, as with consumer purchases, organisational buying decisions follow a sequence. But, whereas in consumer buying the steps usually occur within the mind of an individual buyer, the organisational buying decision process involves discussions between different members of the DMU. These discussions are often formal, involving committees, minutes, written specifications, purchase orders and so on.

Six steps can be identified in the organisational buying decision process (see Figure 6.9) and these are discussed below.

NEED RECOGNITION

As with consumer purchases, the first step in the organisational buying process is the recognition of a need. This state of affairs could be the result of internal events such as the problem caused by a breakdown of machinery or the regular need to order materials. On the other hand, the need could be recognized as a result of external stimuli such as the suggestion of an outside consultant or the marketing communications of potential suppliers, either of which could demonstrate opportunities for improving the organisation's performance.

DETERMINATION OF PRODUCT SPECIFICATIONS

Having recognized a need, internal discussion usually takes place with the objective of generating alternative solutions to the problem. For major purchases, quite a few people could be involved at this stage. As a result of these deliberations, the DMU will reach a consensus on the best way to proceed. Suitably qualified personnel will then draw up a detailed specification for the product or service required.

INFORMATION SEARCH

The next step is to identify and approach potential suppliers. Some buyers may have formal procedures for identifying suppliers but many will simply contact suppliers who spring to mind with most prominence or those easiest to identify. If there is a large number of potential suppliers a brief initial appraisal may follow, perhaps based only on their literature, after which a shortlist of three or four suppliers may be drawn up.

EVALUATION OF SUPPLIERS

Extensive discussions may be held with this small number of potential suppliers, as the buyer assesses the relative benefits of their product or service. The suppliers will probably then be requested to submit a formal quotation.

Evaluation will be based partly on the suppliers' quotations, partly on objective analysis of their respective product or service, and partly on subjective feelings about their likely performance as suppliers. (If the buyer has done business with a supplier in the past, this last factor will be more objective, based on actual performance.)

From these various factors a buying decision is made and a supplier selected.

Decision category	Newness of the problem	Maximum	Consideration of alternatives
New task	High	Maximum	Always
Modified rebuy	Medium	Moderate	Usually
Straight rebuy	Low	Minimal	Periodic

Figure 6.10   Decision categories in organisational buying

NEGOTIATION OF A PURCHASE ORDER

Once the supplier has been selected details regarding delivery dates, terms of payment, penalty clauses and so on are specified. Extensive negotiations may take place before a purchase order is finally placed.

EVALUATION OF PRODUCT AND SUPPLIER PERFORMANCE

Many organisational buyers have developed formal procedures for the evaluation of suppliers. In many routine areas of purchasing, some kind of performance review is the most important factor in determining the choice of future suppliers. This evaluation may vary from formal vendor rating systems to the memory of the relevant manager; it will elicit a range of views from accurate appraisals based on detailed records to purely subjective perceptions.

Whatever the basis of this performance rating, and as we have already seen, perception is reality: it is the basis on which the customer makes purchase decisions.

Complexity of Purchase: Organisational Buying

Organisational markets also have high and low involvement purchases, but these are categorized as 'new task' purchases and 'straight rebuys' (see Figure 6.10).

In fact, it is generally accepted that the organisational buying situation should be split into three basic types. We look briefly at each of these three below.

NEW TASK

A new task purchasing situation is one that is outside the buyer's past experience. The buyer's uncertainty over the outcome of the purchase will be at its height. At this stage, extensive problem-solving abilities are required and much information will be assessed before a decision is made. In this situation the DMU is likely to be at its largest, the decision-making process at its longest and the final decision maker a member of senior management.

Although it is usually associated with the purchase of large capital items, a new task purchase can also be defined as the purchase of any product or service not previously experienced. For example, a company computerizing a process for the first time is in a new task situation; this is so whatever the cost of the system, as the consequences of a bad decision could be dire. Equally, a company using a new material (such as plastic rather than steel) for a component is involved in a new task purchase. The main implications for customer satisfaction measurement will be the extended DMU, which must be fully covered, and the timing of the survey.

New task purchases suit a post-transactional survey which ascertains customers' levels of satisfaction whilst the purchase/installation process remains fresh in their minds. This type of customer satisfaction measurement would therefore be carried out on a continuous basis, shortly after each transaction, rather than at a given point in time such as once per annum.

To track performance, results are aggregated and a moving average monitored. If there is long-term contact between supplier and customer, perhaps for training, servicing or consumables, customer satisfaction in these areas is measured in the normal way through a periodic survey of a representative sample of customers.

MODIFIED REBUY

A modified rebuy is a purchase not totally outside the buyer's experience but also not totally within it. In this situation DMU members may agree that significant benefits are to be derived from seeking new information and re-evaluating their alternatives.

Modified rebuy decision making can best be described as 'limited problem solving'. Although members of the DMU probably have had considerable experience of buying this type of product, some change in the supply environment (such as technological advance or a supplier's marketing initiative) has made them uncertain as to which supplier best meets their needs. A straightforward information search and reappraisal of suppliers will usually result in a relatively quick decision.

STRAIGHT REBUY

In a straight rebuy situation the buyer will have extensive experience of purchasing the product or service. Considerable knowledge of the market for such products and substantial information on most, if not all, suppliers and the products they offer will be to hand.

These routine purchasing decisions are most likely to be handled by the purchasing department with little or no involvement from other departments; the DMU may be very small and the decision taken very quickly. As long as past purchases of the product in question have remained satisfactory buyers will often seek no new information but will simply re-order the product when necessary from the same supplier. In some companies straight rebuys have become so systematic that a computer re-orders automatically as stocks of the product fall to a certain predetermined level.

Products or services categorized as modified rebuy or straight rebuy are suited to snapshot customer satisfaction measurement requiring a periodic survey of a representative sample of customers.

Conclusions

- Customers' pre-purchase expectations and their purchase experience can have a significant effect on their ultimate satisfaction level. Organisations must therefore have a detailed understanding of the way in which customers make their purchase decisions and must consider its implications for customer satisfaction research.
- The buying processes of individuals tend to be more subjective with consequent scope for customers to hold mistaken views about a supplier's performance. However, the customer's perception is reality since it is this reality on which purchase decisions are made.
- The most significant difference between individual and organisational buying is the involvement of a decision-making unit in organisational purchases. Any customer satisfaction measurement exercise must therefore identify the types of people involved and their role in the decision-making process if a representative sample is to be surveyed.
- The complexity of purchases varies from routine rebuys to high involvement and/or high risk transactions. Whether in consumer or organisational markets, customers' satisfaction with high involvement or new task purchases which occur only infrequently is best measured on an ongoing basis using a post-transactional survey.

7 EXPLORATORY RESEARCH

AIMS

By the end of this chapter you will:
- Understand the role of exploratory research in the design of a meaningful survey.
- Be able to design and undertake depth interviews.
- Know how to use focus groups and projective techniques to explore customers' hidden attitudes and perceptions.

The purpose of the exploratory stage in any research project is to ensure that the researcher understands enough about the composition and attitudes of the target population to draw an accurate sample and to design an appropriate questionnaire.

In other words, the purpose of exploratory research is to ensure that:

- the right questions are asked;
- in the right way;
- to the right people.

The Role of Exploratory Research

Crucial to the success of the exploratory phase is the researcher's ability to probe very deeply into all aspects of the relationship between customer and supplier, uncovering those factors that influence customers' choice of and satisfaction with suppliers.

Very often this probing will rely on the use of techniques to stimulate ideas and help customers express attitudes and beliefs which they may have difficulty in articulating. Later in this chapter we consider how depth interviews and focus groups can be used to reveal customers' deepest beliefs, but first we must clarify two specific objectives which are achieved by the use of exploratory research techniques: the composition of the survey population and the component elements of customer satisfaction.

COMPOSITION OF THE SURVEY POPULATION

Even for the simplest customer perception survey, the composition of the population to be surveyed will rarely be straightforward. As we saw in the previous chapter, consumers' decisions on which product to buy, which suppliers to buy it from, their expectations from the purchase and their subsequent satisfaction with it, are frequently influenced by other people.

To really understand the customer–supplier relationship a hospital, for example, would need to interview patients' relatives as well as the patients themselves in its exploratory research.

In business-to-business markets the decision-making process and the decision-making unit are almost always complex. Exploratory research must therefore probe the make-up of the DMU, the 'roles' played by its members and the relative influence of each DMU member on the organisation's level of satisfaction with the supplier. A quality manager, for example, may be responsible for maintaining formal records of supplier performance, producing ratings for each supplier on a regular basis. However, other colleagues (such as the production manager) may in practice be far more influential in determining that company's level of satisfaction with suppliers and in deciding whether or not to remain with existing suppliers or switch to new ones.

Your exploratory research, therefore, must question customers in some depth about how they make purchase decisions and evaluate their outcome. It must also identify who else is involved and their relative influence on the decision making. Without a very detailed understanding of customers' buying behaviour you can never be confident that the sample selected for your survey is truly representative of customers as a whole.

COMPONENT ELEMENTS OF CUSTOMER SATISFACTION

If you plan to measure your own customers' level of satisfaction with your organisation you need to determine precisely what it is that you are measuring. There are many different factors which combine to produce customers' level of satisfaction, referred to in Chapters 4 and 5 as the customer value package. Exploratory research needs to define what these factors are and it must also clarify the relative importance of the various component elements. This latter point is often overlooked and is particularly important if your survey method will not allow for a long questionnaire. In that case there is a limit to the number of component elements of satisfaction that you can include, so you need to be very confident that you are covering the factors that make the most significant contribution to customers' overall level of satisfaction.

Exploratory research also allows customers an opportunity to set the agenda, to explain what matters to them in their relationship with the supplier. If the way to competitive advantage lies in 'doing best what matters most to customers' it is surely important to let customers define what matters most to them. Far too many organisations leap straight into a customer satisfaction survey having defined the relevant performance criteria themselves, without consulting customers. This could be very misleading as research shows that managers do not have an accurate grasp of customers' priorities and certainly not the relative importance of those priorities.

So, the purpose of this exploratory phase is to probe your customers' priorities, attitudes and beliefs in order to develop a full understanding of the customer–supplier relationship from the customers' perspective. Firstly, you need to understand how customers make and evaluate their buying decisions and who gets involved in those processes and, secondly, what are the component elements of customer satisfaction and the relative importance of those factors.

The remainder of this chapter examines the two exploratory research techniques used to develop this understanding: depth interviews and focus groups.

Depth Interviews

Depth interviews are one-to-one interviews. In business markets they are usually conducted at the respondent's premises; in consumer markets in the home. The interview usually lasts for about one hour, sometimes up to 90 minutes, and is the usual way of conducting exploratory research in organisational markets.

There are two aspects to consider.

Firstly, since the objective is to develop a very broad understanding of the customer–supplier relationship, respondents need to represent the widest possible spectrum of opinion. We will therefore examine which people should be chosen for depth interviews. Secondly, you must consider how to structure depth interviews in order to derive the greatest possible benefit from them. Since the interview will attempt to draw out attitudes and beliefs which respondents find difficult to articulate, well practised interview skills and a good understanding of appropriate interview techniques will be necessary.

Let's rehearse how depth interviews should be approached.

RESPONDENTS FOR DEPTH INTERVIEWS

In planning your depth interviews you will need to consider the following: customers; experts and influencers; and sampling.

Customers

Ensure that your depth interviews cover the full range of customer types as attitudes and priorities can vary considerably between different customers.

In consumer markets you will need to consider segments according to:

- age;
- gender;
- income or socio-economic group;
- family life-cycle;
- lifestyle;
- product usage.

You may not need to segment your customers according to all the criteria listed but you will need to identify which groupings result in the biggest differences in the component elements of customer satisfaction. For example, a restaurant might identify age and family life-cycle as two important determinants of variations in customer satisfaction. Younger diners will place a high value on a lively atmosphere, music, large servings and an unusual menu; priorities for older customers might be a quiet atmosphere, comfortable furnishings, quality of the food and a familiar menu; families with young children will look for a welcoming attitude, high tolerance levels towards young children, play facilities, a suitable menu, provision of high chairs and so on. All these benefits may be in stark contrast to those required by so-called 'empty-nest families' seeking much more peaceful surroundings.

In other industries different segmentation variables have a far greater impact on customer satisfaction. A manufacturer of sports or outdoor clothing and equipment would probably find that product usage is far more meaningful. People buying the manufacturer's products for very serious and testing uses, such as mountain climbing or marathon running, would display very different components of customer satisfaction from more casual participants in the sport, and they in turn would have different priorities from people buying the products merely as fashion accessories.

Suppliers in organisational markets need to adopt these same principles but have to accommodate totally different segments to encompass the full range of variables affecting customers' satisfaction. Segments may include:

- size of customer (small or large organisation);
- amount or frequency of usage;
- type of usage;
- customer's industry;
- geographical location;
- supply chain variables (direct purchase or through distributors);
- individual position/role within DMU.

A manufacturer of envelopes, for example, would find a big difference in priorities between trade customers who buy a wide range of envelopes very frequently to sell on and end users who buy for their own consumption. Even amongst end users customers from different industries will often base their satisfaction on different criteria. A life assurance company might be very concerned about quality and image whereas a utility company using envelopes for billing may prefer to concentrate on unit cost and the envelopes' suitability for highly mechanized mailings.

In whatever way organisations are segmented, you must always bear in mind that it is individuals, not companies, who are interviewed. Ensure adequate coverage of DMU variables – the priorities and perspectives of the purchasing manager will usually differ from those of the production manager. One of the purposes of depth interviews is to understand the composition of the DMU and the differing roles and priorities within it. Therefore, whilst you should make every effort to include representatives of all known DMU variables within your exploratory research, depth interviews themselves may identify additional DMU members who should be included in the main survey.

Outside experts and influencers

To broaden your understanding still further it can be very useful to cast your net beyond customers when recruiting respondents for depth interviews. There are many experts who have a considerable amount of knowledge about all kinds of markets and frequently influence customers' expectations and purchase decisions: these include editors and journalists of relevant trade magazines, staff of trade associations, consultants specializing in the industry, or experts in the field. Experts may range from a university professor for a company manufacturing medical laser equipment to leading climbers or employees at an outdoor centre for a manufacturer of outdoor clothing and equipment.

Sampling

In an ideal world, exploratory research would encompass every conceivable input into customers' decision-making processes plus an impressive array of outside experts but, of course, the real world always dictates a compromise between coverage and cost.

Compromise means drawing a sample believed to be as representative as possible within the constraints of time and cost. Sampling is fully covered in Chapter 8 and is a far more important exercise for the survey itself than it is for the exploratory research. At this stage a judgemental sample is used; it does not purport to statistically cover the different segments of a market-place, and may not even be totally objective, but it does cover the widest range of opinion which can be encompassed within the number of depth interviews allocated to the exercise.

The number is guided by the size and variety of the customer base. In a mature industrial market with a small number of large customers, six to ten depth interviews should be adequate to meet exploratory research objectives, provided the respondents are well chosen. You could use a matrix, as in Table 7.1, to ensure that coverage of customer variables is as thorough as possible. In this example, which is based on a survey of raw materials supplied to the paper industry, the chief variables are the customer's process (the type of paper each customer makes), the size of the customer in terms of volume usage and the role of the individual respondent in each of the companies' DMU.

These eight customer interviews should provide sufficient information to guide sampling and questionnaire design for the main survey.

Customer satisfaction surveys in mass markets, whether business-to-business (say, office equipment) or consumer (hotels) will often be more complex as they require a larger number of depth interviews to cover the full range of variables.

For example, a hotel would need to consider:

- age groupings;
- males and females;
- usage groupings:
  - individual business use
  - group business use
  - personal use
  - family use
  - holiday use
- frequency groupings;
- nationalities;
- special interest groupings (say, leisure centre users).

Table 7.1   Sampling plan for depth interviews

	Customers' product	**Usage**	**Respondent's role in DMU**
Interview 1	Tissue	Large user	Buyer
Interview 2	Tissue	Medium user	Technical Manager
Interview 3	Manilla	Large user	General Manager
Interview 4	Manilla	Small user	Technical Manager
Interview 5	Board	Medium user	General Manager
Interview 6	Board	Small user	Production Manager
Interview 7	White copier	Large user	Production Manager
Interview 8	White copier	Medium user	Buyer

The longer the list, and more complex the customer satisfaction variables, the more cost effective it becomes to conduct exploratory research through focus groups, where six to eight customers can discuss their views together. (Focus groups are discussed later in this chapter.)

In the hotel example we would advise use of focus groups rather than the fairly large number of depth interviews which would be required.

CONDUCTING DEPTH INTERVIEWS

Recruiting respondents

The first thing you need to do is to recruit your respondents. This issue is fully covered in Chapter 13 for the main survey and the approach is very similar for depth interviews. The main difference is that depth interviews take longer – at least 30 minutes and preferably an hour and this time commitment should be clearly stated when the approach is made. You should also point out that the interview will take the form of a wide-ranging discussion and list topics that you wish to examine. As well as providing respondents with an opportunity to think about the issues in advance, it is useful to highlight the discursive nature of the session since most people will have preconceptions of a much more formal interview following a set questionnaire.

Suggested approach for depth interview

As depth interviews are relatively unstructured and there is a lot of note taking a decision has to be made regarding tape recording interviews and/or making handwritten notes.

Interviewers have to guide the discussion and also participate in it, whilst at the same time making quite detailed and intelligible notes – not an easy task, so recording interviews is advantageous in that nothing is missed. However, tape recording does create a considerable amount of additional work after the interview. Transcribing tapes is heavy on secretarial resources and the interviewer has to check and read the transcript in order to make summary notes on the interview's main points; alternatively, the interviewer can make summary notes from listening to the tape, but this takes even longer.

Moreover, there is no doubt that some people, especially managers worried about divulging sensitive information, will be inhibited by the tape recorder. There is a widely held view in the market research world that tape recording of interviews is normal and that respondents expect it, so you just produce your tape recorder at the outset of the interview as though it were the expected norm. Our view, however, is that whilst the tape recorder generally presents no problem in consumer interviews, we would not use it in business-to-business markets. In our experience it is perfectly satisfactory, and least time consuming, to take brief scribbled notes during the discussion and to go through them, adding details and filling in gaps where required, immediately after the interview. If you are conducting several interviews on the same site, allow time between interviews to review your notes.

Let's assume you are conducting a business interview and therefore not using the recorder. You should start by introducing yourself, reminding the respondent of the topics to be covered and the unstructured nature of the interview (even though this has previously been explained by letter) and establishing any time constraints. The golden rule is to start with tangible topics which the respondent will find easy, leaving the more difficult issues until later.

Begin the interview by asking the respondent some questions about their business and marketplace before moving the discussion on to their company's usage of the product or service in question, again starting with tangible issues such as what it is used for, when it is used, how much is used, and so on. Having established a good rapport with the respondent you can then move on to the more substantive topics which will cover your exploratory research objectives.

TOPICS FOR DEPTH INTERVIEWS

Depending on the purpose of the interview there are, of course, a multitude of topics to choose from. For our purposes we identify below seven which are typical.

1 The purchase decision and the DMU

The first serious topic for discussion should be designed to explore the customer's purchase decision for the product in question. This is often best achieved by asking the respondent how his or her organisation would approach the task of selecting a supplier for a new product or service which had not previously been purchased. This topic of discussion enables the interviewer to probe the full sequence of the purchase decision from initiation to the ultimate placing of the order, identifying all the members of the DMU as the decision unfolds.

If the respondent appears to be missing any steps or overlooking any staff who might be involved in the decision, the interviewer draws the discussion back by using a 'What about?' question: 'What about checking out the prospective suppliers' quality systems? Is that something you would do? ... How would it be done? ... Who would get involved?'

2 Supplier evaluation

Now you move on, asking how a new supplier would be evaluated. This should complete the identification of DMU members and will begin to explore the customer's expectations and priorities.

3 Purchasing criteria

You must fully explore what is important to the customer when he or she is selecting and evaluating a product similar to your own. Sometimes respondents reply in very general terms, citing quality, delivery or service and the like. But do probe more deeply; ask questions such as, 'When you say that service is important, what kind of things would a supplier have to do to be rated highly for service?' … and 'What sort of problems arise as a result of suppliers performing badly on delivery?' As the discussion progresses build a list of criteria that are important to the customer, criteria the supplier must get right if the customer is to be satisfied.

4 Priorities

Having established those factors which are important to the customer it is now necessary to clarify which are the most important. Some respondents may be inclined to say that they are all important. They probably are, but some will be more critical than others and these must be highlighted. This is best achieved initially by using the forced trade-off approach. You might ask, 'I realize that short lead times and reliable deliveries are both important to you, but which would cause more problems: a supplier that offered a slightly longer lead time than you requested or a supplier that promised to meet your lead time but was a little late with the delivery?'

In this way you can force a number of trade-offs to identify the factors that are most crucial to the customer. You can then use these factors as benchmarks, asking the respondent to rate other criteria against them, perhaps by giving each a mark out of ten.

Most respondents are able to generate a criteria list of around twenty factors at this stage and it is valuable to establish these as 'unprompted front-of-mind' issues. It is likely that many more factors or elements can be identified by conducting internal research, asking employees what they believe to be important to customers, and by studying corporate literature to identify product features or services the company claims to offer its customers. You should prepare such a list before commencing the exploratory study so that after the unprompted stage of the interview the respondent can be asked to rate all the factors.

This list is best structured in a logical sequence so that it covers the range of involvement between client and supplier. For example, there could be several factors connected with seeking information, then product features, placing orders, order fulfilment, invoicing, communication, training, service support, company image, attitude and so on.

The prepreprepared list, which may contain up to sixty factors in several sections, should fit on no more than three A4 sheets. Any factors from the respondent's list which are not already on your large list should be added before asking the respondent to rate all the factors in the following way.

Place the sheets of factors in front of the respondent and ask him or her to read through them all before starting to rate them. Ask if there is anything they do not understand or would like to add (perhaps from a list of criteria against which the company officially measures suppliers) and then ask them to select the single most important factor from anywhere in the list. Give this a rating of ten and ask the respondent to identify 'a handful' of other factors which they would consider of almost equal importance. The reasoning here is that whilst we do not wish to restrict the respondent in identifying the most important factors we do not wish to have half the list rated as vital since it is not only unlikely to be realistic but it will not fulfil the objective of establishing factor prioritization. It is also acceptable to suggest ratings of ten because in reality it is not the scores that matter but the order. The main research phase will accurately establish importance ratings for each of the final factors chosen.

Once they have selected between five and a dozen 10s suggest that they now have a 'handful' of 9s and these may be placed against the factors which are almost as important as the 10s. Incidentally, it is acceptable to most respondents that they write in the score themselves and whilst they are doing so you should note down any comments or explanations they may offer concerning their reasoning. You should actively ask for clarification on any factors which may not be entirely clear. Sometimes a respondent may be unwilling to rate aspects of the relationship where they have little or no involvement, but if you explain that it is their perception of the importance of the factor you are looking for it will generally be forthcoming so try to leave as few blanks as possible.

It is difficult for some respondents to focus on identifying their needs and resist the temptation to talk about any problems they have experienced with the supplier. You should reassure these people that you will talk about their satisfaction later and remind them occasionally that this is all about how important these factors are to them, regardless of who the supplier may be.

Go through the same process for 8s and then introduce a change by suggesting that factors of low importance should now be identified and perhaps scored anywhere between 1 and 4. This method is better than asking the respondent to rate each factor in turn from 1 to 10 because it is easier and more interesting to select factors of similar importance.

By this time the respondent has been over the list a number of times and is very familiar with it, so they will be able to rate any remaining items from 5 to 7 quite easily.

When all the factors have been given a rating ask the respondent if there is anything they wish to change so that the final list is a true reflection of their needs. Very few people will change anything at this stage but they must be given the opportunity so that you can be certain of the validity of the result.

This process is likely to take around 15 minutes but we have not finished with the list yet. Whilst for the purposes of designing the main questionnaire we have achieved our objective, the respondent will be disappointed if they have no opportunity to talk about their satisfaction with the supplier. As well as being good PR it is very useful to gather early information about issues which may arise in the main survey.

5   Supplier performance

It is not, however, necessary or advisable to obtain a satisfaction score for each factor on the list. The respondent will lose interest in the process if asked to rate things they do not consider important and in any event the data gathered here is qualitative and will not form part of the final quantitative result. What we advise is that you ask the respondent to consider the list again and identify any areas where they are not satisfied with the supplier's performance or where it could be considerably improved. Always ensure that the notes you make can be referred back to the factor under discussion.

6   Relative performance

The purpose of customer satisfaction measurement is to rate your company's performance so that you can identify areas where you need to improve in order to increase customer satisfaction. But in today's fast-changing world where good suppliers are constantly getting better it is very dangerous to rate your own company's performance in isolation.

Customers' perceptions and expectations will be affected by what other suppliers offer, so if you are going to anticipate how well you may have to perform in the future you must benchmark yourself against other suppliers – and customers' perceptions provide the ideal starting point.

The luxury of the added time afforded by depth interviews means that you can explore a number of techniques in your efforts to really understand how your company is regarded and how it is compared with other suppliers. Rather than try to compare other suppliers' performance on each factor, it is preferable to adopt a more qualitative approach since this will provide greater insight into customers' thinking and you will not generate any valid quantitative data from such a small number of depth interviews.

There are two approaches to this and you probably have time to use both of them during a one-hour depth interview. Firstly, ask the respondent to compare your company with 'best practice' suppliers. Ask the respondent to nominate his or her best supplier, find out the name of the company (if the respondent is prepared to divulge it) and explore in some depth the performance attributes that make that company such a good supplier. You can then ask the respondent to compare your company with that best practice model, because that is the standard to which you must aspire and which you will have to attain sooner or later.

The best practice supplier may not be a competitor or even be a comparable business to your own. If so, that should be seen as a positive as you can often learn more by comparing yourself with the best outside your own industry.

What you also need to do at this exploratory stage is to encourage the respondent to reveal the images which your company and its competitors present. This can be very difficult to achieve since many respondents will produce little more than a few vague generalizations if you ask them directly to describe your image and those of your competitors.

You must therefore adopt a different approach, using so-called projective techniques. These techniques are more frequently employed in focus groups, and will therefore be explained in more detail in the next section. Very briefly, projective techniques are based on the principle of asking indirect questions and using the answers to gradually draw out the respondent's attitudes. A projective technique which works very well in one-to-one interviews is 'creative comparisons'. To use that technique in this situation you might ask the respondent to imagine that your company and all your main competitors were famous sports or TV personalities. If so, who would they be? It is important to give a choice of personality types. Some people will relate readily to sports personalities, others more easily to TV personalities. Our experience is that virtually everyone is comfortable with one or the other.

The answers can be very enlightening. In a recent interview the respondent labelled two very large chemical companies (with virtually indistinguishable images) as Tony Blair and Gordon Brown. His reason was that whilst both companies were top quality, very professional and very good at what they do, the 'Tony Blair' company was more friendly, more approachable, whereas the 'Gordon Brown' company was more aloof, less customer oriented and more difficult to build a relationship with. Of course, it doesn't matter whether in real life the real Tony Blair is friendly or whether Gordon Brown is aloof. The character descriptions may be totally false. What matters is *why* the respondent chose the two personalities. He had described the image of the two chemical companies in a way that he probably would not have done if he had been asked a direct question.

Comments like these are of immeasurable value in building a picture of the images of competing suppliers, especially where they are very similar organisations, both good performers and perhaps supplying undifferentiated products.

7 Future trends

Although it is not strictly concerned with customer satisfaction measurement, a depth interview provides an ideal opportunity to ask respondents to look into the future and explain any changes they foresee in their organisation or their industry. This question will often provide exactly the kind of information that companies need to anticipate changes they will have to make to keep their customers satisfied in the future.

At the end of the interview always ask if there is anything that has not been covered and explain that as a result of these interviews a shorter questionnaire will be developed and it may be that their views will be sought again as part of a larger sample and you would very much like them to be included in the final result. We make a habit of explaining that when the results are complete they will be informed about the findings and about what will be done as a result in order to further improve their satisfaction. Thank them for their time.

Focus Groups

More commonly used in consumer markets than in business markets, focus groups are discussions involving around six to eight customers led by an experienced facilitator. They last for up to two hours, take place at neutral venues such as a hotel or specialist studio and are often recorded or videoed.

The purpose of focus groups is exactly the same as depth interviews: to improve your understanding of all aspects of the customer–supplier relationship. For that reason, the topics covered are very similar (see Table 7.2). In using focus groups rather than depth interviews the differences you will need to contend with are recruiting the groups, selecting a venue, and running the groups. Each of these is discussed below.

RECRUITING FOCUS GROUPS

Because of the time commitment you are asking a respondent to make which, in business markets especially, may be considerable once travel to and from the venue is taken into account, recruiting focus groups requires much time and effort. In business markets it is difficult to persuade people, especially more senior managers, to give so much time for the benefit of another company's research. One way to overcome this problem is to combine the focus group with corporate hospitality, such as a day at a sporting event. Time seems to become miraculously available for such outings and it is not usually a problem to request earlier attendance at the venue or at a neighbouring hotel in order to conduct the focus group.

Table 7.2   A comparison of depth interviews and focus groups

Depth interviews	Focus groups
• One-to-one interviews	• Group discussions with 6-8 people
• Typically used for B2B	• Typically used for B2C
• Held at respondent's premises	• Held in hotel, studio or meeting room
• No fee for respondents	• Incentive for participants
• Costly on interview time	• Costly on recruitment
• Medium skill level required	• Skilled facilitator essential
• Few respondent reservations	• Some inhibitions initially
• 60 minutes' duration	• 90 minutes' duration
• Some projective techniques feasible	• Ideally suited to projective techniques
• Usually interviewer driven	• Usually driven by group dynamics
• Can be recorded on audio	• Can be videoed and viewed

Consumers are easier to recruit though some encouragement may be required. Offer a modest incentive, such as £35 or a more valuable incentive for some difficult to recruit groups – such as social class AB men.

If your own product or service is of interest to consumers, that in itself can be an incentive thus maximizing its perceived value to the respondent whilst keeping down company costs, e.g. vouchers from a restaurant chain. Customers are normally recruited by telephone, using your own database to draw a representative sample. If customers visit your premises they could be recruited on site in a retail environment for example. Alternatively you could use targeted databases sending a mailed invitation with reply card or using the telephone to contact them. Door-to-door recruiting may be used if significant screening is required to identify precisely targeted groups; alternatively, advertising in special interest magazines which accurately reach your target segment is a possibility, although there is always a risk that a self-selected group will be biased toward special interests.

Always qualify respondents before inviting them, especially when you are not using your own database. Keep in mind that consumers without sufficient experience of using a given product or service (occasional flyers for an airline company) may be unable to make a worthwhile contribution to the group. By naming the focus group it becomes more meaningful to respondents. A 'Customer Advisory Panel', 'Customer Council', or a 'Customer Think Tank' not only have in themselves good PR value but will also raise the perceived importance of participants' contribution to your business.

Sampling should follow the advice which was given earlier regarding depth interviews in order to ensure that different customer groupings are represented. It is important that you avoid the worst forms of convenience sampling, such as asking friends or close business contacts to take part, just because they are easier to recruit. On the other hand, you do need to exercise some judgement when selecting participants because someone who will be unable or unwilling to articulate their views in a group setting is of no use. In business markets, participants can usually be screened from personal knowledge, but in consumer markets they will need to be qualified. This can be done by explaining to respondents the workings of a focus group and making certain that they are confident about participating.

You will also need to segment your focus groups for maximum effectiveness especially in consumer markets. A group whose participants have wildly differing attitudes and priorities can slide into negative argument rather than positive brainstorming. If you are going to run several focus group sessions you can use a quota sample for recruitment. (See Chapter 8 for a full explanation of sampling methods, including quota sampling.)

Focus groups do tend to suffer from a large number of withdrawals and no-shows and this can be a problem. Allow for this by recruiting more people than you need – up to twice as many. To some extent you can be flexible with numbers so as to accommodate response levels. If you want 8 participants, invite 12. If as few as 50 per cent turn up you can proceed with the minimum 6 participants. A higher than expected response rate allows you to increase the size of the group to a workable maximum of 12 participants, thus accommodating a response rate of 100 per cent.

Telephone respondents the day before the focus group to confirm their attendance. If the problem of too few participants arises you then still have time to transfer participants from other groups or from a reserve list. In deliberately over-recruiting you are more likely to have a problem with over-attendance, in which case you can deter some respondents, perhaps by placing them on the reserve list for future focus groups.

In organisational markets, too, problems with last-minute withdrawals occur, so you still need to over-recruit. However, be more businesslike in your handling of over-attendance since it is not acceptable to inform busy managers at the last minute that they are not required. The safest strategy for organisational markets is to plan two simultaneous focus groups. If you are using an external agency there will be no problem sourcing two experienced facilitators. With a good turnout you can run the two groups as planned but where attendance is very low you simply run one group with two facilitators, and your customers will never know that attendance was poor.

Finally, focus group recruitment is made easier next time if you retain respondents' names, addresses and telephone numbers, having asked them if they would be prepared to participate in future research. This is particularly valuable when your own specialized customer base is difficult to identify or to access.

ARRANGING THE VENUE

The venue should be on neutral ground. It should be perceived by participants as an attractive place to go and must offer a comfortable, relaxing environment for conducting the focus group. Hotels are commonly used as venues as they can meet most catering requirements and provide suitable meeting rooms. Providing refreshments on arrival helps to break the ice. Always check the venue facilities beforehand as some hotels are too austere to provide the right kind of relaxing atmosphere for consumer focus groups. For business focus groups this is less of a problem as most managers are accustomed to attending meetings in hotels.

It is possible to hire purpose-built studios in London and some provincial cities. These provide relaxing sitting room-type surroundings and have facilities to record and video the proceedings. They also tend to have viewing rooms behind one-way mirrors enabling staff from your company to view the proceedings live if you wish!

To maximize attendance the venue must be convenient for the participants. This means within 30 minutes' drive for business people and no more than 15 to 20 minutes for consumers. For socio-economic groups assumed to have no car the venue must be accessible by public transport or have a taxi service provided. If a business focus group is linked to a hospitality event travel distances can, of course, be much greater. The timing of the event needs consideration as evenings and weekends are generally more convenient for many customer groups.

CONDUCTING FOCUS GROUPS

As with depth interviews, always brief focus group participants before the event. This can be done in writing, which allows participants to think about the issues. The session starts with a buffet, a few drinks and an informal chat to allow everyone to meet.

The facilitator begins the focus group with a formal welcome to the participants. The agenda is outlined and the respondents are briefed as to what is expected of them (total frankness, all ideas expressed however silly they may seem) and explanations are given regarding any technical aids to be used, such as video recording. The facilitator should also explain why the focus group is being held, what feedback participants can expect and when they will receive their incentive for attending!

The facilitator should also point out that there will be a representative from the company available at the end of the session to deal with any individual queries. If you don't do this, some respondents will want to spend a considerable amount of time on personal complaints and experiences and this can soon eat into a ninety-minute focus group. By referring participants to the company representative after the session the facilitator will be able to minimize such distractions. It is important, by the way, that the company representative is not present during the focus group since this might inhibit some of the more critical comments.

As in all research exercises it is best to start the discussion with easy topics, subjects on which all participants will have views, preferably quite strong ones. This will tend to stimulate discussion within the group, allowing the facilitator to sit back and let group dynamics take over before possibly interjecting with a few prompts when it is time to move the group on to the next topic. A focus group of small business owners meeting to discuss their satisfaction with accountancy services might start with the question, 'What are the things you like most and least about your dealings with your accountant?'

It can sometimes be useful to divide the session into two parts and withhold the identity of the supplier until the second part. This enables early discussion of generic matters without the distraction of having a particular supplier in mind. Topics include what matters to customers and the relative importance of those factors as components of customer satisfaction. Explore those levels of performance which participants expect from suppliers and how this might change in the future. Stimulating group ideas is assisted if participants have been asked at the briefing stage to come to the focus group prepared to talk about their own experience, of wonderful or diabolical service in the relevant market-place. Having identified customer experiences and priorities, move on to a comparison of suppliers. This is more objective if the identity of the sponsoring organisation has still to be revealed.

Finally, identify the supplier and focus the remainder of the session on participants' views and experiences of that supplier.

One great advantage of focus groups is their suitability for the use of projective techniques. When probing participant attitudes the best way to elicit the required information is not to ask a direct question but to approach the matter indirectly.

Allow respondents to develop and express their views in a less self-conscious manner. In its early stages this technique was sometimes referred to as the 'friendly Martian' method. A group (or an individual) might be asked how they would advise a friendly Martian (who, of course, had no knowledge of the subject) on, for example, the best method of heating a house. Faced with this, respondents would go back to basics, explaining to the Martian how to go about the task, explaining in the process their own beliefs and attitudes. Had they been asked the direct question, 'How did you decide upon the best method of heating your house?' the respondents would have taken much more for granted and may even have been less honest in their appraisal.

More recently, many group techniques have been developed using this friendly Martian principle. Some are discussed below.

Drawing pictures

'Thematic apperception' is based upon the assumption that it is easier and more accurate for people to describe their real feelings in pictures rather than words. In their book, *Qualitative Market Research*, Gordon and Langmaid described the results of a survey into attitudes towards TV companies in which 50 respondents were asked to draw four UK television stations as if they were people: BBC1 was a rather dignified old lady, with a high neck blouse, tweeds, pearls and knitting in her lap; BBC2 a serious and academic man of middle age wearing a corduroy jacket; ITV a loud-mouthed money-grabbing yob; and Channel 4 a split personality, wearing a Walkman playing opera in one ear and rock music in the other.

Such portraits paint clearer pictures of how TV stations are perceived than you would get if people were asked to describe them in words. This is apparent in the exercise carried out by the manufacturer of Domestos bleach who wanted to find out what people thought of the brand. Respondents were asked to draw Domestos as a person. One drew a knight in shining armour, another drew Mrs Thatcher. The results apparently reassured Domestos about the accuracy of their brand image.

Marketing executives are not always happy with the results of similar research. In one survey, respondents tended to draw a sick child in bed when asked to visualize Lucozade. Thereafter, in an effort to strengthen brand image and to widen its market, the company recruited Olympic decathlon champion Daley Thompson to star in its Lucozade advertising.

Creative comparisons

Very similar in principle to drawing pictures, creative comparisons endow companies and brands with personalities by linking them with easily recognized people or things. The technique of anthropomorphizing companies as sports or TV personalities was mentioned earlier. A similar technique, very successful in customer perception exercises, is using cars to symbolize the personalities of different companies.

In one of our market standing surveys, a large, well known British company was facing growing competition from a recently arrived Japanese competitor. The British company was described as a Volvo, trundling up the inside lane of the motorway, well within the speed limit, very safe, very reliable, not exciting or innovative but you knew it would always get there in the end. The Japanese company was a BMW, very good quality, high profile and very aggressive, flying up the outside lane of the motorway and about to overtake the Volvo. The only problem was, you were never totally sure that the BMW was going to stay on the road and reach its destination. The implication here was that there might be continuity of supply problems with the Japanese company.

Psychodrama

Sometimes called 'role play' or 'fantasy situations', psychodrama asks respondents to imagine they are products. Individuals describe and discuss their feelings about being used as the products are used or act out the process of being used.

In one set of psychodrama exercises, groups of typical consumers of pain killers were asked to act out the process of a person's headache being cured by a pain killer. In each group of three people one person had to be the sufferer, another had to be the pain and the third was to represent the pain killer. After a brief discussion of how they would do it, most groups came out and showed the pain ruthlessly dominating the sufferer until the pain killer burst upon the scene and aggressively fought and subdued the pain, making the sufferer smile again. Some groups acted out different plays. They still showed the pain dominating the sufferer but they showed the pain killer soothing the pain from the sufferer, being assertive but not violent. In the group discussions which followed the mimes, respondents were asked to put brand names to the two different types of pain killer which had been portrayed. The fighting pain killer presented people with no problem, many of the well-known brands being mentioned in this category. But the soothing pain killer was much more difficult, people finding it difficult or impossible to put a brand name to it. But, interestingly, there was a lot of support for the idea of a soothing pain killer.

Had the researcher identified a group of consumers with an unsatisfied need? Yes! Before long Nurofen was being positioned as the pain killer which soothes away headaches.

Psychodrama can also be used very effectively for exploratory research for customer satisfaction measurement, particularly where large organisational suppliers are involved in consumer markets. To give a health service example, one actor might be a large NHS hospital with a second participant acting as a patient, whilst third and fourth participants act out the relationship a patient has with a small private hospital. The whole group then discusses the role plays during which customer perceptions are described and explained.

CUSTOMERS' PRIORITIES

Having used some of the techniques outlined above to identify a long list of things that are of some importance to customers, the remainder of the focus group needs to become much more structured. First list on a flipchart all the customer requirements that have been mentioned in the discussions during the first half of the focus group. See if anybody can think of any more to add, then ask all participants to nominate their top priority as a benchmark and give it a score out of ten. This should be done on an individual basis, not collectively as a group. It is best to give out pencils and answer sheets enabling everybody to write down their individual views.

Having established everybody's top priority each participant can read down the list and give every customer requirement a score out of ten, to denote its relative importance compared with their top priority. Having completed all the groups you can work out the average scores given by all the participants. The requirements that are most important to most customers will receive the highest scores and should be used in the questionnaire for the main survey.

Conclusions

- It is arrogant, and almost always mistaken, to assume that you know enough about what matters most to customers to design a questionnaire without first undertaking exploratory research.
- Exploratory research must achieve two specific objectives:
  - it must identify the full extent of the population to be surveyed, which may need to include those people who influence the purchase decision and its evaluation as well as the buyers themselves. In business markets the decision-making unit can be large and complex;
  - it must define the component elements of customer satisfaction; in other words, exactly what it is that determines how satisfied, or dissatisfied, customers are after a purchase (referred to elsewhere as the customer value package).
- Depth interviews are the most usual way of carrying out exploratory research for customer satisfaction measurement, especially in business markets.
- Focus groups are more successful at uncovering and explaining deep seated attitudes and beliefs but are time consuming and costly to organize. They afford a very suitable environment for using projective techniques to stimulate ideas and facilitate customer articulation of attitudes which may be difficult to express in words.

8 SAMPLING

AIMS

By the end of this chapter you will:
- Appreciate the importance of accurate sampling.
- Understand the different methods of drawing a sample.
- Be able to select the most appropriate sampling method for your own situation.

On completion of exploratory research a good understanding will have been gained as to what types of question need to be asked to what kinds of people. At this stage, a sample of people to interview can now be drawn up, decisions taken on how the survey will be administered, and the questionnaire itself designed.

The Importance of Sampling

Most markets contain far too many customers to undertake a census where everybody is interviewed. It is only feasible and only necessary in most cases to interview a small proportion of people who make up the 'total population' in a market. The purpose of sampling is to select a small number of 'units' from the target 'population' in such a way that the sample is *truly representative* of the total population being surveyed.

To defend the validity of the results of your survey as the basis for taking important and perhaps costly management decisions, accurate sampling is absolutely essential. The easiest and most effective way for obstructive colleagues or a cynical superior to cast doubt on the validity of your findings is to claim that your small sample is not representative of the views of customers as a whole. They may use anecdotal evidence to support their argument, generalizing wildly from the particular. Such tactics, if aggressively advanced, can be very powerful in meetings. Your most effective defence against such tactics is to demonstrate a sound sampling methodology as outlined in this chapter.

SAMPLING RELIABILITY

The reliability of a sample is judged on repeatability. If you did exactly the same survey again but with a different randomly selected sample of customers, would you get the same result? This is primarily determined by sample size. The larger the sample the more reliable the result will be, but this general assertion can be broken down into three specific aspects of sample reliability: precision, confidence level and variance.

Precision

The precision of a survey result can be defined in general terms as its accuracy. If you surveyed 100 people and asked them if Great Britain should bid for hosting the Olympic Games and 38 per cent said 'yes', 40 per cent said 'no' and the remaining 22 per cent said 'don't know', you might find that the precision of your result is +/– 5 per cent. That means that if you conducted the same survey with a different sample the result for the 'yes' vote could be anywhere between 33 and 43 per cent. With a much larger sample, e.g. 1000, you would achieve much better precision, say +/– 1 per cent. Research textbooks call this concept the confidence interval, but in view of the potential confusion with the confidence level, we prefer the term precision.

Confidence level

You can calculate the precision of your sample at various confidence levels. Absolutely critical research such as medical research is typically conducted at 99 per cent confidence level. If our sample for the Olympic Games survey had been designed to 1 per cent precision at 99 per cent confidence level, it would mean that if you conducted the survey 100 times you would expect a result within +/– 1 per cent on 99 of those occasions. In other words, the risk of the result differing by more than 1 per cent from a census is 100:1 against. It is normal for samples for commercial market research to be based on 95 per cent confidence levels, meaning that you can be confident that the result would fall within your stated precision at least 19 out of every 20 times that the survey was conducted.

Variance

The precision that you can expect from a specific sample size at a given confidence level can still differ considerably depending on the variance of views held by the respondents. Common sense dictates that if you question people about a topic on which almost everybody holds the same view (e.g. 'Should murdering people be against the law?'), you would expect a virtually identical result however many times you conduct the survey. So the lower the variance (the range of views expressed), the more reliable any sample size will be at any confidence level. In our Olympic Games survey the variance was much higher. Roughly half of those with a view felt we should bid for the Games, with the other half holding the opposite opinion. Since reliability declines as variance increases, larger sample sizes are needed for surveys where respondents' views differ considerably. Since the variance will never be known with certainty until after the survey has been undertaken, many

Table 8.1   Standard statistical table

Required precision (+/–%)	Standard deviation assumed						
	0.5	0.75	0.1	1.25	1.5	1.75	2.0
5	4	9	15	24	35	47	61
4.5	5	11	19	30	43	58	76
4	6	14	24	38	54	74	96
3.5	8	18	31	49	71	96	125
3	11	24	43	67	96	131	171
2.5	15	35	61	96	138	188	246
2	24	54	96	150	216	294	384
1.5	43	96	171	267	384	523	683
1	96	216	384	600	864	1176	1537
0.75	171	384	683	1067	1537	2092	2732
0.5	384	864	1537	2401	3457	4706	6147
0.25	1537	3457	6147	9604	13830	18824	24586

The table shows required sample size against various levels of standard deviation and precision. For example: if variation in the sample is small (low S.D. of 0.5) and required precision is within 1%, a sample of 96 will suffice. If variation in the sample is large (high S.D. of 2.0) and required precision is within 1%, a sample of 1537 will be needed.

researchers use standard statistical tables like the one shown in Table 8.1 to determine the required sample size based on an anticipated degree of variance. Based on our experience of conducting a very large number of customer satisfaction surveys, we know that the variance for that type of survey is lower than it is for many types of market research, so sample sizes can be rather lower for customers' satisfaction surveys.

DETERMINING THE SAMPLE SIZE

How then is the sample size to be determined to ensure that it is 'truly representative'? One easy answer is to carry out a census survey, especially in many business-to-business markets where there is a relatively small number of large customers. More realistically, you might undertake a census of larger users, covering a large proportion of sales in the market-place, with a sample of the many smaller users. More guidance on 'stratified sampling' is given in the following two sections of this chapter.

It is not feasible for most businesses to undertake a census survey, so a sample will have to be drawn, but how large should it be? It is not the total size of the customer population that matters but the actual size of your sample. For example, if Company A has 100 customers and Company B has 100000 customers, Company B will not need 1000 times as many respondents to achieve a sufficiently accurate sample. In practice, once a sample size exceeds 200 in a customer satisfaction survey (whatever the size of the total population) it is likely to give an acceptable degree of accuracy provided it is random and representative (see next section). With

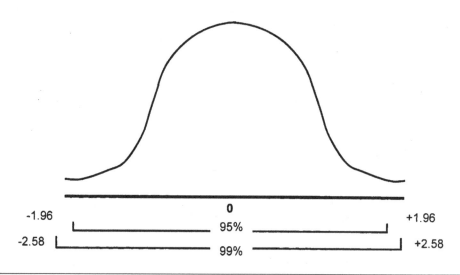

Figure 8.1   A normal distribution curve

a sample size in excess of 200 the data generated by the survey will conform with the normal distribution curve as shown in Figure 8.1.

Most responses will not deviate far from the arithmetical mean and the small proportion of less typical responses at either extreme will not be sufficient to skew the overall result.

Most samples for customer satisfaction surveys would fall in the range of 200–500 respondents. Based on our experience this will yield precision of around +/– 1 per cent at the 95 per cent confidence level for the vast majority of CSM surveys. Increasing the sample size would improve the accuracy but at a very high cost. Typically, to double the precision (for example from +/– 2 per cent to +/– 1 per cent) you would have to increase the sample size by four times, quadrupling the cost of your survey.

The only reason for increasing sample size is when several distinctive segments exist and you need to be confident that responses for each segment are representative. For example, a mail-order seed firm serving 50 000 customers in the course of a year carries out a telephone survey to measure customer satisfaction. A sample of 200 customers would provide an acceptable level of accuracy for identifying satisfaction even though it is only 0.4 per cent of the total population. However, should the seed firm wish to establish the relative levels of satisfaction of customers buying different product categories or customers in different age groups, it would need a sample of 100 for each segment to be confident of the accuracy of the results. A sample of 50 per segment is said to be the absolute minimum.

Companies, therefore, serving relatively small numbers of customers will need to survey quite a high proportion of the total population to be confident that the results are representative. Census surveys are consequently very common in industrial markets. Companies in mass consumer markets often do not need larger sample sizes than those in industrial markets unless they wish to segment their customers into a larger number of sub-groups (which they often do).

Even in consumer markets, samples of 500 customers usually allow plenty of scope for demographic and behavioural segmentation. There is only one situation where organisations need consider sample sizes larger than 500 – multiple outlets. Retailers, banks, industrial distributors and many other organisations often have multiple outlets, sometimes several hundred. Using the example of a large supermarket, a randomly selected national sample of 500 customers would provide a very reliable overall guide to customer satisfaction with the company across the UK generally, but satisfaction could vary considerably by outlet. In fact, the best way for organisations with multiple outlets to improve customer satisfaction overall is often to focus on improving satisfaction at the poorest performing outlets rather than trying to address company-wide PFIs (priorities for improvement) across all outlets. For organisations with multiple outlets the most effective CSM programmes will survey customers from all outlets and produce a result at outlet level. For the outlet result to be reliable, at least 100, and preferably 200, customers should be surveyed from each one. Clearly this can lead to some very large samples at the national level. A multiple with 500 outlets surveying 200 customers from each would end up with a total sample size of 100 000.

But, before we leave the subject of sample size, it is worth reflecting that in the UK more and more organisations are sending out more and more questionnaires. It would not be uncommon for a large bank, for example, to send out over one million customer satisfaction questionnaires per annum. We must also remember that the bank's customers are also the customers of many other organisations such as airlines, insurance companies, utilities and building societies to name but a few; and these other organisations, too, want to measure their customers' satisfaction, often by using self-completion postal questionnaires. There is already evidence that the British nation is beginning to suffer from questionnaire fatigue, reflected in falling response rates, especially in London and the South East. It is in everybody's interest in the long run to keep sample sizes down. Our advice is to carry out a more thorough survey with a small, carefully selected sample rather than sending out thousands of questionnaires in the hope of getting enough back to form a reasonable sample. A high-quality, low-quantity approach will improve the detail and accuracy of your results, removing any doubt of bias in sampling and contributing to a reduction in everyone's questionnaire fatigue!

Sampling Options

There are two types of sample: random and non-random. We will look briefly at each in turn, with the full range of sampling choices illustrated in Figure 8.2.

RANDOM SAMPLES

Also known as a probability sample, random sampling must give every unit in the survey population an equal chance of being included in the sample.

A unit would usually be one individual in a consumer survey but in organisational markets it could be a company or an individual respondent.

Simple random sampling

To draw a simple random sample, the researcher starts with a complete list (the population or sample frame) of the market or group to be surveyed. The size of the sample is determined and chosen from the complete list on a random basis, which means that each individual in the sample frame has the same likelihood of ending up in the sample. One way of achieving this would be to use a computer to draw out names or numbers at random. Another method would be to draw a systematic random sample as in the following example.

In a limited geographical area a researcher has a population of 10 000 in the sample frame. The survey sample is 200. Dividing 10 000 by 200 produces an answer of 50. There are thus 200 equal groups containing 50 people in that population.

The researcher chooses at random a number between 1 and 50; say, 37. The next step is to identify the 37th, 87th, 137th, 187th, 237th, etc., person on the list of 10 000 people. This

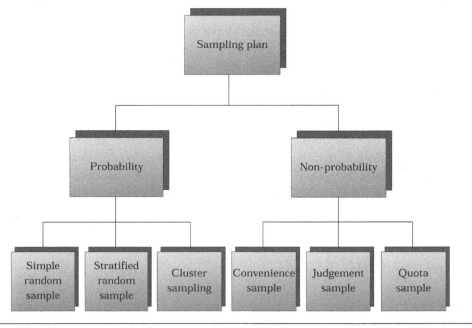

Figure 8.2   Sampling methods

produces a systematic random sample of 200. Using statistical techniques the researcher can calculate the level of certainty with which results obtained from the random sample can be used to predict results for the total population of 10 000. The larger the sample the higher the degree of accuracy.

Stratified random sampling

Random sampling can sometimes distort results in markets where some customers are more important than others. In this case stratified random sampling is used. The method involves weighting the sample on the basis of the importance of various segments making up the market. Imagine a company with 6 200 customers segmented as: 5 000 light users accounting for £3m turnover; 1 000 medium users accounting for £20m turnover; 200 heavy users accounting for £25m turnover. A randomly chosen sample of 200 would not be fully representative of the company's business. Since the heavy users account for half the company's turnover they should also make up half the sample, the medium users representing 40 per cent of turnover should be 40 per cent of the sample and the light users, although half the population, make up only 10 per cent of sales and should therefore form no more than 10 per cent of the sample. Thus, the 'strata' of the stratified sample would be: 100 heavy users randomly chosen from the heavy user population of 200; 80 medium users randomly chosen from the medium user population of 1 000 and 20 light users randomly chosen from the population of 5 000.

Cluster sampling

The third and less costly method of producing a random sample, is cluster sampling. It reduces the cost of research by concentrating the sampling in one or several representative areas and is widely used in consumer markets. A random sample drawn nationally would involve interviewing small numbers of respondents in scattered locations. For personal interviewing this would be time consuming and costly. Random samples are therefore often drawn from a small number of tightly defined locations (clusters) deemed to be typical of the target market in question. This method is considered to be of sufficient statistical accuracy for most commercial market research involving the general public.

NON-RANDOM SAMPLES

Non-random (non-probability) samples are quicker, easier and cheaper to carry out but they may not be as representative of the market as a whole and statistical techniques cannot be legitimately used to apply levels of certainty to the results. The three main types of non-random sample are discussed below.

Convenience samples

This would involve gathering data from any convenient group, for example, passers-by in a street interview situation. Supermarket shoppers are more easily contacted in a supermarket than at some other place, but those recruited on any single occasion do not necessarily represent all shoppers of all stores at all times. Sampling needs to be structured to reflect the target population. If the sampling method is not clearly specified there is always a danger that the person responsible for the survey will take the easy option, interviewing close contacts, friends or even family members. Quite clearly, convenience samples taken in this way are unlikely to be representative and, if used, could invalidate an entire survey.

Judgemental samples

Here respondents would be selected on the basis of the researcher's (or interviewer's) belief that they were representative of the target market being studied. The more knowledgeable the person who selects the respondents the more accurate it is likely to be. For exploratory research a judgemental sample is perfectly acceptable since the research is qualitative and will be used only to design the main survey and not as a basis for management decision making. The main survey will be quantitative and its results will be used to make definitive statements about the priorities of customers in general and their views on the performance of an organisation. For the findings to be taken seriously, especially as a sound basis for management decisions, people must be convinced that the results do accurately reflect the views of the market as a whole. A judgemental sample, however objective and sound it is in the eyes of the sampler, will never be sufficiently convincing.

Quota samples

Quota controlled samples are frequently used by commercial market research agencies to minimize the cost of fieldwork. The research agency initially uses secondary sources to divide the population into groups. In the case of consumer research these groups will often be based on social grade and age. The research agency, using as a basis published statistics, decides on controlled quotas (or groups) of respondents for each interviewer in the field. For example, the interviewer might be told to question 20 females aged between 20 and 35 years, 15 females aged between 36 and 50 years and 25 females aged 51 years and over. Using this method the agency can be certain that the quotas are an accurate reflection of the population being surveyed. However, there is no guarantee that the individuals within those age bands will represent an accurate sample of all females within that age band. The interviewer will simply question the first 20 females who agree to be interviewed in the 20- to 35-year-old age band. This method is very commonly employed in commercial research simply because it is often considered to be the most cost effective way of producing data of sufficient accuracy.

DRAWING A SAMPLE

In order to draw a sample for your own customer survey follow the steps described below.

Step 1: Survey objectives

The first consideration is whether you are carrying out a customer perception survey or a market standing survey. If you are only surveying your own customer base, Step 2 will almost certainly be much easier than it will if you have to draw an accurate sample of all the buyers in the market-place. Objectives may also range from continuous tracking to a full strategic baseline survey. For continuous tracking, non-probability, even convenience samples may be perfectly acceptable. For example, a dental practice might rely on the views of the small proportion of patients who complete a post-treatment questionnaire for its continuous tracking; or, an office equipment servicing company may survey the first 20 firms who can be contacted by telephone from a list of customers receiving service visits during the previous week.

On the other hand, an annual baseline survey – which will have to re-benchmark customers' priorities and fully assess an organisation's performance – must be based on a truly representative sample.

Step 2: Define the sampling frame

Whatever your survey population, you will now need to define it in terms of an accessible list of names (a sampling frame) from which you can effectively draw a sample.

For most organisations carrying out a customer perception survey the sampling frame will be obvious – it will be your own customer list. Most companies now capture data on their customers, but if your organisation doesn't know who its customers are you will have to use a quota sample. For example, a retailer could set a quota sample of customers visiting its stores. A manufacturer selling through distributors would have to gain the cooperation of the distributors if it wanted to survey end users. (And the distributors themselves would form a valid population for customer satisfaction measurement, but that would require a separate survey.)

For a market standing survey, the population encompasses all the buyers of that product in the market-place. In many mature industrial markets all the buyers, customers and non-customers alike, will probably be known to the supplier. They are probably visited by the sales force, so a comprehensive sampling frame can be compiled even if it does not exist on the computer. For markets with larger numbers of customers a list such as a relevant directory or *Yellow Pages* could be used. It probably will not include every single company that buys the product but will usually be sufficiently comprehensive.

In consumer markets the electoral roll is the most comprehensive list but to target by segment there are many commercial lists available for the population as a whole or for special interest groups. But remember that to draw a random sample you will need a list on which to base it.

Step 3: Identify the strata

If you wish to segment the market into a number of customer types or strata you need to identify the strata. The more you stratify the population the larger your sample will need to be if it is going to be truly representative of each segment as well as the population as a whole. If you need to use a stratified quota sample you will have to define the segments on which the quotas will be based.

Step 4: The value of different units

In most consumer markets the value of each individual unit (customer) within the sample frame is similar. An affluent family tends to have a higher average spend at the supermarket than a poor family, but the difference in value to the supermarket between higher and lower spend customers is not sufficiently great to be worthwhile including as a variable in the sampling: the supermarket's sampling frame considers each individual customer (unit) to be equal.

The value of individual customers in industrial markets is normally far from equal. The value of the largest customer (defined in terms of purchasing power) may be 1000 times or even 10 000 times greater than that of the smallest customer. In such cases your sample would not be truly representative of the market if you assigned an equal value to each customer in the sample frame. You would therefore need to draw a stratified random sample as described in the previous section and determine the values (typically based on usage rates) which will be used to assign customers to the different strata or segments.

Step 5: The DMU and other sampling variables

In most surveys in consumer markets each customer will be adequately represented by one individual. Sometimes a family decision-making unit will be involved (for example a major household purchase), in which case the sample should include a representative mix of both partners, not just the individual who signed the order.

For business markets, as we saw in Chapter 6, the decision-making unit is often much larger and more complex and this needs to be reflected as accurately as possible in the sample of individual respondents drawn for your survey. As well as accurately reflecting the individual involved in the purchase decision your sample may need to accommodate other variables such as end-user industry in business surveys and social grade or family life-cycle grouping in consumer surveys.

Many surveys need to reflect regional variations. Multiple branched depots, dealerships, service centres or sales districts must be taken into account at the sampling stage. When results of your survey are national, staff at individual branches or service centres will tend to say, 'That's all very well, but these results are for the whole country. They don't reflect what our customers think of us in this region.'

Therefore, your results must be meaningful to the most local units that create customer satisfaction and can do something about improving it where necessary. Consequently, if you have multiple branches, dealerships and so on, and need to relate the survey results to the performance of each one, the size of your total sample may be increased considerably in order to cover each outlet adequately.

Step 6: Determine the sampling method

You now have all the information you need to decide on a sampling method and draw your sample. The first decision is whether or not to opt for the most accurate type of sample, a random sample, or whether it is not possible or cost effective to do so.

It is our belief that you should use a random sample whenever feasible as long as it is not prohibitively costly. This procedure makes it far easier to defend your findings as a sound basis for decision making. Sometimes, where the identities of individual customers are not known, it will be impossible to draw a random sample. In such cases a quota sample will be the best option and its accuracy can be maximized by using published statistics to define the quotas so that the sample reflects the known composition of the market as accurately as possible.

In organisational markets it should always be possible to draw a random sample for a customer perception survey and it will usually be feasible to identify or compile a sufficiently comprehensive sampling frame to draw a random sample (often a stratified random sample) for a market standing survey. This will be a random sample of customers and each customer will be an organisation. Having determined which organisations will be surveyed you will have to select the individual respondents. At this point there is considerable difficulty maintaining the random nature of your sample. With many organisations having large and complex DMUs it will be prohibitively costly, and often impossible, to compile a comprehensive sampling frame of individuals. You will therefore have to compile the best list of names that you can (and companies with a large sales force can often produce surprisingly long lists of contacts) and then draw a random sample from that list. Even though the sampling frame cannot be relied on to be comprehensive, its random sampling will ensure that your closest contacts stand no more chance of being included in the survey than individuals whom you know far less well.

Drawn in this way your sample will be as truly representative as it is practical to make it. The next section illustrates this sample type, using a worked example.

WORKED EXAMPLE

ABC Supplies is a typical industrial company supplying a raw material used in various process industries. As with many industrial markets a large proportion of the consumption is accounted for by a very small number of heavy users (see Figure 8.3).

To simplify the matter, we will assume that a sample size of 100 has been adopted. Since this is a business-to-business example, the composition of the sample should reflect purchasing power. Thus: the four large users who represent one-third of the market should form one-third of the sample; the 40 medium users the next third; and the 40 small users the final third.

If a simple random sample were used the four large users would have to provide 33 respondents,

Value segments	Interviews	Respondents
Large users: 4 companies = 40k tonnes Medium users: 40 companies = 40k tonnes Small users: 400 companies = 40k tonnes Total market = 120k tonnes	Large users: 20 interviews Medium users: 40 interviews Small users: 40 interviews Total sample = 100 interviews	Industry Paint = 60% Textiles = 30% Paper = 10% DMU Production = 30% Purchasing = 30% Technical = 20% Quality = 10% General = 10%

Figure 8.3   Worked example, drawing a sample for ABC Supplies

a tall order even for such large companies operating from several sites. It is far more practical and just as accurate to use a disproportionate random sample which involves applying a variable sampling fraction to the different strata.

Thus, the medium and small users would provide one respondent for each tonne used whilst the large users would provide one respondent for every two tonnes used. The under-representation of the large users can be corrected at the analysis stage by doubling the value of their scores. This would give the equivalent of 40 respondent values in the large user sector and 120 respondent values altogether, with each stratum contributing one-third of the values in line with usage.

The large and medium user companies do not need to be samples. All will be included in the survey. The 400 small companies, however, will provide only 40 respondents so 1 in every 10 should be selected. This is done by printing a list in tonnage-only of small users, drawing a random number between 1 and 10 and using that number to select the first member of the sample. So, if the number 6 were generated, the 6th, 16th, 26th, 36th and so on companies on the list would be included in the sample.

The number of respondents from each company is now clarified. The medium and small users are straightforward. Each medium user and each small user drawn in the sample will provide one respondent. The four large users, however, need to provide 20 respondents. These should not be divided equally between them but should reflect their consumption, resulting in the split of respondents shown in Table 8.2.

The next step is the necessity to ensure that the sample reflects the usage by industrial sector: 60 per cent of the product is used in the paint industry, 30 per cent in textiles and 10 per cent

Table 8.2   Distribution of respondents in the large user segment

Company	Usage	Number of respondents
A	16 tonnes	8
B	10 tonnes	5
C	8 tonnes	4
D	6 tonnes	3

Table 8.3   Randomly ordered list of DMU members

Original list	Randomly ordered list
1 Production	3 Production
2 Production	9 Quality
3 Production	8 Technical
4 Purchasing	5 Purchasing
5 Purchasing	4 Purchasing
6 Purchasing	1 Production
7 Technical	10 General
8 Technical	7 Technical
9 Quality	6 Purchasing
10 General	2 Production

in paper production. The large and medium segments therefore will inevitably reflect usage by industry segment. Check that you will have 72 respondents from the paint industry, 36 from textiles and 12 from paper – not forgetting to double the actual number of respondents for each company in the large user segment. If the split does not come out exactly right the problem will be in the small user segment.

Let's assume that you have ended up with 73 respondents from paint and only 35 from textiles. You should pick at random one of the small users that you have selected from the paint industry and remove it from your sample. Again at random, select an additional small user from the textile industry and add it to the sample. You now have a sample which accurately reflects purchasing power and the split by industry segment.

The final task is to reflect the composition of the DMU as accurately as possible. It is here that an element of judgemental sampling will inevitably creep in. In Figure 8.3 the composition of the DMU and the relative influence of its members has been gleaned from the exploratory

Table 8.4   Accurate coverage of the DMU

Company	Respondent	Position of respondent
A	Respondent 1	Production
	Respondent 2	Quality
	Respondent 3	Technical
	Respondent 4	Purchasing
	Respondent 5	Purchasing
	Respondent 6	Production
	Respondent 7	General
	Respondent 8	Technical
B	Respondent 1	Purchasing
	Respondent 2	Production
	Respondent 3	Production
	Respondent 4	Quality
	Respondent 5	Technical
C	Respondent 1	Purchasing
	Respondent 2	Purchasing
	Respondent 3	Production
	Respondent 4	General
D	Respondent 1	Technical
	Respondent 2	Purchasing
	Respondent 3	Production

research, but with quite a small number of depth interviews carried out, a considerable element of judgement must be included to arrive at the outcome shown.

Having arrived at what you believe to be the closest possible representation of the DMU you must ensure that it is reflected as accurately and as objectively as possible in your sample, by adopting the following procedure. Firstly, list the members of the DMU using frequency of mention in the depth interviews to reflect their relative influence as shown in the left-hand column of Table 8.3. Next choose numbers 1 to 10 in a random order (for example, pull them out of a hat) and re-list the members of the DMU in that order, as shown in the right-hand column.

Place the randomly ordered list next to the companies you have drawn in your sample, listing the multiple respondents for the larger user companies as shown in Table 8.4.

The companies in the sample drawn from the medium and small user segment, each of which will have one respondent, should be listed in tonnage order, with the randomly ordered list of

DMU members placed alongside and repeated eight times to cover the 80 respondents required from medium and small users. In some smaller companies there may be problems where there is nobody with, for example, the title 'Technical Manager'. In such cases you have to use the closest equivalent, that is, the person responsible for technical matters.

If you have more contact names than you need for a given company (for example, Company D has more than one person responsible for production) the selected respondent must be chosen randomly.

There is one final factor which might yet affect the accuracy of your sampling – refusals. If you follow the guidelines in Chapter 13, refusals can be minimized, but you may get some. If so, complete the interviews with all the willing companies so that you know exactly how many replacement respondents you need, and from which segments. If you are missing one small user, and it must be from the paint industry, you select one at random from an alphabetical list of uncontacted small users from the paint industry. If you have a refusal from the medium user segment and you don't have an uncontacted company from that segment promote the largest of the small users into the medium user segment.

Conclusions

- It is of vital importance that sampling is made as accurate as possible since it will be a key factor in justifying the validity of survey findings.
- A sample does not have to be large to be accurate. A sample of 200–500 will be adequate for most customer surveys.
- Results and consequent PFIs from a customer satisfaction measurement study must be owned by the people who will have to implement changes. Sampling must accommodate all these people which may necessitate a considerably increased sample size if multiple branches, service centres, and so on are involved.
- If possible use a random sampling method.
- In business markets a series of steps must be taken in order to arrive at a truly representative sample, typically by customer value, business sector and DMU role.

9 SURVEY OPTIONS

AIMS

By the end of this chapter you will:

- Know how to assess the advantages and disadvantages of the four main survey options for customer satisfaction measurement – personal interviews, telephone interviews and self-completion questionnaires.
- Be able to select the most appropriate survey method for specific purposes.
- Recognize a variety of techniques to increase postal survey response rates.
- Be able to adopt the most suitable approach to measuring the satisfaction of key accounts.

The survey method must be finalized before a questionnaire can be designed.

Personal Interviews

In consumer markets, personal interviews can be conducted in the street, in peoples' homes on a door-to-door basis, on your own premises if your customers come to you or at your distributor's premises if you sell through middlemen. In organisational markets, personal interviews are usually carried out on the respondent's premises but could be at the point of purchase (for example, a wholesaler's trade counter). There are both advantages and disadvantages (see Table 9.1) in the use of personal interviews, some of which we look at below.

Whether in consumer or organisational markets, interviews in the street or at the point of purchase will have to be quite short, usually no more than 15 minutes in duration. This means that questions will have to be mainly quantitative (see Chapter 10) if sufficient data are to be collected in 15 minutes to achieve the objectives of customer satisfaction measurement. Interviews in the home, or at business respondents' premises can be longer, typically 30–45 minutes in duration, providing scope for a more thorough examination of customers' attitudes and perceptions. This allows for the component elements of customer satisfaction to be broken

Table 9.1   Summary of advantages and disadvantages of personal interviews

Personal interviews	
Advantages	**Disadvantages**
1. Should achieve total respondent understanding	High cost especially in business markets
2. Visual prompts possible	Well trained interviewers required
3. Complex questions possible	Personal/sensitive questions difficult
4. Random samples possible for home/office interviews	Street/point-of-sale interviews need good planning and control if an accurate quota sample is to be achieved

down in considerable detail, enables comparisons with competing suppliers to be made, and gives time to ask some open questions, possibly with limited use of projective techniques. (See Chapter 10 for a comprehensive sample questionnaire, 'ABC Ltd: Questionnaire A', for use in a personal interview of 30–45 minutes' duration.)

Other advantages of personal interviews include the opportunity to use visual prompts. These may include show cards – where questions are so detailed and precise that a once-only reading may be insufficient for the respondent to fully assimilate the information – and using photographs or examples of the product or service being surveyed to aid respondent recall and understanding.

The fact that interviewer and respondent have face-to-face communication in a personal interview, enables the interviewer to record observations and to achieve greater understanding of the respondent's answers, particularly to open-ended questions. A good relationship with the respondent can usually be established and this improves the quality and quantity of information gained. In organisational markets, provided a high calibre of interviewer is used, serious discussions can take place, providing considerable insight into customers' priorities and perceptions.

A disadvantage of personal interviews is their high cost, particularly in business markets. In consumer markets the average cost per interview can be as low as £20, but in business markets, due to the extensive travel and higher calibre of interviewer required, the average cost per interview can easily reach £200.

Personal interviews also depend on well-trained interviewers for their validity. It is very easy for an untrained interviewer to unintentionally influence the respondent, introducing bias into the data collected. This risk is particularly acute if the sales force is used to interview contacts with whom they already have quite a close relationship. Professional market research agencies never allow interviewers to conduct an interview with anybody who is known to them.

A final problem with face-to-face interviews is that personal and/or sensitive questions can be more difficult: some respondents have a tendency to distort answers to please the interviewer or to avoid appearing foolish. This risk can be minimized through good questionnaire design and the use of well-trained interviewers.

If interviews are carried out at the respondents' business premises or home, control over sampling is possible. Interviews in the street or at point of sale can, at best, use quota sampling and, when strict controls are not maintained, will easily degenerate into a convenience sample.

Telephone Interviews

Telephone interviews (Table 9.2) strike a good compromise between cost and effectiveness. Costing as little as £10 per interview in consumer markets and between £25 and £50 in organisational markets they provide a lot of data for little money. They do need to be shorter than on-site personal interviews, but 10–15 minutes' duration is quite feasible. In that time there will be little opportunity for open questions, projective techniques cannot be used, and there is a limit to the number of component elements of customer satisfaction that can be measured. This last limitation is caused not just by the short duration of telephone interviews but also by the greater difficulty of maintaining respondents' interest and concentration if the interviewer has to wade through long lists of similar performance attributes.

One of the attractions of telephone interviews is that they eliminate additional costs associated with a geographically diverse customer base. Very suitable for business-to-business markets, for national consumer markets where cluster sampling is not acceptable, and for companies with an international customer base, telephone interviews afford total control over sampling whether a customer perception or market standing survey is being conducted. The quickest method for completing a survey, they can be immediate for companies wanting to track customer satisfaction on a continuous basis.

As with personal interviews, two-way communication enables explanations to be made where necessary so mutual understanding is maintained. Photographs or visual aids, when required, can be sent through the post, although this can result in organisational problems: respondents sometimes do not have them to hand when the interview takes place. Response rates for

Table 9.2   Summary of advantages and disadvantages of telephone interviews

Telephone interviews	
Advantages	**Disadvantages**
1. Quick	Short interviews
2. Low cost	Simple, straight-forward questions
3. Two-way communication allows explanations and prompts	Visual aids are impractical though not impossible
4. Total control over sampling	Good interviews required to maintain respondents' interest and concentration
5 Distance no problem	

telephone interviews are quite good and can be maximized by following the advice given in Chapter 13.

In consumer markets, telephone interviews for customer perception surveys using your own database present few problems provided your database is up to date. Response rates are good, especially if the call is preceeded by an introductory letter.

Market standing surveys in consumer markets are much more difficult as growing numbers of ex-directory and telephone preference (TPS) households make it extremely difficult to compile a comprehensive sampling frame, especially for higher social grades.

Self-Completion Questionnaires

Self-completion questionnaires (Table 9.3) may seem to be the obvious way to assess customer satisfaction, particularly for organisations undertaking the exercise for the first time, and they do have a number of advantages.

They are very low cost since there is no interviewer time involved and also they eliminate all problems associated with untrained interviewers and interviewer-induced bias. They are the least intrusive form of data collection and can offer respondents complete anonymity, which means that some respondents who are reluctant to agree to personal or telephone interviews may be prepared to cooperate with a self-completion questionnaire. In view of the anonymous nature of the exercise there are no problems with sensitive or embarrassing questions. Distance is immaterial and there is a wide choice of methods for distributing questionnaires. In addition to the post, the fax machine can be used in business markets for added speed and urgency especially if overseas respondents are involved. Questionnaires can also be distributed and collected personally either to households door-to-door or by the sales force in business markets. Personal delivery and collection improves response rates and sealable envelopes can be provided to suggest confidentiality (though neither confidentiality or anonymity can be assured if personal collection is used).

Self-completion questionnaires are a particularly useful method of capturing customers' views at the point-of-sale or point of consumption. This is very appropriate for many service businesses such as hotels and restaurants, the simultaneity of service consumption and questionnaire completion obviously contributing to the accuracy of the data collected. Manufacturers who are remote from their customers can use self-completion questionnaires, including them along with delivery notes or instruction manuals as part of product registration/guarantee cards – or spiced up as a competition and printed on packaging.

Despite these many attractions, self-completion questionnaires do have serious disadvantages. The questionnaire has to be reasonably short and questions simple; any perceived difficulty

Table 9.3   Summary of advantages and disadvantages of self-completion questionnaires

Self-completion questionnaires	
Advantages	**Disadvantages**
1. Low cost	Slow response rate (apart from electronic surveys)
2. No interviewer bias	Low response rate
3. Unintrusive and anonymous	Short questionnaires
4. Distance no problem	Simple questions
5 Wide choice of distribution methods	Hurried, possible unreliable responses
6. Point-of-sale surveys for immediacy	Unrepresentative samples

in completing the exercise will have a considerable adverse effect on response rates. They are also very slow with many respondents having good intentions to complete them 'when they get five minutes', but leaving them in pending trays and behind clocks for inordinate lengths of time.

By far the most serious drawback of self-completion questionnaires is the accuracy of the data generated. There are two problems here. Firstly, respondents tend to reply very hurriedly and with little thought: this is a particular problem in business-to-business markets. As a result, questions are often misinterpreted or omitted. Secondly, and more serious, is the effect of very low response rates on the sampling and the problem of 'non-response bias'.

Apart from the fact that low response rates in themselves make it less likely that a sample will be representative there is a strong possibility that the customers who did return the questionnaire are not typical of customers as a whole.

There is much evidence that self-completion surveys with low response rates are skewed towards the extremes of the normal distribution curve. They are more likely to be returned by customers who love you or hate you than by the silent majority of more typical customers. A rule of thumb in the research industry is that a response rate above 50 per cent is sufficient to minimize the problem of non-response bias. The lower the response rate the more biased the sample is likely to be. Response rates below 20 per cent should be treated with the utmost caution. To check the existence or extent of non-response bias, survey a random sample of 200 non-responders using telephone or personal interviews and compare the results with the results generated by the self-completion survey. If there are discrepancies between the two consider a different method of data collection or introduce measures to significantly improve the response rates of your self-completion survey.

Electronic Surveys

There are two options for electronic surveys – web surveys and email surveys. An email survey involves sending questionnaires to customers by email, typically in the form of a file attachment. Customers open the file attachment, in their own time and, typically off line, complete the questionnaire and return it to the sender. A web survey is completed on line by logging onto a specified web site. It would typically be conducted over the internet, but for surveys of internal customers or employees the organisation's intranet can be used. Before they can take part, respondents need to be alerted to the survey and told where the questionnaire is located on the web. For an internal survey or surveys of the general public this could be done using general media such as magazines, newsletters, notice boards or postal letters and this eliminates the need to have respondents' email addresses. However, this approach makes it difficult to control the sample so it is more normal to email customers to invite them to take part in the survey and to include within the email a URL that can be clicked to take respondents straight to the questionnaire location. Respondents can also be given a unique password that gives them access to the survey site and also ensures that they cannot complete the survey more than once. For both web and email surveys basic off the shelf software is available at modest cost.

Web surveys, typically in the form of exit surveys, are useful for e-commerce businesses, especially for measuring satisfaction with the web site itself. However, even for e-commerce businesses that should not be confused with a full measure of customer satisfaction since it would precede order fulfilment and ignore any requirement for after sales service. For a worthwhile measure of customer satisfaction, e-businesses should invite a random sample of customers to complete a web survey that covers all customer requirements. Even then, a web survey with a low response rate will suffer from non-response bias in the same way as a postal survey, especially in B2B markets.

Electronic surveys illustrate the best and worst aspects of self-completion questionnaires. They are extremely quick. Internet surveys will be completed at the time of a website visit and most people respond very quickly to their e-mail. From web or e-mail surveys data can be exported instantly into analysis software. To make things easy for respondents, questionnaires can be designed with invisible routing and interesting graphics can be incorporated. Above all, with virtually zero print and distribution costs they are almost certainly the cheapest way of gathering survey data.

However, at the time of writing it remains virtually impossible to obtain reliable samples in

Table 9.4   Summary of advantages and disadvantages of electronic surveys

Electronic surveys		
Advantages		**Disadvantages**
1.	Low cost	Representative samples impossible in most consumer markets
2.	Quick response	Access to email more widespread than web access for B2B respondents
3.	Zero cost data and comment capture	Low response rates and non-response bias caused by huge volume of junk emails
4.	Good for routing	Short questionnaires
5	Modern image	Hurried, possible unreliable responses

consumer markets using electronic media unless internet users form your target population, e.g. visitors to your website. In consumer markets internet usage needs to increase significantly before reliable sampling will be possible, especially in certain segments such as older customers and lower social grades. Moreover, whilst most organisations have comprehensive records of customers' names and addresses and, usually, good records of their telephone numbers, records of customers' e-mail addresses remain far from complete, especially in consumer markets. Since response to electronic surveys, like all self-completion surveys, is voluntary, the problem of unreliable sampling frames is likely to be aggravated by low response rates and consequent non-response bias.

In B2B markets internet penetration and email usage is no longer a problem apart from some very small businesses (e.g. self-employed tradesman) A much bigger problem is the huge number of emails received by many managers (often over 100 per day), which is increasingly exacerbating the problem of poor response rates and non-response bias.

MAXIMIZING RESPONSE

The more committed an organisation's customers and the more interested they are in a product or service the higher will be the response achieved by self-completion surveys. People who have just bought a new car will respond more readily to a postal satisfaction survey than will purchasers of a lower involvement product. There are variations in response rates for different parts of the country: Scotland responds well whilst London and the South East are particularly poor. The huge growth in poorly targeted direct mail is partly responsible here with many customers failing to distinguish between selling and research mailers. The solution to this problem lies partly in researchers' own hands. A postal satisfaction survey must differentiate itself from promotional mailshots rather than imitating the techniques of the direct marketers with strongly branded envelopes and free prize draws heavily featured.

A postal satisfaction survey should be approached more seriously as befits a very important subject. The respondent should be treated as an individual, not just one of many customers. As well as addressing the letter by name it is even better if it can refer to a specific transaction or other dealings that the respondent has had with the company. This introductory letter is most important and should stress how much customer feedback is valued by the company and how the survey will help to improve service for all customers. Clearly, if it is so important, the letter should be sent from someone very senior, preferably the chief executive. (The PR aspects of the survey are discussed, and a specimen letter is outlined, in Chapter 13.)

As well as the introductory letter, the whole self-completion package must be very user-friendly. The questionnaire itself need not be very short (good response rates can be achieved using four-page questionnaires) but should be well laid out. Ease of completion is crucial to a good response rate. Early questions should be ones that respondents find easy to answer; and you must pilot the questionnaire beforehand to test how easily customers can complete it. As well as being easy to answer, the first few questions should also be interesting to respondents. If necessary, add a few such questions at the start of the questionnaire even if the answers are of no real value.

A reply-paid envelope is essential. Reminders are also very useful for boosting response. An initial reminder letter should be sent after ten days, preferably just to non-responders, once more stressing how highly their views are valued and how the survey will help the organisation to improve customer service. Distinguishing between responders and non-responders can be difficult; despatch of a general letter to serve as a thank you to responders as well as a reminder to non-responders is useful in such circumstances. The first reminder can just be a letter, but after a further ten days a second reminder should include a replacement questionnaire and reply-paid envelope.

Sending two reminders in this way significantly boosts response rates. Some companies also believe in sending out advance notification of the survey which again improves response rates.

The question of incentives is more tricky. Many organisations achieve good response rates without using any incentives, believing that making the customer feel involved is far more important. For more important purchases or for organisations where customers (or members) already feel involved, a non-incentivized approach is usually quite adequate, but there is no doubt that a sufficiently generous incentive can boost response rates and this may be important in lower involvement markets.

However, it is generally felt that certain types of incentive, such as a prize draw, will be more likely to skew the response and to trivialize the survey, often without even improving the response rate. It is better to view incentives as a thank you, and therefore a small gift that is sent to everyone with the original questionnaire or is claimed by respondents is the most appropriate type of incentive. As far as possible a gift should be relevant. Thus, as a universal gift mailed with the questionnaire, a good quality pen is usually effective. The pen can also feature a company name and logo. Vouchers, for use against future purchases, are also effective: they cost less than externally sourced gifts to provide and have a higher perceived value.

Ask respondents to claim vouchers when they return their completed questionnaire rather than mail them to everyone, since this will enable you to raise the value of the voucher. If you expect a 50 per cent response rate, for example, you can double the value of the voucher if it has to be claimed by respondents.

When conducting a large postal survey it is worthwhile testing different approaches. If you need to use an external database it is worth testing alternative lists. You can also test different types of incentive, different questionnaires, and even different packaging. Make sure, however, that you change only one variable between each test or you will never know which change made the impact. You also need samples of no less than 500 for each test. A test involving three different

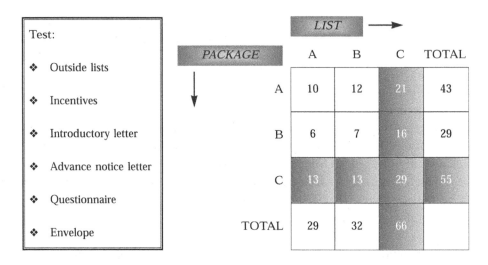

Figure 9.1   Testing different approaches

databases and three different types of incentives gives a total combination of nine different options, as demonstrated in Figure 9.1. Here, list C and incentive C clearly produce the best result and should be adopted for the survey. With careful planning and piloting, then, the total response rate can be boosted quite considerably.

You can also improve from one survey to another if you keep a detailed record of response rates and test ideas for improvement before your next survey.

As you can see from Table 9.5 the sample frame is overwhelmingly the main contributor to response rates. This is compatible with the experience of companies using any kind of direct mail. A good database of customers with a strong relationship with your organisation (for example, a health and leisure club membership list) will achieve response rates more than double (and maybe as great as four or five times) that of a list of occasional customers for a low involvement product or a rented list of product category users. The figures show the maximum percentage by which the techniques listed might improve your response rate. Notice that incentives are well down the effectiveness list. A reply-paid envelope, by the way, is taken for granted. Due to the very low response rates achieved by many postal surveys it is advisable for some customer surveys to consider whether self-completion questionnaires will elicit such a poor response that a more reliable form of data collection should be used.

THE ROLE OF SELF-COMPLETION QUESTIONNAIRES

Unless you have a very responsive customer base it will be advisable to distinguish between baseline surveys and continuous tracking and to use self-completion questionnaires only for the latter.

Table 9.5   Effectiveness of techniques to improve response rates

Sample frame (database)	100%
Introductory letter	30%
First reminder letter	25%
Telephone reminder	25%
High interest questionnaires	20%
Incentive	15%
Advance notice letter	15%
Second reminder letter	12%

Many organisations need continuous feedback on their performance, particularly where high levels of service and support are involved. Hotels often leave self-completion questionnaires in all their bedrooms, though response rates are notoriously low. Rather than being seen as a reliable measurement of customers' satisfaction they should be viewed as an additional complaints mechanism, an early warning of service problems. On that basis they have a useful role to play, and the unrepresentative sampling caused by the low response rate is of less concern if the responses are not used for measurement purposes.

Dell Computers use regular telephone interviews and online surveys to track customer satisfaction on all aspects of the customer experience that are important to customers. As with any tracking the key is to collect and report data quickly so that the company can respond, almost in real time. There's no point collecting customer satisfaction data any more frequently than you can act on it.

Self-completion questionnaires are at their most valuable when used at the point of consumption. In order to secure a high and therefore more reliable response, it is better if staff are trained to encourage customers to complete questionnaires. A waiter might ask diners drinking their coffee to complete a small questionnaire, providing a pen for the purpose. Even with a high response rate, however, questionnaires completed at the point of purchase will often not provide a very reliable guide to future buying behaviour. To pursue the restaurant example, diners filling in a questionnaire at the end of a relaxing evening at the Tuscany Trattoria are likely to be rather generous in their satisfaction ratings unless there is a very good reason why they have not enjoyed their evening. When making a future decision on where to dine out, maybe some weeks or months later, these same diners will compare the relative merits of the Tuscany Trattoria more objectively against those of other restaurants where pleasant evenings have also been enjoyed. Therefore, whilst point of consumption questionnaires provide very useful warning if things are amiss, their use does not achieve the objectives of customer satisfaction measurement as outlined in Chapter 5. So it is necessary to undertake a more detailed 'baseline survey' with a representative sample of customers at periodic intervals, using personal or telephone interviews.

A baseline survey will be carried out less often (probably annually) and will be based on accurate sampling and a comprehensive questionnaire which in turn will have been validated by exploratory research and piloting. For most organisations, self-completion surveys will not prove sufficiently reliable, mainly because of sampling problems. Baseline surveys will therefore usually be administered through interviews conducted fact to face or by telephone. In the UK, for example, Boots have found an effective way of overcoming sampling problems associated with self-completion surveys. Their in-home tracking studies involve 6000 respondents during the course of the year. Instead of using postal surveys, the company employs interviewers to carry out a short personal interview to gather respondents' spontaneous comments; they also leave these respondents a lengthier self-completion questionnaire. This is collected four days later by the same interviewer. The approach can use quota sampling to ensure a representative sample with the personal contact and collection motivating respondents to complete the questionnaire.

Key Account Surveys

As suggested in Chapter 8, sampling should take into account the fact that some customers in business markets will be of more importance than others. The same is true of your choice of survey method. Whilst a brief telephone interview may be suitable for surveying a sample of your small customers, it might not create the right impression with a key account whose annual business with you may be worth millions of pounds. For PR reasons alone personal visits should be made to key accounts and, since sampling is likely to result in several respondents being interviewed from each key account, the visits will be cost-effective.

The Royal Mail uses self-completion postal surveys for its regular tracking of business customers and achieves response rates of 40–50 per cent. Key accounts are interviewed in person and, interestingly, the process is deliberately not anonymous. This means that, in addition to the inclusion of key account scores in the overall report of customer satisfaction, an individual report is prepared for each key account. A draft is sent to the customer for approval prior to being circulated to appropriate Royal Mail staff such as the key account manager, customer services manager, sales director and others. The Royal Mail claims that the vast majority of key account customers are happy with this personalized approach.

You may also wish to consider going further than a personal interview for key accounts. Dell Computers invites its top ten corporate customers to its 'Platinum Event'. This two-day workshop is held on neutral ground and, as well as encompassing all the advantages of a focus group, allows Dell to select a particular theme for each event. The extended time period gives the company an opportunity to explore the theme in considerable depth, with key customers having a direct input into the development of Dell's future strategy.

Conclusions

- Personal interviews are the most costly – but also the most detailed, thorough and reliable – method of collecting customer satisfaction data.
- Telephone interviews offer the best cost–quality compromise for most companies, especially in business-to-business markets. A very quick method of data collection, they eliminate costs and problems associated with distance.
- Self-completion questionnaires are often abused, the low cost of data collection assuming more importance for organisations than accuracy of results. They are useful at the point of consumption for continuous and immediate feedback on customer satisfaction at a superficial level, and are best seen and used as an addition rather than an alternative to periodic baseline surveys by mail or telephone. Companies measuring customer satisfaction in business markets should be very cautious for decision-making purposes about the adequacy of information gained from low response rate self-completion questionnaires.
- Postal survey response rates can be improved through selecting the best database for sampling, including an effective introductory letter, sending reminders and making the questionnaire interesting to respondents as well as easy to complete. Piloting and testing will help improve postal survey response rates.
- Web surveys are very low cost and quick but access problems make sampling difficult in many markets.
- Key accounts should be given special treatment when selecting your survey method in order to afford them the opportunity for more personal and detailed input.

10 QUESTIONNAIRE DESIGN

The Basic Principles of Asking Questions

When judging any question on a questionnaire you need to apply the following tests to it:

- Will the respondent have the information/knowledge to answer it?
- Will the respondent understand the question?
- Is the respondent likely to give a true answer?
- Will the question bias the response?

It is very easy for a question to fail any of these tests so let's examine each of them carefully.

NECESSARY INFORMATION/KNOWLEDGE

People tend to believe they ought to have an opinion on issues. Consequently, when asked a question such as, 'Do you think gas or electricity is better for cooking?' a respondent may answer 'Gas', never having used electricity for cooking. Similarly, a passenger may express an opinion about Virgin Airways having never flown with that airline.

As far as customer surveys are concerned, this pitfall will be minimized by setting very clear objectives at the outset of the project. To take the Virgin Airways example, you may want to measure the satisfaction and explore the attitudes only of knowledgeable people with direct experience of the product. If so you will need screening questions to qualify respondents very carefully before interviewing them. On the other hand you may want to research the attitudes of all air travellers, whether or not they have flown Virgin, because it may be that some customers are deterred from using Virgin by negative perceptions that they have formed despite never experiencing the service. This latter approach would be typical of market standing surveys.

UNDERSTANDING THE QUESTION

There are three problem areas in understanding.

Firstly, there is the loose or ambiguous meaning of many common words. A good example is 'regularly'. A regular habit to one person may seem a very occasional one to someone else. 'Do you eat out regularly?' would therefore mean different things to different people. Rather than try to define such words it is better to avoid them and reword the question: 'When did you last eat out?', or, 'How many times have you eaten out in the last month?'

The second problem is the double question. 'Does washing powder get clothes clean without damaging the fabric?' This one question should be split into two separate questions to accommodate the full range of possible opinions. Sometimes questions use two very similar adjectives: 'Do you find the atmosphere in this restaurant relaxing and informal?' If the researcher sees only one meaning to this question the closer of the two adjectives should be used and the other eliminated.

The third problem is the long rambling question, or definition. Used in a self-completion questionnaire, it results in many respondents not taking the trouble to figure it out, either omitting it altogether or, even worse, ticking any available answer. In telephone surveys, too, the long question is difficult for both respondent and interviewer.

GIVING A TRUE ANSWER

Once again there are three pitfalls to avoid in this area.

Firstly, respondents often find it difficult to articulate their views, especially where attitudes are concerned. They should therefore be given plenty of time to formulate their ideas into words. If a long pause occurs this can be very difficult for interviewers, especially those conducting telephone surveys who have no visual cues to assess the respondent's state of mind. It is to minimize such problems that exploratory research, using unstructured interviews, is undertaken. Questions asking people to describe the image of a company are very difficult to answer without a great deal of thought, hence the use of projective techniques for long personal interviews or attitude batteries for short telephone interviews.

The second potential pitfall is respondents' memory. People may believe they are giving a truthful answer but in reality, due to a defective memory, they are giving an inaccurate response.

For customer satisfaction measurement, where perceptions are reality, this response, inaccurate though it is, will be of no concern whatever to the researcher. For example, the respondent may say that the supplier is very poor regarding on-time delivery, whereas, in fact, for the last twelve months the supplier has the best delivery record in the industry. Nevertheless, it is the respondent's answer that is the accurate one for a customer survey because it is on the basis of such mistaken perceptions that the respondent is making purchase decisions.

Asking questions about past events that require factually accurate answers tests the adequacy of respondents' memories at the exploratory stage. If there is any doubt about their ability to provide sufficiently accurate answers they should be briefed by letter or telephone about the topics in question enabling them to check records or at least give the matter careful thought before the interview.

The third pitfall is more difficult to identify and negotiate. Some respondents may be unwilling to answer truthfully to some questions. This is not malicious. There is no evidence that respondents try to deliberately mislead researchers in customer surveys or any other kind of research but there is evidence that respondents will give what they consider to be an acceptable answer which does not really reflect their views.

As far as customer satisfaction measurement is concerned, these untruthful answers are likely to fall into two areas.

Firstly, most people are eager to please and averse to unpleasantness. They are therefore likely to over-state their satisfaction and under-play any areas of dissatisfaction, as we will see when we look at rating scales later in this chapter. This problem is accentuated if your own staff conduct the interviews and are known to the respondents.

Secondly, people have a tendency to give socially acceptable answers: that is, the answer they feel they ought to give. For example, respondents may not wish to appear irrational (for example, indulging in impulse buying) or unprofessional (a purchasing manager may not want to admit to being influenced by a relationship with a sales person).

WILL THE QUESTIONS BIAS THE RESPONSE?

A fourth reason why you may generate inaccurate data in a customer survey is that the question itself may suggest a form of answer to the respondent. The most likely form of bias in a customer survey is to influence the customer towards satisfaction rather than dissatisfaction.

The following question has a perfectly balanced rating scale but still contains an element of bias. 'How satisfied were you with the cleanliness of your bathroom?':

- Very satisfied.
- Quite satisfied.
- Neither satisfied nor dissatisfied.
- Quite dissatisfied.
- Very dissatisfied.

To avoid any element of bias the question should have read 'How satisfied or dissatisfied were you with the cleanliness of your bathroom?'

It is possible that you may specifically want to explore degrees of customer satisfaction and therefore take a positive decision to introduce a biased scale. An example of a positive biased scale is given later in the chapter.

Piloting

As well as studying the questionnaire and applying to it the tests of knowledge, understanding, truthfulness and absence of bias, you must pilot it to test just how well it works in practice.

Your pilot interviews should be undertaken with members of the target audience who are not part of your sample. In a pilot interview you should do two things: run through the questionnaire, noting answers in the normal way; then note any places where the respondent hesitates or appears puzzled. This straight run through will enable you to verify that the questions do seem to be sensible when you put them to a real customer, that the sequence is acceptable, that the interviewer will have time to write down the answers and that the interview can be completed within the time limits you have set.

On completion of the interview ask the respondent what he or she thought of the interview. Were there any questions that were difficult to answer, any questions that seemed inapplicable to their situation? If the respondent doesn't refer to any of the questions where you noted pauses mention them and ask if there was any reason for their hesitancy. There may be a perfectly reasonable explanation, such as trying to remember the details of a past event.

If the pilot interviews reveal no real problems then you can proceed with the survey itself. If a problem does occur carry out more pilots, asking each respondent about the possible problem area. It may be that the problem is peculiar to one respondent and no one else perceives any difficulty, in which case you should proceed. However, if the other pilots confirm the problem you must rewrite the question and pilot again.

The number of pilots will depend on the size and diversity of your sample. In some business markets with a small customer base it may be unrealistic to do more than two pilots. With a larger business sample, say 200 telephone interviews, carry out around five pilot interviews. Some surveys, for example, users of a local authority's facilities with a large and diverse population, will require more extensive piloting.

Ensure that questionnaires are piloted with all discernible segments since people's understanding of the questionnaire may vary depending on their education, age, beliefs, lifestyle, employment and many other factors.

Self-completion questionnaires and telephone interviews are best piloted initially through face-to-face interviews in order to facilitate discussion of any problematic questions. When difficult questions do arise it is a good idea to ask customers to rephrase the questions in their own words. Having resolved problems in this way, telephone and self-completion questionnaires should be piloted in their precise survey format.

Types of Question

The main distinction between types of question is between the closed and the open question. In the survey itself, where you may have time constraints and where you need to produce quantitative answers for statistical analysis, you will use mainly closed questions.

CLOSED QUESTIONS

Closed questions give respondents a fixed selection of answers to choose from. They are quick and easy to administer and analyse, offer the least scope for interviewer or respondent error and produce quantifiable data. The interviewer (or the respondent in a self-completion questionnaire) need tick only the relevant box.

Closed questions could be dichotomous (see Table 10.1), with only two alternative answers possible. They can be multiple choice, enabling respondents to choose from any number of possible answers. Some questions demand that the respondent selects only one answer (single response), other questions allow selection of all relevant answers (multi-response), as shown in Tables 10.2 and 10.3.

Closed questions can also be linked with a rating scale to qualify the strength of the response, as shown in Table 10.4.

OPEN QUESTIONS

Open questions are used when the researcher does not want to lead the respondent in any way. These questions are more commonly used at the exploratory stage rather than at the survey stage (see Table 10.5).

Table 10.1   Dichotomous closed questions

Are the following facilities important to you when selecting a hotel for an overnight stay on business? Please tick one box on each line		
	yes	no
Fax service		
Satellite TV		
En-suite bathroom		
Gymnasium		
Swimming pool		

Table 10.2   Multiple choice, single response question

Which of the following facilities is the most important one to you when selecting a hotel for an overnight stay on business? Please tick one box only	
Fax service	
Satellite TV	
En-suite bathroom	
Gymnasium	
Swimming pool	

Table 10.3   Multiple choice, multi-response question

Which of the following facilities are <u>essential</u> to you when selecting a hotel for an overnight stay on business? Please tick any relevant boxes	
Fax service	
Satellite TV	
En-suite bathroom	
Gymnasium	
Swimming pool	

Table 10.4   Closed question with rating scale

	Very unimportant	Quite unimportant	Quite important	Very important
How important or unimportant are the following facilities to you when selecting a hotel for an overnight stay on business? **Please tick one box on each line**				
Fax service				
Satellite TV				
En-suite bathroom				
Gymnasium				
Swimming pool				

Table 10.5   Open question

What factors are most important to you when selecting a restaurant for a meal out with a group of friends?

At the survey stage you may wish to use some open questions, particularly for personal interviews, in order to gain totally unprompted responses. If you have done your exploratory research well you will know the types of responses that people tend to give and can therefore make both the interview and the subsequent analysis more efficient by turning the question into an open question, closed response, as shown in Table 10.6.

Note in this question that, firstly, an open question, closed response cannot be used on self-completion questionnaires and, secondly, the instructions spell out your objectives to the interviewer: in this case – 'Do not prompt. Accept up to three responses. Indicate order of response.'

Table 10.6   Open question, closed response

What factors are most important to you when selecting a restaurant for a meal out with a group of friends? *Do not prompt. Accept up to three responses. Indicate order of response.*			
	1st	2nd	3rd
Quality of food			
Price			
Music			
Lively atmosphere			
Quiet atmosphere			
Informal/relaxed atmosphere			
Convenient/local to my home			
Close to night clubs			
Efficient service			
Friendly staff			
Other 1			
Other 2			

Table 10.7   Behavioural question – multiple choice, single response

When did you last eat out in an Italian restaurant? Tick one response	
Within the last week	
Within the last month	
Within the last three months	
Over three months ago	
Never	

Prompting is when the interviewer reads out a series of pre-coded responses to the question. The respondent is constrained to select one of the pre-coded replies. In this question the interviewer must mentally code the response received according to one of the categories listed or, where the response does not fit one of the pre-coded categories, should enter the information under 'other'.

At the data processing stage these other responses are in turn coded. Precise instructions regarding prompting should be given to interviewers in order to guarantee a consistent result.

PURPOSE OF QUESTIONS

Whether the questions are open or closed, they can be used for different purposes, usually to find out about respondents' behaviour, to understand their attitudes, or to gather details about them for classification purposes.

Behavioural questions

Behavioural questions (see Table 10.7) are about what the respondent does or has done in the past. They are both factual and tangible which usually make them easier to answer so they tend to be placed at the beginning of questionnaires.

Attitudinal questions

Although behavioural questions can ask the respondent to dig deeply into his or her memory, attitudinal questions usually require more thought and more decision making and should therefore follow rather than precede behavioural questions. This gives the respondent some time to think about the issues involved. It also provides an opportunity for the interviewer to build rapport – very useful later when the interviewer wants the respondent to make the effort to give proper consideration to any difficult attitudinal questions.

Customer satisfaction measurement is primarily concerned with attitudinal questions. Attitudes towards buying the product and selecting the supplier, attitudes about the performance of the product and supplier and, most difficult of all, attitudes about the image of the supplier, will all come within this category.

In the main, you will not just want to discover the existence of an attitude but also to measure how strongly that attitude is held: not, 'Is the customer satisfied?', but 'How satisfied is the customer?' Your attitudinal questions will therefore be linked with rating scales.

Classification questions

Classification questions (see Table 10.8) are used for the purposes of segmentation. In business surveys sampling will often have been so detailed that the classification data (product usage, industry sector, respondent position, etc.) are known before the interview. In consumer interviews the respondent is asked, in which case it is better to leave the classification questions to the end since they may include details that some people regard as sensitive.

Table 10.8 Classification questions

Sex	Male		Female	
Age	18–24 years	25–34 years	35–44 years	45–54 years
Marital status	Single	Married/ partners	Widowed	Divorced
Occuptation of chief income earner (for assigning socio-economic grade)				

When using a quota sample you may have to ask some classification questions first in order to qualify respondents. Examples of classification questions are shown in the sample questionnaires in Appendix I.

Rating scales

Since customer satisfaction measurement is all about measuring attitudes, the method you use to do the measuring is an extremely important aspect of the exercise. Market researchers have developed several different types of 'rating scale' to measure the strength of peoples' attitudes and here we examine those scales with most relevance to customer satisfaction measurement: Likert scales; verbal scales; semantic differential scales; ungraded scales; numerical rating scales; ordinal scales; SIMALTO scales.

Each type is illustrated by two short questionnaires, demonstrating the two objectives of customer satisfaction measurement. Firstly, to find out what is important to the customer and, secondly, to identify how well a company is seen to perform against those same criteria.

In order to get a feel for the different types of rating scales, and to help you decide which is most appropriate for your own purposes, fill in the short questionnaires. Booking a room in a hotel has been chosen as the subject as this is a process familiar to most readers. The same purchase criteria are used for each type of scale in order to facilitate comparisons.

LIKERT SCALES

Likert scales (Figures 10.1 and 10.2) are designed to measure degrees of agreement with a statement, the wording shown in the example reflecting the Market Research Society's recommended approach. However, some people maintain that it is better to offer only four possible responses, eliminating the middle option.

Importance

Please read the following statements and place an "X" in the box that most accurately reflects how much you agree or disagree with the statement or in the N/A box if it is not relevant to you.

	N/A	Disagree strongly	Disagree slightly	Neither agree nor disagree	Agree slightly	Agree strongly
1. When booking overnight accommodation for business purposes convenience of access by car is very important.	☐	☐	☐	☐	☐	☐
2. When booking overnight accommodation for business purposes speed of response by telephone is very important.	☐	☐	☐	☐	☐	☐
3. When booking overnight accommodation for business purposes ease of booking is very important.	☐	☐	☐	☐	☐	☐
4. When booking overnight accommodation for business purposes flexibility over cancellation is very important.	☐	☐	☐	☐	☐	☐
5. When booking overnight accommodation for business purposes the helpfulness of staff is very important.	☐	☐	☐	☐	☐	☐

Figure 10.1 Likert scale – customer's priorities

Satisfaction

Please read the following statements and place an 'X' in the box which most accurately reflects how much you agree or disagree with the statement, or in the N/A box if it is not relevant to you.

	N/A	Disagree strongly	Disagree slightly	Neither agree nor disagree	Agree slightly	Agree strongly
1. The hotel is convenient for access by car	☐	☐	☐	☐	☐	☐
2. The hotel responds quickly to telephone enquiries	☐	☐	☐	☐	☐	☐
3. It is easy to book a room at the hotel	☐	☐	☐	☐	☐	☐
4. The hotel is flexible over cancellations	☐	☐	☐	☐	☐	☐
5. Staff at the hotel are always helpful	☐	☐	☐	☐	☐	☐

Figure 10.2 Likert scale – supplier's performance

VERBAL SCALES

Similar in principle to Likert scales, verbal scales use words to describe degrees of the attitude being measured. In the case of customer satisfaction measurement, of course, the concepts involved are importance and satisfaction. The scales are shown in Figures 10.3 and 10.4.

Importance

Below are some factors involved in booking overnight accommodation for business purposes. Please place an 'X' in the box that most accurately reflects how important or unimportant each feature is to you, or put an 'X' in the N/A box if it is not relevant to you.

	N/A	Very unimportant	Quite unimportant	Neither important nor unimportant	Quite important	Very important
1. Accessibility	☐	☐	☐	☐	☐	☐
2. Speed of response	☐	☐	☐	☐	☐	☐
3. Ease of booking procedures	☐	☐	☐	☐	☐	☐
4. Flexibility of cancellation policy	☐	☐	☐	☐	☐	☐
5. Helpfulness of staff	☐	☐	☐	☐	☐	☐

Figure 10.3   Verbal scale – customer's priorities

Satisfaction

Below are factors involved in booking overnight accommodation for business purposes at hotel XXX. Please place an 'X' in the box that most accurately reflects how satisfied or dissatisfied you are with each item, or put an 'X' in the N/A box if it is not relevant to you.

	N/A	Very dissatisfied	Quite dissatisfied	Neither satisfied or dissatisfied	Quite satisfied	Very satisfied
1. Accessibility	☐	☐	☐	☐	☐	☐
2. Speed of response	☐	☐	☐	☐	☐	☐
3. Ease of booking procedures	☐	☐	☐	☐	☐	☐
4. Flexibility of cancellation policy	☐	☐	☐	☐	☐	☐
5. Helpfulness of staff	☐	☐	☐	☐	☐	☐

Figure 10.4   Verbal scale – supplier's performance

SEMANTIC DIFFERENTIAL SCALES

Semantic differential scales display an attitude battery between two opposing words. Typically you would allow more options than the four or five given in the Likert scales (the seven shown in the examples in Figures 10.5 and 10.6 would be typical) but you would not label the options in any way. The respondent is left to define the strength of his or her attitude by selecting the proximity to the appropriate adjective.

UNGRADED SCALES

The ungraded scale, shown in Figures 10.7 and 10.8, takes the semantic differential scale to its logical conclusion, replacing the tick boxes of the latter with an ungraded continuum.

NUMERICAL RATING SCALES

A numerical rating scale (Figures 10.9 and 10.10) requires respondents to ascribe a mark, out of 10 for example, to indicate the strength of their attitude. There is no firm rule on the size of the scale. Some companies use a scale of 1 to 5. Federal Express uses a 101 point scale (0 to 100) to measure 'microshifts' in customer satisfaction. In the UK, a ten-point scale works very well. It is understood by respondents who have often grown up with marks out of ten at school and it is wide enough to accommodate a good range of customer opinion.

ORDINAL SCALES

Ordinal scales (Figures 10.11 and 10.12) require the respondent to indicate the relative strength of his or her attitude to the different criteria by ranking them in order of importance, preference and so on. No further qualification is demanded.

SIMALTO SCALES

Standing for 'Simultaneous Multi Attribute Level Trade Off' a SIMALTO profile can be used to collect data on customers' priorities and on their range of expectations, from ideal to unacceptable levels of service, as shown in Figure 10.13. As well as scoring suppliers' performance they can also accommodate the respondent's perceptions of competitor performance as shown in Figure 10.14.

Sometimes known as 'fully descriptive' verbal scales', SIMALTO scales can be used for personal interviews or self-completion questionnaires.

As with the numerical rating scale, competing hotels familiar to the respondent would already have been identified in a personal interview.

Please read the following statements and place an 'X' in the box which most accurately reflects your views on booking overnight accommodation for business purposes

1. The hotel must be accessible by car

   not at all important ❏ ❏ ❏ ❏ ❏ ❏ ❏ *extremely important*

2. The hotel must respond quickly to telephone enquiries

   not at all important ❏ ❏ ❏ ❏ ❏ ❏ ❏ *extremely important*

3. The booking procedures must be easy to follow

   not at all important ❏ ❏ ❏ ❏ ❏ ❏ ❏ *extremely important*

4. The hotel must be flexible over cancellations

   not at all important ❏ ❏ ❏ ❏ ❏ ❏ ❏ *extremely important*

5. Hotel staff must be helpful

   not at all important ❏ ❏ ❏ ❏ ❏ ❏ ❏ *extremely important*

Figure 10.5   Semantic differential scale – customer's priorities

Please read the following statements and place an 'X' in the box which most accurately reflects your views on booking overnight accommodation for business purposes at the ABC Hotel

1. When travelling by car the hotel is:

   very inaccessible ❏ ❏ ❏ ❏ ❏ ❏ ❏ *very accessible*

2. The hotel's response to telephone enquiries is:

   very slow ❏ ❏ ❏ ❏ ❏ ❏ ❏ *very quick*

3. The booking procedures are:

   difficult ❏ ❏ ❏ ❏ ❏ ❏ ❏ *easy*

4. The hotel's terms over cancellations are:

   Very inflexible ❏ ❏ ❏ ❏ ❏ ❏ ❏ *Very flexible*

5. Hotel staff are:

   very unhelpful ❏ ❏ ❏ ❏ ❏ ❏ ❏ *very helpful*

Figure 10.6   Semantic differential scale – supplier's performance

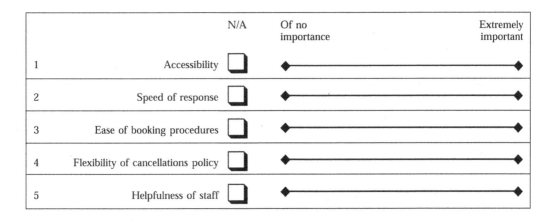

Figure 10.7 Ungraded scale – customer's priorities

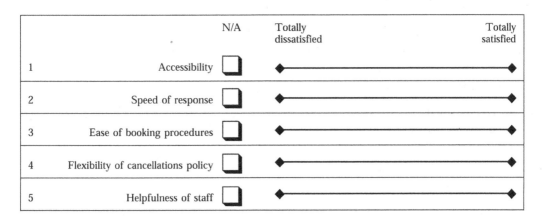

Figure 10.8 Ungraded scale – supplier's performance

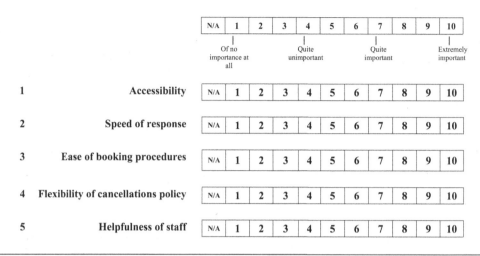

Figure 10.9 Numerical rating scale – customer's priorities

Assessing Rating Scales

All rating scales have their advantages and their application. Likert and verbal scales are very easy to understand and the most respondent-friendly of all the options. Their scale of measurement is not very precise, however, and when translated into quantitative data tends to rely on the researcher assigning numbers (typically 1 to 5 in the examples shown in Figures 10.1 and 10.2) to the positions on the scale. The range of attitudes covered is very restricted, particularly at the positive end of the scale of supplier performance. Effectively, they only accommodate very good performance and good performance. In today's competitive markets, suppliers have to perform to a very high standard, which requires a more detailed rating scale in order to distinguish between them.

In the USA, General Motors analysed this problem using data gathered over ten years of customer satisfaction measurement and involving responses from 100 000 customers.

The GM surveys were carried out using a typical symmetrical five-point verbal scale:

- Very satisfied.
- Somewhat satisfied.
- Neither satisfied nor dissatisfied.
- Somewhat dissatisfied.
- Very dissatisfied.

In the subsequent analysis of its accumulated data, the GM customer loyalty rates did not decline in proportion to reduction in satisfaction levels but fell dramatically if the customer was anything less than very satisfied. Since most customers were 'Very satisfied', and the four points on the scale below 'Very satisfied' are of no value for customer retention, GM came

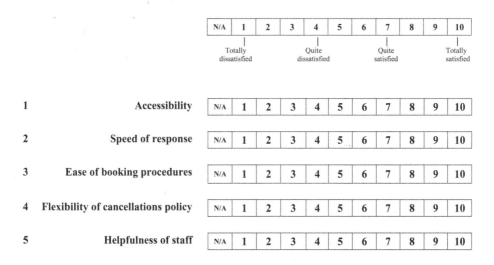

Figure 10.10   Numerical rating scale – supplier's performance

Below is a list of statements describing various aspects of booking a hotel room for business purposes. Please rank them in order of their importance to you by placing the letter accompanying each statement into the appropriate box in the 'Rank Order' column. For example, if you think statement C is the most important one for you, write C in '1st' box in the 'Rank Order' column.

	Booking a hotel room	Rank Order	
A	Accessibility	1st	
B	Speed of response	2nd	
C	Ease of booking procedures	3rd	
D	Flexibility of cancellations policy	4th	
E	Helpfulness of staff	5th	

Figure 10.11   Ordinal scale – customer's priorities

to the conclusion that its symmetrical five-point scale was inappropriate. The real areas of difference that the company wanted to probe were varying levels of positive satisfaction, with the goal being to move customers from satisfied to delighted. GM's exploratory research convinced them that a 'positive biased semantic scale' was the most discriminating form of measure.

An example of such a scale is:

- Delighted: 'I received everything I expected and more.'
- Totally satisfied: 'Everything lived up to my expectations.'

Below is a list of statements describing various aspects of staying in the ABC hotel for business purposes. Please rank them in order of satisfaction by placing the letter accompanying each statement into the appropriate box in the 'Rank Order' column. For example, if you think statement C is the one you are most satisfied with, write C in '1st' box in the 'Rank Order' column.

	Booking a hotel room	Rank Order	
A	Accessibility	1st	
B	Speed of response	2nd	
C	Ease of booking procedures	3rd	
D	Flexibility of cancellations policy	4th	
E	Helpfulness of staff	5th	

Figure 10.12   Ordinal scale – supplier's performance

Importance

Using the table below, please indicate the standards you think a hotel should provide for business use by marking appropriate boxes according to the following key:

I = ideal standard – mark only one box on each row

E = expected standard – mark only one box on each row

U = unacceptable standard – mark all boxes which show unacceptable standards

You can place more than one letter in one box (e.g. if the standard you expect is unacceptable)

If the factor is not relevant to you please place an 'X' in the N/A box.

	N/A	Level 1	Level 2	Level 3	Level 4	Level 5
Accessibility by car	☐	Over one hour out of my way	31–60 minutes out of my way	16–30 minutes out of my way	6–15 minutes out of my way	Up to 5 minutes out of my way
Time taken to answer the telephone	☐	Over 45 seconds	31–45 seconds	21–30 seconds	11–20 seconds	Up to 10 seconds
Ease of making a reservation	☐	Over 10 minutes to make a reservation	6–10 minutes to make a reservation	4–5 minutes to make a reservation	2–3 minutes to make a reservation	Below 2 minutes to make a reservation
Notice required for room cancellation	☐	48 hours' notice	24 hours' notice	Up to 12 noon on arrival day	Up to 6pm on arrival day	Up to 8pm on arrival day
Helpfulness of staff	☐	Often unhelpful	Occasionally unhelpful	Generally helpful	Always helpful	Nothing is too much trouble

Figure 10.13   SIMALTO scale – customer's priorities

- Very satisfied: 'Almost everything lived up to my expectations.'
- Satisfied: 'Most things lived up to my expectations.'
- Not satisfied: 'My expectations were not met.'

A positive biased scale will usually need its ratings qualified as shown above, since the differences between each step are very small. Customers who are not satisfied can be individually followed up to explore the reasons for their dissatisfaction and remedy the situation if possible.

Satisfaction

Using the table below, please indicate the standards you believe to be provided by the ABC Hotel and the ZZZ Hotel by placing an A for Hotel ABC and a Z for Hotel ZZZ in the appropriate boxes. Please mark one box on each row for each hotel. It does not matter whether you mark the same or different boxes for each hotel. If the item is not relevant to you place an X in the N/A box.

	N/A	Level 1	Level 2	Level 3	Level 4	Level 5
Accessibility by car	☐	Over one hour out of my way	31–60 minutes out of my way	16–30 minutes out of my way	6–15 minutes out of my way	Up to 5 minutes out of my way
Time taken to answer the telephone	☐	Over 45 seconds	31–45 seconds	21–30 seconds	11–20 seconds	Up to 10 seconds
Ease of making a reservation	☐	Over 10 minutes to make a reservation	6–10 minutes to make a reservation	4–5 minutes to make a reservation	2–3 minutes to make a reservation	Below 2 minutes to make a reservation
Notice required for room cancellation	☐	48 hours' notice	24 hours' notice	Up to 12 noon on arrival day	Up to 6pm on arrival day	Up to 8pm on arrival day
Helpfulness of staff	☐	Often unhelpful	Occasionally unhelpful	Generally helpful	Always helpful	Nothing is too much trouble

Figure 10.14   SIMALTO scale – supplier's performance

Of the two scales, the verbal scale is more appropriate than the Likert scale for measuring customer satisfaction because its wording is more neutral.

The same problems, of quantifying the results and separating high performing competitors, can be applied to semantic differential scales. The lack of qualifying scale also seems to make them less user-friendly, with respondents often striving to assign values to the points on the scale. This problem is exacerbated with the ungraded scale where the total absence of scoring guidance is often disliked by respondents.

Ordinal scales are very good for clarifying customers' priorities since there can be no equal marks awarded. They are also good for highlighting what suppliers do best and for demonstrating very clearly whether the supplier does best what matters most to customers. However, there are two problems.

Firstly, respondents find ordinal scales difficult to complete and are inclined to lose patience after a while, rushing through the remaining attributes to finish the task. The examples given in this chapter contain only five attributes but most customer surveys seek to measure a higher, sometimes far higher, number. This would be virtually impossible using an ordinal scale. The second problem is quantifying the responses. Assuming a list of ten attributes, the only way to quantify it is to assign a score of 10 to the attribute ranked first down to a score of 1 for the attribute ranked tenth. But this would mean that the supplier's performance is worth only 1, 2, and 3 out of 10 for the lowly ranked attributes, almost certainly a gross injustice to many of today's suppliers who perform well across the full range of attributes.

Only two of the rating scales can meet all of the objectives for customer satisfaction measurement as outlined in Chapter 5. They are the SIMALTO scale and the numerical rating scale (see Figure 10.15).

Of these two, the SIMALTO scale provides the most information. It is more precise than any of the other scales, assigning unambiguous performance levels to each attribute which also allows accurate comparisons to be made on future updates, although it copes less well with attributes which cannot be quantified precisely, such as helpfulness of staff. It is also very flexible, allowing different measures (for example, supplier and competitor(s) to be recorded on the same questionnaire). The zone of tolerance (ideal, expected and unacceptable level of service) would be far more difficult and time consuming to establish using any of the other methods.

However, as you may have concluded from Figures 10.13 and 10.14, SIMALTO scales are not easy to fill in. They are impossible to use in telephone surveys and, although they are used as self-completion questionnaires, there is a high risk that respondents will misunderstand or lose patience with them. SIMALTO scales depend on extensive exploratory research to identify the right entries for the various service levels, the questionnaires are often difficult to design and they need very careful piloting, all of which means that most companies would have to use a professional research agency. Finally, due to the format of the questionnaires, the results are laborious and difficult to communicate to colleagues within an organisation.

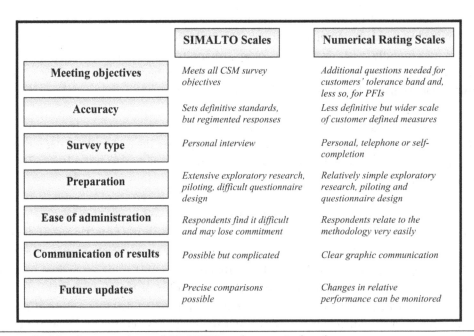

	SIMALTO Scales	Numerical Rating Scales
Meeting objectives	*Meets all CSM survey objectives*	*Additional questions needed for customers' tolerance band and, less so, for PFIs*
Accuracy	*Sets definitive standards, but regimented responses*	*Less definitive but wider scale of customer defined measures*
Survey type	*Personal interview*	*Personal, telephone or self-completion*
Preparation	*Extensive exploratory research, piloting, difficult questionnaire design*	*Relatively simple exploratory research, piloting and questionnaire design*
Ease of administration	*Respondents find it difficult and may lose commitment*	*Respondents relate to the methodology very easily*
Communication of results	*Possible but complicated*	*Clear graphic communication*
Future updates	*Precise comparisons possible*	*Changes in relative performance can be monitored*

Figure 10.15 A comparison of SIMALTO and numerical scales

This leaves the numerical rating scale which, in our opinion, is the best option. It is very respondent-friendly, can be used for personal or telephone interviews and self-completion questionnaires, and lends itself very readily to statistical analysis and visual communication of the results, especially in the key area of doing best what matters most to customers (see Chapter 12). Using a ten-point scale (marks out of 10) is familiar to respondents and provides enough gradations to accommodate the likely range of performance. For future updating the numerical scores can be easily tracked and you can monitor the gaps between your performance and customers' priorities and between your own and your competitors' performance.

Structuring the questionnaire

We can now review the structure of an effective customer satisfaction measurement questionnaire in the form of a step-by-step guide linked with the specimen questionnaires shown in Appendix I. Using business-to-business examples, we start with a personal interview questionnaire, which could be quite long, say 20–30 minutes, ideal for a market standing survey.

Later in this section we consider how the structure and design of the questionnaire would have to be modified for telephone of self-completion options where ten minutes would be the maximum time advised.

PERSONAL INTERVIEWS

Step 1: Ice breaker

To begin a conversation and to quickly build rapport with the respondent, start with topics that he or she will find easy and interesting, such as talking about their company and their own role within it. It does not matter if you are not going to use the information gathered, and you can see that this step (bottom half of first page) is left totally unstructured since you might want to take a completely different approach with some respondents. If the respondent's office displays a sports trophy, a certificate, an interesting photograph or an indication of a football team supported, it may be better in building a relationship to pursue one of these as a subject of conversation.

Step 2: Awareness of competing suppliers

An easy factual question which will form an effective lead in to the following two questions regarding the priorities of customers.

Step 3: Open question on customers' priorities

A question which fulfils three purposes. Firstly, it invites respondents to start thinking about their expectations when sourcing packaging; secondly, it will clarify the terminology used by the respondent (which you must note if your own subsequent questions use slightly different words); and, thirdly, it may isolate a priority which was not identified during your exploratory research, although this would be unusual. Little space has been allocated to this question as the answers are unlikely to be used for analysis purposes.

Step 4: Top priority

You now ask the customer what is the most important single requirement to him or her. The purpose of this question (as you will see when reading the introduction to the next question) is to use the respondent's top priority as a benchmark; this will help him or her decide how to score the detailed list of supplier selection criteria which follow.

Step 5: Closed questions on customers' priorities

This is the first important question and you can see that the interview has built up gradually towards it so that the respondent should now be well positioned to answer it accurately. A personal interview gives time to cover a long list of supplier selection criteria and these are grouped into categories, starting with the performance of the product itself. You may find it helpful with a list of this length to print a separate sheet listing the supplier selection criteria (reducing the type size if necessary to fit it onto one page), so that the respondent can read the points rather than having to rely on listening to the interviewer and then remembering each point.

Step 6: Closed questions for supplier performance ratings

The list of performance criteria is, of course, the same as that used in the previous question, enabling respondents to refer to the prompt sheet they have already been given. Since this is a market standing survey the interviewer will also be seeking scores for key competitors. The competitors to be included should be selected by the respondents, who will choose the ones they know the most about. It does not matter if the mix of suppliers rated changes slightly from one interview to another. You will also now see the additional value in the early question on supplier recall which suggested the names of competitors who could be included at this stage in the interview and started the respondents thinking about the relative merits of different suppliers.

The approach is to move down the list of criteria, eliciting a rating for ABC, and then for any competitors included before moving on to the next point. Any customer dissatisfaction should be probed in order to provide detail on the causes of problems.

Step 7: Open question on future trends

Although customer satisfaction measurement looks back from the present, evaluating past performance, the key purpose of the exercise is to help your company perform better in the future. It is therefore valuable to gather any information which might help to anticipate future customer requirements.

Step 8: Open question on PFIs

Although data already gathered at Steps 5 and 6 will provide quantitative evidence for PFIs, it is worthwhile adding an open question to gather some qualitative views from the respondent.

Both the wording of the question and the fact that it is separated from rating the performance of ABC should prompt the respondent to consider the matter afresh and, hopefully, to produce innovative ideas. Distinguish between the short term and the long term to draw out important strategic areas for improvement as well as urgent priorities to overcome any current problems.

Step 9: Classification information

You will have noticed that this sample questionnaire placed respondent classification data at the beginning, but that it was not mentioned at the start of the interview. In this type of market, respondent details would be known and already filled in before the interview. If details are not known, and particularly if they are sensitive (for example, annual spend in business markets or annual income in consumer markets), classification questions should be asked at the end of the interview.

TELEPHONE INTERVIEWS

If telephone interviews are used instead of face-to-face interviews, ABC's questionnaire would need to change; this is shown in Questionnaire B. The problem here is the shorter time scale, exacerbated by the lack of face-to-face contact making it more difficult to build a relationship and impossible to use a prompt sheet for the list of performance criteria. Some of the steps will therefore have to be eliminated and the approach modified for some of the remaining questions.

The first step to be eliminated is the ice breaker; you just haven't got time for it. Steps 3, and 4 can remain, with a very similar approach (though less discussion time for Step 3): they need not consume much time and they do make a strong contribution to the accuracy of responses for Steps 5 and 6. Exploratory research will have given a good indication of customers' priorities, so some of the less important criteria can be eliminated leaving the list shown in Questionnaire B. Any dissatisfaction with ABC should still be probed in a telephone interview since identifying its causes is a key objective.

SELF-COMPLETION QUESTIONNAIRE

In this type of market-place a self-completion questionnaire would not be advisable for the reasons outlined in Chapter 9. However, were a self-completion questionnaire to be used it would have to focus on the central issues of customer priorities and supplier performance, Steps 5 and 6. The open questions at the beginning (Steps 1 to 4) would not be effective on a

Table 10.9   Summary of questionnaire types

Steps	Customer satisfaction measurement objectives	Personal interviews	Telephone interviews	Self completion
1	Ice breaker	✔		
2	Awareness of competing suppliers	✔	✔	
3	Open questions on customer's priorities	✔	✔	
4	Ordinal scale on customer defined priorities	✔	✔	
5	Closed question on customer's priorities	✔	✔	✔
6a	Closed question on supplier's performance ratings	✔	✔	✔
6b	Probing dissatisfaction with ABC	✔	✔	
7	Projective question on image	✔		
8	Open question on future trends	✔	✔	✔
9	Open question on PFIs	✔		
10	Classification data	✔	✔	✔

self-completion questionnaire and would have to be replaced by a longer explanation of how to complete the first question, which is now Step 5. Open questions requiring open answers tend not to work very well on self-completion questionnaires because respondents lack the commitment to compose a response which requires some thought. However, you could include Steps 8 or 9 or even both and would probably get a few useful responses. The resultant questionnaire is shown as Questionnaire C.

Self-completion questionnaires are at their most useful when used at point-of-sale – and especially point of consumption for businesses providing a service. It is still advisable to undertake a more thorough customer survey with a controlled sample on a regular basis, but a short self-completion questionnaire can form a very useful ongoing indicator of any serious dip in service levels. The sample questionnaire, shown as Questionnaire D, is therefore very brief and concentrates solely on Step 6, supplier performance. It does not find out what is important to the customer and therefore cannot lead to the identification of PFIs. Nor does it shed any light on the supplier's relative performance against competitors. These issues would have to be addressed through a much more serious customer satisfaction measurement exercise, perhaps conducted on an annual basis.

Concise presentation on a small card will also make the questionnaire seem less daunting and therefore improve response rates.

The best way to maximize response rates is to ask customers to complete the questionnaire rather than simply making copies available. Using the example for the restaurant shown in Questionnaire D, the waiter could ask diners to complete the questionnaire whilst their bill is being processed and, to thank them for their trouble, could provide a complimentary pen bearing the restaurant's name and telephone number.

SUMMARY OF QUESTIONNAIRE TYPES

This section has demonstrated the wide gulf between the quantity and quality of information which can be gathered from personal interviews at one extreme and self-completion questionnaires at the other, with telephone interviews occupying a middle position. Table 10.9 summarizes the objectives that can be achieved through the different types of questionnaire.

Conclusions

- Questionnaires should be put through the three tests of knowledge, understanding and truthfulness.
- Always pilot questionnaires before carrying out surveys.
- Open questions are more useful for exploratory research and closed questions must be used if quantifiable answers are required.
- Always start a questionnaire with factual, behavioural questions before moving on to the more difficult attitudinal questions and, where possible, leave classification questions to the end.
- Rating scales lie at the heart of customer satisfaction measurement. Only SIMALTO scales and numerical rating scales can achieve the full range of customer satisfaction measurement objectives and of these two, numerical rating scales will prove the more practical for most companies.
- Be realistic about what can and cannot be included in questionnaires. Personal interviews can be very comprehensive, telephone interviews must be briefer and self-completion questionnaires need to be very concise and easy to follow.

11 INTERVIEWING SKILLS

AIMS
___

By the end of this chapter you will:
- Know how to conduct personal and telephone interviews.
- Have learned a number of techniques for encouraging people to participate, particularly in telephone surveys.

As the approach to personal interviews has already been considered in some detail (see Chapter 7 on conducting depth interviews and Chapter 10 on the survey interview), in this chapter we will concentrate on the behaviour of the interviewer.

Personal Interviews

In a controlled sample, typical of business markets, a personal interview will usually take place at the respondent's premises. An appointment will have been made, the respondent will be expecting the interview and will have been briefed beforehand, probably by letter. In consumer markets some interviews take place in the home but more often are conducted in the street; the respondent is unlikely therefore to have been briefed beforehand. In either eventuality, the starting point is always to brief the respondent as to the purpose of the survey, the format of the interview and the length of time it will take.

It is best not to rely on the memory of the respondent who was briefed some weeks before; they seldom remember what was said in the introductory letter sent to them earlier. It is always good practice to carry a copy of the briefing letter to show to the respondent as they may have mislaid or forgotten about their own copy.

For longer interviews in the respondent's home or at the office – as we discussed in the last chapter – it is a good idea to start with an ice breaker (often taking your cue from your surroundings) in order to build rapport. In shorter interviews, particularly those held on the street, you will not be able to afford the time for such luxuries as ice breakers.

It is unlikely that you will want to tape record even the longest of structured survey interviews. The personal interview questionnaire shown in Appendix I does not require a large amount of writing and would be typical of questionnaires at the survey stage which need to be highly structured if quantifiable data are to be gathered. In consumer markets the proportion of closed questions (or at least closed answers) is likely to be even higher. But, if you do tape record an interview, now is the time to introduce the recorder. Be confident about it, as though it is normal practice, and also introduce a benefit for the respondent saying it will speed up the interview by eliminating your slow writing. Of course, if the respondent displays any misgivings about the recording it should be abandoned immediately. In our experience it is far better to train yourself to write more quickly rather than use a tape recorder because it is far more efficient. Transcribing tapes after the event is extremely time consuming.

Most surveys start with easier, behavioural-type questions designed to put the respondent at ease even if there has not been time for an ice breaker. The interviewer should do everything possible to encourage the respondent at this stage through use of positive body language (smiling, nodding) and by making complimentary remarks about early answers. It's human nature for individuals to become more committed to a task if they think they are doing well at something – and respondents are no different from the rest of us!

In structured interviews it is particularly important to be as consistent as possible from one interview to the next. This means adhering to the form of words used on the questionnaire. When explanations or prompts are required they should be identified at the pilot interview stage and scripted into the questionnaire. Of course, there is a difference between consistency and reading questions like a robot. An interviewer operating on automatic pilot will often give the impression of not being interested in the survey or, even worse, not fully understanding the subject matter. Interviewers therefore need to develop the ability to maintain consistency whilst, at the same time, using natural, conversational speech patterns. Above all, they need to appear interested in both the interview itself and in the answers which the respondent is spending time and effort to supply.

Where the interview is not being recorded the interviewer should make every effort to capture as much as possible of what the respondent says, especially answers to open questions. This is applicable also to an open question, closed response, where the temptation just to tick appropriate boxes must be resisted. In this type of question the respondent will often think out loud, elaborate, qualify responses. The interviewer should try to always add interest to the findings at the reporting stage. Even closed questions will often elicit additional respondent comments and these should be noted whenever possible in the questionnaire margins or on a separate pad.

Once the survey is completed, thank the respondent. It is customary in consumer markets also to thank the respondent officially in writing. This is done by way of a thank you leaflet or card which also explains, in general terms, the purpose and authenticity of the research (Figure 11.1).

The Leadership Factor

Taylor Hill Mill
Huddersfield
HD4 6JA

Tel: 01484 517575

Thank you for taking part

Why was I asked to help?
On most research jobs we have to talk with a cross-section of the public; people from all walks of life and all ages. Sometimes we have to talk to people who either have something specific like a microwave oven or have done something specific like having a holiday in a particular place or country. Sometimes people are asked to help because they work in a particular place. All of this is to make sure that the people whose opinions we collect are representative of the rest of the population.

How can I be sure that someone is a genuine market reasearcher?
The researcher is wearing a badge with his/her name and the name of the company for whom he/she is working. Also you can telephone the company on the above number. They will confirm that the researcher is genuine.

Is the information confidential?
The survey is for market research purposes only and in no circumstances will the information, or details about you be passed on to any other party.

Finally, we would like to thank you once again for sparing some of your time to help us

---

Figure 11.1 Thank you note for consumer markets

Suppliers conducting customer surveys in business markets will often want to thank respondents individually with a letter and a small gift (see Chapter 13). As soon as possible after the interview, go through the questionnaire checking your comments and adding details where necessary. During the interview there is time only to scribble rough notes when the respondent makes comments; your notes therefore may appear unintelligible if left for some days (and after more interviews have taken place). By checking them immediately, or as soon as possible after the interview, comments made during conversations will still be fresh in your mind and you will be able to fill in any gaps or re-write the scribble.

Telephone Interviews

Telephone interviews benefit considerably from thorough preparation beforehand. A well organized contact sheet (Table 11.1) clearly showing names, telephone numbers and any classification data required for quota purposes should be prepared. Each entry includes a large space for noting suggested call-back dates and times – important for surveys in business markets where managers will often be very difficult to contact.

With the contact sheet a systematic procedure can be adopted after each call: check your questionnaire (if an interview was successfully completed) or note a possible call-back date and time; then scan down your contact sheet and immediately telephone the next entry on the list who might be available that day.

Assuming you have organized yourself, the next challenge is getting through. If it is a controlled sample respondents will have been invited to participate, usually by letter, which also provides brief details of the nature and purpose of the survey. If you are working from a quota sample in a business market, perhaps using a list from a directory or *Yellow Pages* (which is quite possible for a market standing survey), you will have no contact names and the people you need to interview will not be expecting your call or to be asked to take part in a research survey. To overcome these barriers your approach will therefore have to be very professional.

In organisational markets you never know who is going to answer the telephone. In a large company it will usually be a receptionist; in a small firm it could be anybody from the owner downwards. Whoever it is, you have never spoken to them before, nor they to you. In this situation, one little phrase works like magic: 'Can you help me please?'. Use it every time as it generally results in a positive response and the beginnings of a rapport with the person answering your call.

You can then explain, 'I am trying to contact the person responsible for production. Do you know who that person is?'. There are two things to note here. Firstly, don't use a job title – it will vary from one company to another even for people with identical responsibilities. Secondly, your style of question should elicit a name: 'Oh yes, that will be Mr Smith, shall I

Table 11.1   Contact sheet

Project:			Interviewer:				
Name of respondent	Company	Tel. No.	Date & time when called			Outcome	
			1st call	2nd call	3rd call	interview achieved	Reason for non-interview

put you through?'. If a name is not mentioned try to find it out before you are connected so that you can greet Mr Smith. Should you be asked why you wish to speak to Mr Smith, say that he has been chosen to take part in a customer satisfaction survey – which sounds better than 'a market research survey'. In circumstances where the supplier's name can be disclosed, and especially if it is likely to impress, use it: 'He has been chosen by AB International to take part in a customer satisfaction survey'.

It may be that you will experience further difficulties in getting through to the person you want, or be told that it is against company policy to take part in surveys. Do not persevere in such a case, it is more productive to leave it and move on.

When you have successfully made contact with Mr Smith, start in exactly the same way: 'Good morning/afternoon Mr Smith, my name is Jim Alexander from The Leadership Factor. I wonder if you could help me please?'. This approach will, we hope, receive a positive response from Mr Smith. You continue: 'Am I right in believing that you are responsible for production?'. You receive a second affirmative from Mr Smith. Now you have an opportunity to put the big question: 'I'd like to invite you to participate in a customer satisfaction survey organized by AB International. It takes only ten minutes over the telephone. Is it convenient to do the interview now or would you prefer me to make an appointment to ring you back at a better time?'

Here, of course, you have offered Mr Smith two options, both of which suit your purpose. Although this is an old trick, the old ones are usually the best and it often works. Mr Smith may say that he is not a customer of AB International, in which case you must explain that the survey is to identify the needs and assess the satisfaction of a cross-section of all buyers or users of whatever the product or service is. When inviting Mr Smith to participate you must communicate a very positive attitude. Be confident, sound interested, don't hesitate. Most people will decide within the first 15–20 seconds if they are or are not going to cooperate.

If you follow the approach outlined above, you will have received two positive responses from Mr Smith before you ask the big question. There is no other method of contacting cold, unknown prospects which will achieve a higher success rate. It is very helpful to script and rehearse your entire introduction, especially if you are carrying out your own survey and you or your interviewers are not experienced in telephone research.

Utilize a similar approach when contacting consumers at home. If you use the telephone directory you start with the advantage of knowing the respondent's name. In consumer markets it is easier to make contact than it is in business markets, and also easier to secure participation in most circumstances. An important factor in consumer markets is identifying the best time of day to make the approach. It is not always what you would expect. Self-employed people in the building trade, for example, are often best contacted in the two hours between arriving home from work and going out in the evening. Despite strong competition from activities such as eating meals, showering and watching Coronation Street you have to try to contact potential respondents between 6.00 p.m. and 8.00 p.m because you probably won't succeed at any other time.

Having secured participation for a telephone interview launch straight into the questionnaire. It is important to pilot telephone questionnaires to make sure that the questions are easily assimilated by respondents. Long questions and unfamiliar words will cause serious problems. The difference between personal and telephone interviews is the greater need to encourage and motivate telephone respondents. They have never met you and they can't see you. Your relationship with them is very tenuous so you must work hard to maintain their interest and commitment. Tell them how interesting and useful their answers are, agree with them and if any opportunity arises have a laugh. You should also give the respondent feedback on progress ('only two more questions now'), especially if you are nearing the end of your stated time span. A clock or stop watch on the desk is very useful for monitoring interview duration. At the end of the interview always thank the respondent and check through your questionnaire before moving on to the next interview.

Conclusions

- Always brief respondents on the purpose, format and duration of the interview, even if they have previously received details by post.
- It is better not to rely on tape recording interviews. As well as being time consuming after the interview, tape recorders will make some respondents feel uneasy. Check through the questionnaire immediately after the interview to overcome problems caused by hurried writing.
- The interviewer should always be conscious of the need to encourage respondents and provide feedback in personal as well as telephone interviews.
- Recruiting respondents for telephone interviews, particularly from cold lists, relies on a very positive and well rehearsed approach.
- Telephone interviewers should prepare a contact sheet with spaces left open for recording call-back dates to avoid losing time between interviews.

12 ANALYSIS AND REPORTING

AIMS

By the end of this chapter you will:

- Appreciate the advantages and disadvantages of analysing the results of your survey manually or by computer.
- Understand basic statistical techniques for the interpretation of survey data.
- Be aware of the appropriate techniques for analysing different types of rating scales.
- Be able to 'code' open questions to organize large volumes of seemingly unstructured comments.
- Appreciate a variety of techniques to display survey results.
- Be able to define and make use of an overall 'Customer Satisfaction Index'.
- Develop effective ideas for communicating survey results internally and involving colleagues in determining the implications of the results.
- Understand the advantages of conducting an internal survey.

Choice of Software

This is not a book about the relative merits of specific software packages but we will briefly outline the main software options for analysing customer satisfaction data.

There is a wide choice of specialist computer software for analysing survey results. One of the most common packages is 'SNAP', developed by Mercator Computer Systems. Designed to be user-friendly, the program allows you to enter results as though you were writing them on the questionnaire. Statistical analyses are displayed in table or chart form. Pinpoint by Logotron is similarly aimed at market researchers, and SPSS by SPSS (UK) Ltd is a sophisticated statistical analysis package. Details of suppliers of specialist software are provided in Appendix 4.

Until recently, it was an unwelcome compromise to use anything other than the type of specialist software mentioned above. Now, the leading spreadsheet packages are able to provide all the statistical analysis you are likely to need for customer satisfaction measurement.

The big advantage of using a well-known spreadsheet package is that most organisations use them and employ people with the necessary operating skills. There are, too, advantages for reporting since spreadsheets offer a wide range of graphical options for displaying results and can link into sister packages for word processing reports or producing slides for presentations. Compared with the specialist research packages, the only disadvantage is that a spreadsheet database has to be compiled for each survey, with columns appropriately labelled to cover each question, one row assigned to each respondent and appropriate analyses programmed in to the columns at the foot of the spreadsheet itself. However, for anyone with reasonable spreadsheet skills this is a very simple task. Microsoft Excel now makes this easier by providing a data entry form, pivot tables for cross tabs and an extra module (the Analysis ToolPak) with extra statistical procedures.

Analysing Numerical Scales

Having interviewed a representative sample of customers to measure their individual satisfaction levels, there are several statistical analyses that should be carried out if you are to draw accurate conclusions about the satisfaction of the customer base as a whole.

AVERAGE

More accurately defined as the 'arithmetic mean', the average of a string of values is the most commonly used measure to define overall customer satisfaction. It is easy to communicate and widely understood provided a suitable rating scale (for example, a ten-point numerical scale) has been used.

However, this commonsense average can occasionally provide misleading results, so it is prudent to supplement the arithmetic mean with some additional analyses to confirm the validity of conclusions.

Table 12.1 is based on the personal interview questionnaire shown in Appendix I. Column headings refer to individual questions in the 'Field Sales Performance' category. These are:

- Frequency of visits.
- Technical capability of representative.
- Commercial capability of representative.
- Interpersonal skills of representative.
- Empowerment of representative.
- Accessibility (available when needed) of representative.

Using Excel, the analyses are based on:

Table 12.1   Sample spreadsheet

Field sales performance						
Respondent	Frequency	Technical	Commercial	Personal	Autonomy	Access
1	9	7	8	10	9	10
2	9	7	10	10	9	10
3	8	8	8	4	8	10
4	10	7	9	9	10	9
5	10	10	1	5		6
6	8	7	8	8	7	10
7	9	7	9	10	9	6
8	9	9	8	9	6	7
9	8	7	9	4	8	9
10	10	7	8	9	7	7
Average	9	7.6	7.8	7.8	7.8	8.4
High	10	10	10	10	10	10
Low	8	7	1	4	6	6
Standard deviation	0.77	1.02	2.36	2.36	1.31	1.62
Median	9	7	8	9	8	9
Mode	9	7	8	9 and 10	6, 7, 8, 9	10
Base	10	10	10	10	9	10

AVERAGE	=	**the arithmetic mean**
MAX	=	**the largest value in a list**
MIN	=	**the smallest value in a list**
STDEV	=	**the population standard deviation of a list**
MEDIAN	=	**the middle value in a sorted list**
MODE	=	**the most frequently occurring value in a list**
COUNT	=	**the total number of non-blank cells in a list**

RANGE

Whatever the rating scale it is useful to know the range of marks given as well as the average. An apparently satisfactory average score of 8.6 out of 10 could hide a wide range of individual scores possibly including a small minority of highly dissatisfied customers. In a spreadsheet, the range will be shown by displaying the highest and lowest scores in the column of values.

The range is not a very satisfactory measure since it is based on only two of the values in the entire list of numbers. This could be misleading if either the highest or the lowest values are untypical, extreme scores, as shown in the values in the 'Commercial' column of Table 12.1.

Comparing the scores for commercial capability with the scores for interpersonal skills shows the danger of relying on the range as a measure of dispersion. Both have a similar average score, but the range of values in the 'Commercial' column (1 to 10) suggests a more diverse spread of opinion than the range in the 'Personal' column (4 to 10). In reality, the views of most respondents on the representative's commercial capability are quite close, with one extreme value resulting in an untypically wide range of 1 to 10.

STANDARD DEVIATION

The standard deviation is less affected than the range by extreme and untypical values. It is a very accurate measurement for showing how closely the values in a list cluster around or diverge from the average. The standard deviation is lower if the values cluster closely around the mean and becomes higher the more they diverge from it (see Table 12.2).

For the mathematically inclined, the standard deviation is defined as the square root of the variance, or

$$\text{Standard deviation} = \sqrt{\frac{\Sigma(x - \bar{x})^2}{n}}$$

Using the list of values from the 'commercial capability' column, Table 12.2 shows how to calculate the standard deviation.

Comparing the 'Commercial' capability values from Table 12.1 with the values for interpersonal skills shows the limitation of the range indicator and the usefulness of the standard deviation. Although the range of commercial capability scores is 50 per cent greater (9 compared with 6), the 'Standard deviation' is the same. This is produced by the greater number of values (4s, 5s and 10s) that diverge from the mean in the interpersonal skills column. In fact, if Table 12.1 showed a more typical sample size (100 respondents) a single extreme value such as the 1/10 in the commercial capability column would have far less impact on the standard deviation. However, if the bipolar pattern (that is, people either like or dislike the representative, with very few respondents occupying middle ground) shown in the interpersonal skills column, were repeated over a much larger sample size, the 'Standard deviation' would remain similar. This is a useful feature in customer satisfaction measurement for demonstrating when the average score may be an unreliable measure because customers cluster into two or more groupings. This will not usually occur on rating the supplier's performance, although measures such as rating representatives' interpersonal skills are more likely to display the characteristic since there are several different representatives and therefore several different levels of performance.

Even if the results were isolated for each individual territory, you might expect a higher standard deviation because of the subjectivity of the measure.

Table 12.2 Calculating the standard deviation

Value		Variance is difference between value and average value	Variance squared
	(x)	(x-x)	$(x-x)^2$
	8	0.2	0.04
	10	2.2	4.84
	8	0.2	0.04
	9	1.2	· 1.44
	1	-6.8	46.24
	8	0.2	0.04
	9	1.2	1.44
	8	0.2	0.04
	9	1.2	1.44
	8	0.2	0.04
Totals	78	0	55.60
Averages	7.8		5.56
The standard deviation is the square root of 5.56, i.e. 2.36			

A high standard deviation may also show up in the section on customers' priorities. For example, buying at the lowest possible price may be very important to some customers but far less important to others. This variance in customers' priorities can be a very effective way of segmenting markets according to customer needs.

MEDIAN

The median is the true middle score – the middle of a list of numbers when all the values are arranged in order or magnitude. The median is sometimes preferred to the mean as a true average if a very small number of wayward values significantly distort the arithmetic mean.

Let's take as an example, overdue deliveries. A firm may have recorded ten late deliveries in the previous month as shown in Table 12.3. Typically, overdue deliveries are one, two or at most three days late but the occasional delay with a bought-in component or a design problem will exceptionally result in a seriously overdue delivery. In this example the median lateness is clearly more representative of the real situation. In customer satisfaction measurement, however, it is unusual for the median value to be a more useful indicator than the arithmetic mean. One reason for this is the relatively narrow range of the commonly used rating scales, making it impossible for exceptional values to diverge as excessively as the example shown in Table 12.3. Another problem with the median for customer survey analysis is that it will typically be a round number, and with suppliers tracking very small shifts in average scores the median is unable to provide the required accuracy.

MODE

The mode is simply the value with the highest frequency, i.e. the greatest number of mentions. The advantages and disadvantages associated with the median also apply to the mode. This measure is not generally used in satisfaction measurement but is very useful when dealing with shoe or clothing sizes which do not deal in decimal points

BASE

The final row in Table 12.1 uses the COUNT function to simply count the number of cells in which a value exists. This will demonstrate if large numbers of respondents have been unable to answer a particular question, which may point to a problem area. For example, if a significant number of respondents felt unable to rate the supplier company on environmental management and the company has passed the ISO 14000 standard, it clearly has a need to educate its customer base however high the average score of those respondents who did express an opinion. The count function can also be very useful on market standing surveys where the number of values for some minor suppliers will be very low, possibly to the point of rendering the data meaningless.

CROSS-TABULATIONS

One of the most interesting and revealing analyses to undertake is the cross-tabulation which extracts and compares subsets of data. This enables, for example, comparison between the

Table 12.3   Mean and median averages

Overdue deliveries		
Delivery number	Despatch date	Days overdue
21680	04/10/99	1
21698	05/10/99	1
21731	09/10/99	1
21731	20/10/99	1
21696	09/10/99	2
21720	13/10/99	2
21721	13/10/99	2
21760	18/10/99	2
21784	25/10/99	3
21582	26/10/99	48
Mean lateness = 6.3 days Median lateness = 2 days		

Table 12.4   Frequency distribution

	Very satisfied	Quite satisfied	Neither satisfied nor dissatisfied	Quite dissatisfied	Very dissatisfied
Opening hours	34	27	6	21	12
Queuing time	4	18	48	19	11
Courtesy of staff	47	31	20	2	0
Knowledge of staff	16	26	28	23	7
Friendliness of staff	32	24	23	10	1
Appearance of staff	40	44	16	0	0

priorities of purchasing managers and production managers or young versus older customers. It also enables the supplier to see if it is rated more highly in some market segments than in others, to consider why it is rated more highly in its stronger segments and to use those conclusions for strategic decision making. Cross-tabulations can be used to examine any type of segment, provided respondents have been appropriately classified.

There is a strong argument for including as many classification categories as possible at the survey design stage since the cross-tabulation function can be used to isolate any number and permutation of respondent groupings during analysis. Very often the results will be of little interest, but sometimes they can be very revealing. Cross-tabulations on customers' priorities can even help companies to redefine their segmentation of the market and can serve as the basis for loyalty segmentation.

Analysing Verbal Scales

If verbal-type scales, such as the verbal or Likert scales shown in Chapter 10, are used for questionnaires, the results must be analysed using a frequency distribution – in other words, how many people said what. A frequency distribution is shown in Table 12.4. The numbers are usually percentages, so in the example shown, 34 per cent are very satisfied with the opening hours and 27 per cent are quite satisfied. It is a totally accurate summary of the results, but it does not make a very strong impression.

Table 12.5   Changing verbal to numerical scales

Strongly agree/very satisfied	+2	or	5
Slightly agree/quite satisfied	+1	or	4
Neither agree nor disagree/neither satisfied nor dissatisfied	0	or	3
Slightly agree/quite dissatisfied	+2	or	2
Strongly disagree/strongly dissatisfied	+2	or	1

It would be possible to produce charts for individual attributes, each with five bars showing varying levels of satisfaction or importance by attribute. However, the real problem is the absence of a single average score for each attribute. For example, it is not possible to make a direct comparison between the importance score for opening hours and the satisfaction score for opening hours, so you cannot carry out a gap analysis to arrive at the PFIs. That is a major disadvantage of using a verbal-type scale because what you can do with the results is very limited compared with the numerical scale.

Some people look at the data they get from verbal-type scales, recognize its limitations and realize that it would be much more useful to have numerical average scores. They then immediately solve the problem by changing the points on the verbal scale into numbers and carry on as though they had used a numerical scale from the outset. People change five-point verbal-type scales into various numerical scales as shown in Table 12.5.

The numerical data in Table 12.5 illustrates one of the problems. Once you decide to change the information given to you by the customers into something else, what do you change it into? The two sets of numbers shown in the table will not give the same result. Even if everybody standardized on the 5-4-3-2-1 scale, how can you be sure that a customer who responded 'quite satisfied' would have scored 4 on the numerical scale. As a general rule, it should never be the researcher's role to change any answers provided by respondents. However, there is an even bigger problem caused by changing verbal responses into numerical scales. It is not statistically valid, as illustrated by Figure 12.1.

Strictly speaking a numerical scale is known as interval scaling and it is statistically valid to average the scores given by customers because all the points on the scale are equi-distant and assume equal proportions in the respondent's mind. With a verbal-type scale, strictly called a categorical scale, the points on the scale do not assume equal proportions in respondents'

Interval and categorical scaling

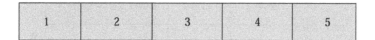

Interval scaling = means and standard deviation

Very poor	Poor	Average	Good	Excellent

Categorical scaling = frequency distributions

Figure 12.1 Interval and categorical scaling

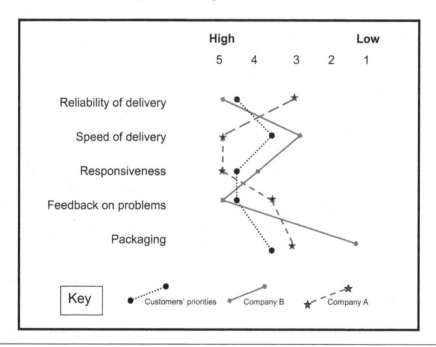

Figure 12.2 Performance profiles

minds, as shown in Figure 12.1. For that reason it is only considered to be statistically valid to analyse a categorical scale using a frequency distribution like the one shown in Table 12.4.

PERFORMANCE PROFILES

An alternative way of displaying results which is often used for ungraded and semantic differential scales, but can also be used for verbal or numerical scales, is profiling. Using this method, the number of points on the scale is displayed across the top of a grid with the

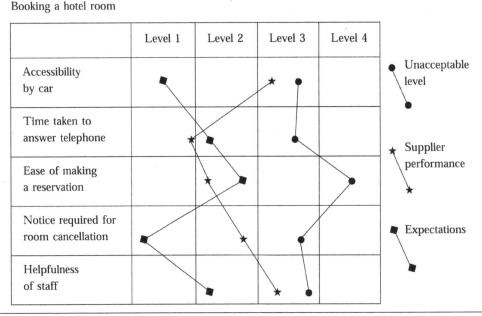

Figure 12.3   Performance profiles for SIMALTO scales

performance criteria down the side. The average scores are then plotted against the scale resulting in 'profiles' or 'maps', as shown in Figure 12.2.

The more closely the supplier's profile tracks the customer priorities profile the better its performance is. In the example shown, Company A is clearly meeting customers' needs more closely than Company B. The technique does relate very well to ungraded and semantic differential scales and also facilitates comparisons: for example, your organisation's performance profile against customers' priorities and/or against competitors' performance. However, many people do find performance profiles difficult to assimilate and it is our belief that the combination of tables and bar charts provides a more effective method of communicating results.

A similar principle is often applied to analysing and reporting SIMALTO scales (see Figure 12.3), but the outcome can be complex, especially if there is a large number of questions. Imagine the problem of colleagues trying to figure out your slide when you are presenting the result.

Coding

Using open questions (such as questions 3–5 in the ABC Ltd personal interview questionnaire in Appendix I), generates a large volume of unstructured information which requires organizing if you are to draw meaningful conclusions from it and to report the findings in a concise form. The

Table 12.6   Coding

Environmental trends	Number of mentions
Environmental legislation	31
Eco-labelling	23
Pressure from direct customers	22
Pressure from consumers	16
Environmental pressure groups	8
Pressure to achieve ICO 14000	5
Total mentions	105
Total respondents	68

most commonly used technique to achieve this objective is coding. In Chapter 10 we considered the technique of using open questions with closed, unprompted responses. Although it feels like an open question to respondents, researchers can analyse it as efficiently as a closed question.

The objective of coding is to reach the type of outcome shown in Table 12.6, but to do this *after* rather than *before* the interviews. This is achieved by scanning through all the completed questionnaires, reading the responses to just one question on each pass. As you scan the responses make a list of the points made by each respondent. The points can then be grouped into categories and the number of mentions for each category recorded. Though a time-consuming process it is worth doing accurately. If in doubt, have more rather than fewer categories. Comments with a different emphasis are kept separate rather than lumped into one category for the sake of simplicity. For example, many respondents might have mentioned environmental trends in response to question 4 in the ABC Ltd questionnaire, but to simply code all as 'Environmental trends' could be too simplistic. Subdivide the category as shown in Table 12.6, which still enables an overall total for the number of environmental mentions to be recorded.

Since an individual respondent could have mentioned more than one of the specific environmental trends noted in Table 12.6 it is important to record how many of them mentioned anything to do with environmental trends.

Open questions are particularly useful for generating interesting quotations, especially questions such as 3 and 5 in the ABC Ltd questionnaire. Quotations are always of interest to your audience and should therefore be included in reports and presentations. They can easily be collated separately, whilst post coding open questions, and should always be referenced to add authenticity. If respondent anonymity was promised, references will refer to respondent type: for example, 'Production Manager, Paint Industry' or '35–44 year old C2 male, married with 2 children'.

The Basic Results

Whether for a report or a presentation, results need to be displayed in a form which enables the audience to quickly and easily assimilate the information without over-simplifying it.

Using the ABC Ltd questionnaire and focusing on the two core questions, importance to customers and suppliers' performance, presenting the basic results is outlined below.

IMPORTANCE

Different people relate more easily to different forms of presentation. For example, some people easily assimilate tables of numbers whilst others are more comfortable when presented with a graphic. It is therefore best to convey information in more than one format in order to maximize audience understanding.

As a starting point we recommend a simple table showing customers' priorities in the form of their average (arithmetic mean) score, as shown in Table 12.7. The tabular format accommodates data in a single table, even when many customer satisfaction criteria are involved. The table gives an overview but we would not recommend adding any additional detail (e.g. standard deviation) since this would detract from the picture at this stage. Detail can be included as appendices.

Table 12.7   Customers' priorities in tabular form

Product performance	Importance score	Field sales performance	Importance score
Consistency of product quality	9.33	Frequent calls	4.66
Technical performance of product	9.66	Technical capability of representative	7.50
Comprehensive product range	4.16	Commercial capability of representative	8.50
Supplier must have good quality systems	8.00	Inter-personal skills of representative	8.66
Supplier must have high standards of hygiene	7.50	Adequate empowerment/autonomy	8.83
Other documentation (e.g. health and safety)	6.33	Accessibility	9.16
Delivery and service performance		**Pricing performance**	
Reliability of delivery	9.50	Supplier must offer the cheapest price	8.00
Speed of delivery	8.00	Price negotiation or handling	6.75
Packaging	6.60		
Ease of ordering	5.00		
Feedback, especially on problems	9.50		
Confidence in continuity of supply	7.83		
Technical service performance		**Environmental performance**	
Ability to innovate/R&D expertise	7.50	Supplier must be environmentally responsible	6.0
Design expertise	8.50	Supplier has recycling capability and expertise	5.2
Responsiveness on technical service	8.50		

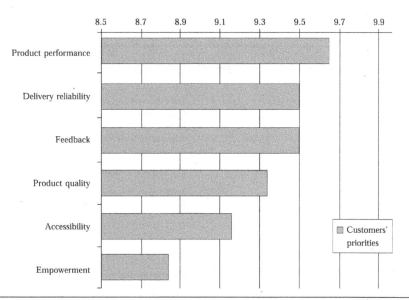

Figure 12.4 Customers' top priorities in bar chart form

You should then provide exactly the same information as a graphic. Although software will produce all kinds of clever and complicated graphs, a simple bar chart (for example, Figure 12.4) is by far the best for easy assimilation. However, a bar chart showing all the results that were included in the table may be too crowded in which case the information should be broken down. We would start by showing customers' top priorities in order of importance and then show each category (product, delivery, etc.). This is an extremely important chart since it encapsulates all the areas where you can most easily upset customers. If you have low scores on any of these factors they will become PFIs and must be addressed urgently. Even those criteria where you have good scores are potential drivers of dissatisfaction. They represent areas where maintenance of performance is essential and may be headed 'Service Recovery Priorities'. The latter are areas where you need to get it right first time but even more right the second time. In other words, if you do make a mistake or receive complaints in these areas you must have good service recovery procedures in place. These procedures must resolve the problem and you should, ideally, present customers with a bottle of wine or bunch of flowers so that their enduring memory is the way you resolved the complaint rather than the complaint itself.

PERFORMANCE

The results for customers' level of satisfaction with your own performance can now be shown in exactly the same way starting once more with the full table as shown in Table 12.8. In a market standing survey, we would not introduce competitor scores at this stage. Let the audience assimilate your own performance first.

Table 12.8   Supplier performance in tabular form

Product performance	Average	Field sales performance	Average
Consistency of product quality	8.23	Frequent calls	9.57
Technical performance of product	8.71	Technical capability of representative	8.00
Comprehensive product range	7.71	Commercial capability of representative	9.00
Supplier must have good quality systems	8.43	Inter-personal skills of representative	9.83
Supplier must have high standards of hygiene	8.57	Adequate empowerment/autonomy	8.83
Other documentation (e.g. health and safety)	8.33	Accessibility	9.17
Delivery and service performance		**Pricing performance**	
Reliability of delivery	8.57	Supplier must offer the cheapest price	8.33
Speed of delivery	9.14	Price negotiation or handling	7.66
Packaging	8.80		
Ease of ordering	9.20		
Feedback, especially on problems	8.42		
Confidence in continuity of supply	8.57		
Technical service performance		**Environmental performance**	
Ability to innovate/R&D expertise	9.00	Supplier must be environmentally responsible	9.57
Design expertise	8.66	Supplier has recycling capability and expertise	9.48
Responsiveness on technical service	8.50		

The Satisfaction Index

It is very useful for internal purposes, such as monitoring service improvement, motivating staff and bonuses to have a figure which represents your customers' overall level of satisfaction. This is known as the satisfaction index. Since numerical scales must be used to calculate mean scores, the ten-point numerical rating scale will be used for our explanation of developing a satisfaction index.

The simplest way of arriving at a satisfaction index is to average all your performance scores. That would not be ideal because some things are more important to customers than others, and their most important requirements influence their satisfaction judgement more than those that are less important to them. An accurate satisfaction index therefore has to work in the same way. It has to be more strongly influenced by the attributes with the highest importance scores. In other words it must be a weighted average satisfaction score, which requires a two-step process for its calculation.

STEP 1: CALCULATING THE WEIGHTING FACTORS

The importance scores are used to calculate the weighting factors. The first column of data in Table 12.9 shows the average importance scores from a fictitious supermarket survey. To calculate the weighting factors simply total all the importance scores. In this example they add up to 68.6. Then express each one as a percentage of the total. Using 'staff appearance' as an example, 7.3 divided by 68.6, multiplied by 100 produces a weighting factor of 10.64 per cent.

Table 12.9   Calculating the weighting factors

	Importance score	Weighting factor
Location	9.4	13.70%
Range of merchandise	9.2	13.41%
Price level	9.1	13.27%
Quality of merchandise	8.9	12.97%
Checkout time	8.5	12.39%
Staff helpfulness	8.3	12.10%
Parking	7.9	11.52%
Staff appearance	7.3	10.64%
TOTAL	**68.6**	**100%**

Table 12.10   Calculating the Satisfaction Index

	Satisfaction score	Weighting factor	Weighted score
Location	9.2	13.70%	1.26
Range of merchandise	7.9	13.41%	1.06
Price level	8.8	13.27%	1.17
Quality of merchandise	9.1	12.97%	1.18
Checkout time	7.4	12.39%	0.92
Staff helpfulness	7.7	12.10%	0.93
Parking	8.6	11.52%	0.99
Staff appearance	8.5	10.64%	0.90
Weighted average		8.41	8.41
TOTAL			**84.1%**

STEP 2: CALCULATING THE SATISFACTION INDEX

The second step is to multiply each satisfaction score by its corresponding weighting factor. The first column of data in Table 12.10 shows all the average satisfaction scores and the second column shows the weighting factors that were calculated in Table 12.9. Taking staff appearance as the example again, the satisfaction score of 8.5 multiplied by the weighting factor of 10.64 per cent produces a weighted score of 0.9. The overall weighted average is determined by adding up all the weighted scores. In this example they add up to 8.41, so the supermarket's weighted average satisfaction score is 8.41 out of 10. It is normal to convert that score into a percentage and say that the satisfaction index is 84.1 per cent.

In this example, the satisfaction index shows that the supermarket is 84 per cent successful in satisfying its customers. To demonstrate the mathematical basis of the formula, imagine that the supermarket was such a wonderful supplier that all the customers surveyed insisted on giving satisfaction scores of 10 out of 10 for every one of the customer requirements. In that eventuality the average satisfaction scores would all be 10. The weighting factors would all stay the same because they come from the importance scores, and the weighted scores in the right hand column of Table 12.10 would all be different from each other, but they would all add up to precisely 10.0. That is how the formula works. Total customer satisfaction on all their requirements would produce a satisfaction index of 100 per cent.

UPDATING THE SATISFACTION INDEX

You must be able to update the satisfaction index so that it provides you with a comparable measure of satisfaction that you can monitor in the years ahead, even if the questions on your questionnaire change to suit customers' requirements. Basically, the satisfaction index answers this question:

**'How successful are we at satisfying our customers according to
the *n* things that are most important to them?'
(where *n* = the number of attributes on the questionnaire)**

If the questionnaire changes in the future because customers' priorities have changed, the satisfaction index remains a measure of the same question:

**'How successful are we at satisfying our customers according to
the *n* things that are most important to them?'**

That comparability also applies for organisations with different customer groups who might have to be asked different questions in the same year. Provided that the exploratory research has been correctly undertaken, the satisfaction indexes from two or more surveys asking different questions are directly comparable.

The Outcomes

DOING BEST WHAT MATTERS MOST

The first outcome of a customer satisfaction survey is produced when you put the importance and the performance scores together and ask that very simple but absolutely fundamental

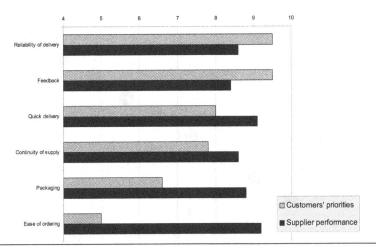

Figure 12.5   Gap analysis to highlight PFIs

question, 'Are we doing best what matters most to customers?'. The answer to that question is shown in Figure 12.5. By comparing the importance and satisfaction scores you can use 'gap analysis' to identify PFIs (priorities for improvement). Not rocket science, gap analysis indicates that if the performance bar is shorter than the importance bar the company may have a problem! But that is the main strength of the chart. It is clear, simple and obvious. Anybody in the organisation can look at it, understand it and draw the right conclusions.

The biggest gaps between importance and performance highlight where the company is failing to meet customers' requirements and these are the attributes it needs to focus on if it wants to improve customer satisfaction. These are the PFIs, the priorities for improvement. The bigger the gap, the bigger the problem. However, there are other factors to consider when deciding what the PFIs should be.

DETERMINING THE PFIs

We would say that typically on a ten point scale any gap above 1 is significant and gaps in excess of 2 are serious but, by definition, it is not feasible to have too many priorities for improvement. When deciding which gaps are the most serious and should be adopted as PFIs five factors should be considered.

Factor 1: Size of gap

The most important factor is the size of the gap. Normally a greater gain in customer satisfaction will be achieved by closing a large gap rather than a small gap.

Factor 2: Stated importance

Almost as significant as the size of the gap is the importance of the issue to customers, whose satisfaction judgement is more heavily influenced by their most important requirements.

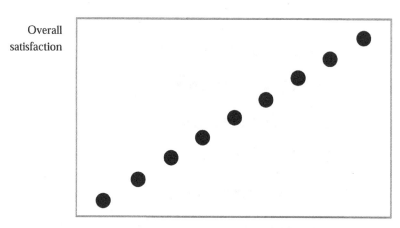

Figure 12.6   +1 correlation

Closing a slightly smaller gap on something that is a top priority to the customer may therefore generate more satisfaction gain than addressing a larger gap on an issue of lower importance.

Factor 3: Derived importance

Stated importance scores are often said to overemphasize the givens. For example, if you ask customers direct questions about the relative importance of a list of attributes concerning air travel, they will invariably give a high score for 'safety'. Nobody will say that the safety of the aircraft is unimportant. By comparison, most customers will give a lower importance score for 'the quality of food' served during the flight. It is, of course, important that aircraft are safe, but safety is a given. It is essential that all airlines perform well on safety simply to be allowed to operate in the market.

Differentiators are attributes where the suppliers in a market do not all perform equally and therefore help to distinguish between suppliers. In the air travel example, food can be a differentiator, especially on long-haul flights. A very good or a very bad experience with the food may therefore have a disproportionate influence on the customer's overall satisfaction judgement and future choice of supplier. Since stated importance scores can sometimes overlook these 'drivers of satisfaction', an alternative measure is required. This is known as derived importance.

Derived importance is identified statistically, using correlation, rather than by asking direct questions to customers. To calculate derived importance, a simple question on overall satisfaction must be inserted on the questionnaire. Each individual respondent's scores for the individual attributes are then correlated with their overall satisfaction score, and those that correlate highly are said to be the 'drivers of satisfaction'. The theory is illustrated in the diagrams. Figure 12.6 shows a perfect correlation.

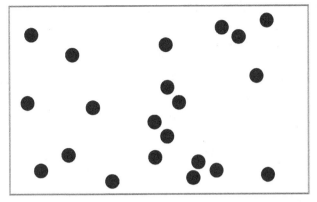

Satisfaction with location of store

Figure 12.7   Zero correlation

Table 12.11   Comparing stated and derived importance

Requirements	Stated importance	Derived importance
Cleanliness of store	9.27	0.48
Choice of products	9.19	0.59
Prices	9.16	0.55
Quality of products	8.84	0.50
Speed of checkout	7.80	0.51
Opening Hours	7.40	0.44
Layout of store	7.19	0.39
Helpfulness of staff	6.84	0.61
Staff appearance	6.12	0.38
Base		500

Customers who are extremely satisfied with 'helpfulness of staff' are extremely satisfied overall with the supplier. Those who are very dissatisfied with 'helpfulness of staff' are very dissatisfied overall. 'Helpfulness of staff' must therefore be a very strong driver of customer satisfaction.

The second example, Figure 12.7, shows the lowest possible correlation, 0.0. Of the customers who are highly satisfied with the 'location of the store', some are extremely satisfied overall but others are very dissatisfied with the supplier overall. By contrast, some customers are very dissatisfied with the location but very satisfied overall whilst others are dissatisfied with both the location and the company overall. The 'location of the store' shows no correlation with overall satisfaction and is therefore not a factor which is significantly influencing customer satisfaction for that company.

The way to use derived importance is to compare the rank order of attributes according to stated importance and derived importance. Some organisations place more reliance on derived importance than stated importance. This is misguided. Stated importance should always be given prominence since it reflects what the customers are saying. It is not sensible to believe that you know the customers' minds better than they do just because you have used a few clever statistical techniques. However, derived importance should be used to supplement stated importance scores because the stated importance scores might overlook one or more strong drivers of satisfaction. Table 12.11 shows that, for the company concerned, 'helpfulness of staff' is clearly a driver of satisfaction and this should be reflected in the company's decisions about its PFIs.

Factor 4: Business impact

However important customer satisfaction is, it should not be bought at any price. Ultimately, the decision to invest in customer satisfaction improvement has to be a trade-off between the cost of making those improvements and the potential gain from doing so. To clarify that business impact decision it is helpful to plot the potential satisfaction gain against the cost and difficulty of making the necessary improvements. A hypothetical business impact matrix is shown in Figure 12.8.

The most positive business impact will be made by adopting PFIs which will generate the greatest possible gains in customer satisfaction at the lowest possible cost. Based on categorizing customer requirements into three broad bands according to the cost and difficulty of making improvements, the business impact matrix illustrates where the most cost-effective gains can

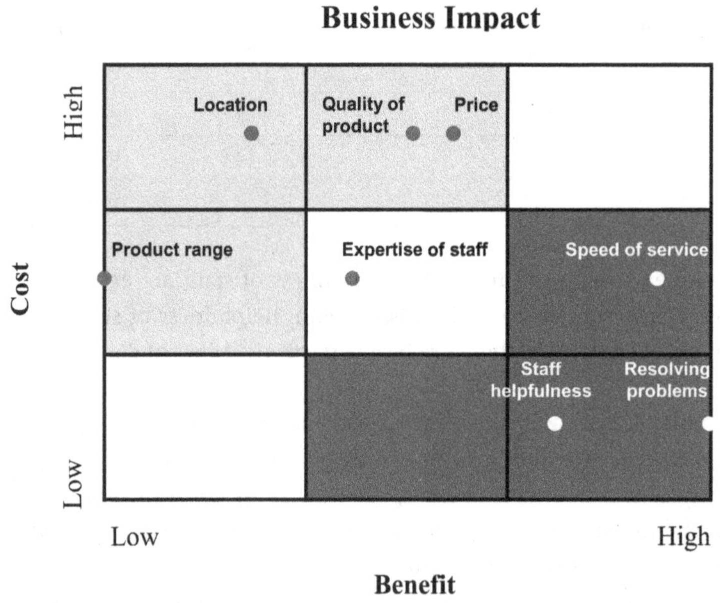

Business Impact

Figure 12.8 Business impact matrix

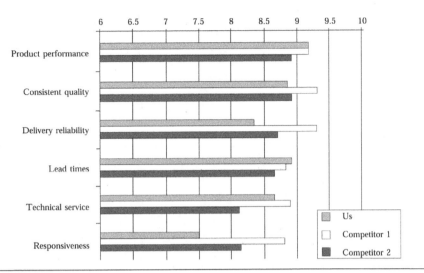

Figure 12.9   Bar chart showing comparison with competitors

be made. As shown in the figure, some requirements, particularly those in the cells in the bottom right hand corner, such as range of merchandise and staff helpfulness, should bring high returns due to their large satisfaction gaps, and relatively low cost. However, requirements in the top left hand corner, such as parking, would bring little benefit, due to low or non-existent satisfaction gaps and high relative cost. We are certainly not advocating avoidance of the difficult issues, but we do believe it is important to adopt at least one PFI which can be addressed relatively easily – a quick win. It is very helpful if both customers and employees can see prompt action being taken as a direct result of the survey.

Factor 5: Policy/Regulations

Some organisations may be constrained from closing some gaps by circumstances beyond their control such as regulations or by a deliberate corporate strategy which is contrary to customers' wishes. A public sector or government regulated organisation may have several aspects of its relationship with customers dictated by such constraints. In the foreseeable future a supermarket can do little about the location of its individual stores even if customers were dissatisfied with 'convenience of store location'. A company whose strategy is to be a premium priced supplier may choose not to close a gap on price. All of these positions are perfectly valid, but whenever there are gaps that the supplier cannot, or chooses not to, close it must work particularly hard to close any remaining gaps. You need to give customers enough reason to go the extra mile to the less convenient location or to pay the price premium.

Based on the five criteria outlined above, senior management must quickly determine the PFIs for their organisation. Speed is of the essence. Once the survey results are known, every day that passes is another opportunity lost to improve customer satisfaction and, maybe, another lapsed customer. Senior management should schedule their meetings to review customer

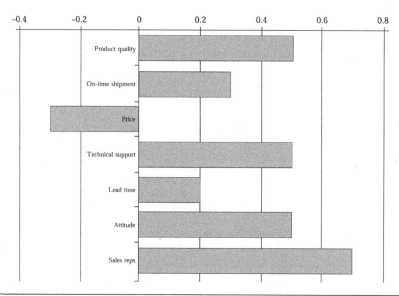

Figure 12.10 Positive-negative bar chart showing differential against competitors

survey results and set PFIs well ahead, as soon as they know when the survey results will be available. They should also schedule the next critical phase of the process well in advance – disseminating the results and the action plan to other staff in the organisation.

COMPARISONS WITH COMPETITORS

For a market standing survey you can produce similar results. There will be only one set of importance scores but a set of performance scores for each supplier. The suppliers' performance scores can be shown using a simple bar chart in the same format as before – see Figure 12.9. An alternative method is to focus on the differences rather than the scores themselves. Use a horizontal bar chart (Figure 12.10) and a scale showing negative as well as positive values – unless you are better at everything! You can only use this method to compare your performance against one competitor at a time or, as in the Figure 12.10 example, against the average scores for all competitors.

The best solution is probably a combination of both charts, Figure 12.9 used to show your performance and that of each competitor with a positive–negative chart used to provide an overview of differentials. As a matter of interest, the values shown in Figure 12.10 are authentic values from a real survey conducted by Milliken Industrials in the market for industrial textiles. The company is achieving a price premium for its superior performance in customers' other priority areas.

If you have undertaken a market standing survey it is possible to produce a league table of competing suppliers' performance as rated by customers. To do this you have to weight the

Table 12.12   Weighting customers' purchase criteria

Customers' purchase criteria	Average	Weighting
Product	8.99	0.171
Delivery	8.70	0.165
Price	9.06	0.172
Continuity of supply	9.29	0.177
Communications	8.55	0.162
Technical service	8.08	0.153

customer satisfaction criteria according to their importance to customers, as shown in Table 12.12.

As explained in the previous section, the importance weightings are calculated simply by totalling the six purchase criteria listed, giving a total of 52.67 in the example shown, and then expressing each individual customer priority as a proportion of the total. Thus, taking reliable delivery, 8.70 divided by 52.67 gives 0.165. As you would expect, the sum of all the weighting factors will be 1. It is then a simple matter to multiply the supplier performance scores for each company by the weighting to give a weighted average, as shown in Table 12.13. Each supplier's weighted averages can then be totalled to give an overall weighted average score out of 10, showing their relative market standing as defined by customers.

Reporting Internally

Reporting internally involves more than simply producing a few tables and bar charts although these will make a strong contribution to effectively communicating the results. The chief medium for disseminating the results internally will be a report. This may be circulated, but its impact will be increased if a formal presentation of its findings is made to appropriate staff.

REPORT AND PRESENTATION

If a presentation is to be made the audience should include as many staff as can possibly be accommodated. The report and the presentation need to be as closely linked as possible and should both adhere to the following format:

- Introduction
- Sampling

Table 12.13 Calculating competing suppliers' market standing

Customers' requirements	Weight	Company A		Company B		Company C		Company D	
		Average	Weighted average	Average	Weighted average	Average	Weighted average	Average	Weighted average
Product	0.171	8.14	1.39	8.33	1.42	8.66	1.48	7.94	1.36
Delivery	0.165	8.02	1.32	8.96	1.48	8.90	1.47	7.25	1.20
Price	0.172	6.82	1.17	7.64	1.31	7.44	1.28	7.08	1.22
Continuity of supply	0.177	7.79	1.38	8.59	1.52	8.77	1.55	7.86	1.39
Communications	0.162	7.75	1.26	7.87	1.27	8.54	1.38	6.06	0.98
Technical Service	0.153	7.41	1.13	8.31	1.27	8.65	1.32	8.08	1.24
TOTALS	1.00		7.65		8.27		8.48		7.39

- Research methodology
- Survey results
- PFIs.

Introduction

Taking no more than one page this should simply outline the mechanics of the exercise such as dates of the exploratory research and the survey; the number of customers interviewed; the method of interview/data collection and so on. The following two sections will explain these mechanics in more detail and justify the methods used.

Sampling

As suggested in Chapter 8 a customer satisfaction survey must be based on a truly representative sample if it is to have credibility. The purpose of this section of the report and presentation is to establish that credibility. Therefore, enough detail should be provided to explain the sampling method used, stressing its randomness if it is a random sample, or its objectivity if it is a non-probability sample. If quota sampling has been used, substantiate the breakdown of the survey population, perhaps by using population statistics from the local authority or the census in a consumer market; or by using authenticated sources, such as a trade association or a well respected directory in a business market.

Research methodology

Having demonstrated that you have included the right businesses/people in your sample, demonstrate that you asked them the right questions.

This means explaining your methodology and results of the exploratory research before moving onto questionnaire design. Here it will be worth highlighting the cornerstone of the methodology – that is, establishing customers' priorities and rating your company's performance against the same criteria.

The final element of this section is the survey method. Here you will need to explain why the method was chosen and how it was implemented. If your own staff were used for interviewing mention any training they undertook and any measures adopted to ensure objectivity.

The final part of this section should explain how the survey was introduced to customers (see Chapter 13). Appendices can be added to give the full questionnaire and a copy of any introductory letter to customers.

Survey results

The main results of the survey can be reported using the bar charts suggested in this chapter, with just brief explanatory comments for each one. Any open questions can be post-coded and reported.

Computer analysis tends to yield large volumes of data, particularly if cross-tabulations have been used to extract data for different customer groupings. You will need to be selective on how much of this information you report. If it will not add anything to your colleagues' understanding, don't include it. A good test for whether or not to include any additional breakdowns is to ask what conclusion you would draw from the information. If you can't draw a worthwhile conclusion, leave it out. In some organisations it may be politically necessary to include all your results. If so, include a complete set of results as an appendix but keep the body of the report for a concise overview of the main results.

When presenting the results, clarity and simplicity are paramount. You should therefore consider all possible ways of simplifying the results. One way is to focus solely on the gaps rather than communicating importance and satisfaction scores. You can also use the traffic light principle in charts: red for danger – i.e. large satisfaction gaps and major PFIs; yellow for areas which are not major problems but could be better, and green for customer requirements which are being met or exceeded. An example is shown in Figure 12.11.

Another reporting issue concerns organisations with multiple outlets. Where these exist, the best way for the organisation as a whole to improve customer satisfaction is often to raise the standards of the poorer performing outlets rather than addressing a standard set of PFIs across all outlets. It is therefore very important to have a sufficiently large sample to produce results, including gaps and a satisfaction index for each outlet. You can then produce a league table but must decide whether the results are linked to each outlet (everybody knows who is top and who is bottom) or whether they are anonymous, as shown in Figure 12.12. The darker bar (84&) shows the overall company index.

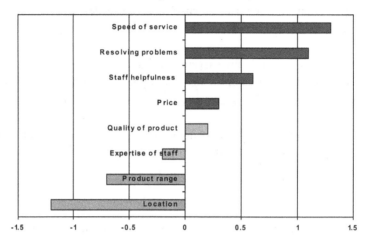

Figure 12.11 Gaps chart

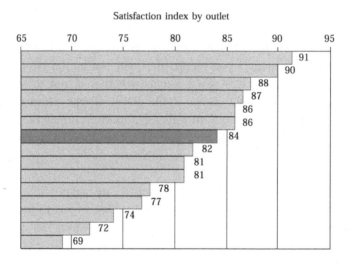

Figure 12.12 Satisfaction index by outlet

Once you are tracking satisfaction over time, it is especially important with multiple outlets to monitor and communicate improvements, or regression. Due to differences in their product offering which are beyond their control (e.g. store size or location), or to differences in the type of customers which they serve, it may be difficult for some outlets to aspire to head the league table. An outlet close to the foot of the league table which makes a significant improvement in its satisfaction index may therefore have achieved more than one near the top whose customer satisfaction has fallen slightly. A good chart for highlighting such differences is shown in Figure 12.13.

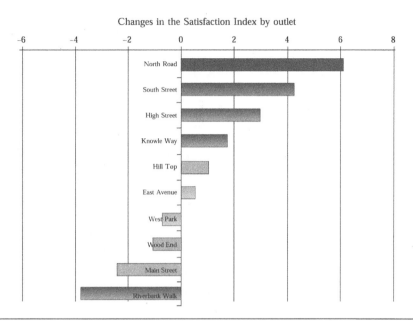

Figure 12.13   Changes in the satisfaction index by outlet

PFIs

As a researcher you draw conclusions from the results of your survey. In the case of customer satisfaction measurement these conclusions will be PFIs. It is not normally the researcher's domain to go on to recommend how the PFIs should be addressed, but simply that they must be addressed.

Again, clarity is essential, and when it comes to PFIs, the main source of confusion is likely to surround responsibility for their implementation. Since different departments and teams have different roles and responsibilities they will not all have an equal ability to affect the PFIs. In the case of multiple outlets the PFIs will vary between outlets. To be effective, people need a very clear indication of what they are responsible for. Senior managers also need to be able to see at a glance where responsibility lies for addressing the PFIs and improving customer satisfaction (see the action map in Figure 12.14). Again, you can use the traffic light principle, with red blobs for major PFIs, yellow ones for minor PFIs and green blobs where there is no problem or that particular department cannot have any impact on addressing that particular PFI.

So far, the presentation should have faithfully followed your report and you may need all the available time to simply convey that information and handle any questions. However, if you have more time available the group can begin the discussion of how PFIs should be addressed. In a small group this discussion can proceed informally, but if you have a larger audience you will need to programme a breakout session where staff can discuss in small groups the implications of the survey and report back to the plenary session with their ideas

| | | ACTION MAP: Region 1 | | | | | | | | | | | | |
| | | Central functions | | | | | | | | | Stores | | | |
Requirement	Size of gap	Marketing	Merchandising	Customer service	Product dev.	Personnel	Training	Purchasing	Facilities mgt	I.T.	Leeds	Hull	Huddersfield	Harrogate
Cleanliness of store	−1.82													
Stock availability	−1.68													
Choice of products	−1.36													
Layout of store	−1.21													
Speed of checkout	−1.19													
Prices	−0.87													
Special offers	−0.52													
Quality of products	−0.21													
Loyalty scheme	+0.38													
Helpfulness of staff	+1.03													
Opening hours	+1.14													
Café/restaurant	+1.28													

● Major PFI   ◌ Minor PFI   ◉ All Clear

Figure 12.14 Action Map

for the way forward. Correctly handled, this will be the first step towards the organisation as a whole taking ownership of the results and taking decisive steps towards addressing the PFIs.

Internal Survey

Whilst carrying out a customer survey it is a good idea to take the opportunity to administer the survey to a sample of your own staff, using the core sections of rating customers' priorities and your own performance for the internal survey (sometimes called a mirror survey).

This exercise demonstrates how well your own staff understand what matters most to customers and how your organisation is perceived to perform. Almost invariably, the results will demonstrate that your organisation's understanding of what matters to customers is far from perfect. This in itself provides a useful internal lesson, demonstrating that everyone needs to work harder at understanding customers' needs. More importantly, it may also provide some ideas for how you can begin to address PFIs and improve customer satisfaction since the attitude of your own staff will often be a key factor in the level of service provided by your organisation. If staff have the wrong ideas about what matters most to customers they may be focusing their efforts in the wrong areas.

A good example of this problem was identified by a customer survey carried out for Thai Airways. Managers were seen to be more concerned than customers about some aspects of service (employees' appearance, for example) but under-estimated the importance to customers of other aspects, such as the regular provision of information and care during delays. This is a good example of the type of service gap discussed in Chapter 2. Identifying such gaps is a major step towards improving customer satisfaction and it is only through administering questionnaires internally as well as externally that a confident diagnosis can be made.

Since you are likely to draw important conclusions from your internal survey it is important that it is accurately carried out. As well as using exactly the same wording as on the customer questionnaire, it is important to ensure the accuracy of the sampling. If it is not feasible to conduct a census, the sample must be random and also must faithfully reflect different departments and levels within your own organisation. The sample should cover all staff, not just those with direct customer contact since staff apparently remote from customers can often have a significant impact on customer satisfaction.

One final point on the accuracy of an internal survey concerns the method of data collection. Ideally, the method should be the same as that used for the customer survey. In practice, a self-completion questionnaire will often be used internally even if personal or telephone interviews were used when surveying customers. This is acceptable, since the main argument against self-completion questionnaires (the poor response rate sabotaging sampling accuracy) can be overcome internally through the imposition of a 'three-line whip'. But self-completion questionnaires used internally must be completed seriously and carefully. The importance of the exercise must be stressed and staff also must complete questionnaires individually, not in groups or pairs where their responses may be influenced by colleagues. Moreover, if they are to be totally honest (e.g. about where they think the organisation is performing very poorly), the questionnaires must be anonymous and confidential. This means placing them in a sealed envelope and, ideally, allowing employees to return them direct to an objective third party such as a research agency.

Questionnaire A in Appendix I provides an example of an internal survey questionnaire.

Conclusions

- Modern spreadsheets such as Microsoft Excel are perfectly adequate for analysing customer satisfaction data, are very good at turning data into tables and charts and have the added possibility of linking with sister packages, for example for the production of presentation materials.
- Means and standard deviations are used to analyse numerical scales, frequency distributions are correct for verbal scales.

- Open questions require careful coding with broad response categories broken down into subsections in order to retain the full range of respondent views.
- A combination of tables and bar charts will be the most effective method of displaying survey results.
- A satisfaction index will help to guide and motivate staff towards the objective of improving customer satisfaction.
- A report and internal presentation should start with a brief introduction followed by sections on sampling, research methodology, survey results and PFIs.
- An internal survey should be conducted in parallel with a customer survey since this will often identify important service gaps.

13 PR ASPECTS

AIMS

By the end of this chapter you will:

- Be able to introduce the survey to customers in a way which will maximize participation.
- Appreciate the importance of providing post-survey feedback to customers and understand how to produce a report of the survey findings for an external audience.
- Understand the need, under certain circumstances, to modify customers' perceptions and develop techniques to do so.

In this section we examine the introduction of the customer satisfaction survey from the initial announcement within an organisation through to the arrangement of appointments for customer interviews.

Introducing the Survey

Most customers are prepared to cooperate with a customer satisfaction survey provided it is introduced in the right way.

INTERNAL ANNOUNCEMENT

The first step is to inform your own people what's happening. This step is very frequently overlooked or performed inadequately by management.

Your own staff need to know:

- that the exercise is taking place;
- its purpose;

- the form and timing of the survey;
- how to respond to customers if asked about it.

If your organisation has team briefing it provides the ideal channel for informing all staff and giving them the opportunity to ask any questions. If you don't have an effective method of personal communication it should be done in the form of a circular (email, internet, memo as appropriate) with all staff encouraged to raise any questions with their superiors.

It is particularly important to discuss the survey at the exploratory stage with colleagues who are going to be responsible for taking action on PFIs after the survey. If the exercise is to be successful in the long run, staff such as the distribution manager, the production manager and the sales office manager must be on your side rather than against you. There are two ways of ensuring this. Firstly, the chief executive must be totally behind the survey and must be seen to be its strongest supporter. Secondly, you must involve key colleagues in the planning of the survey so that they will take ownership of its methodology and consequently its findings. Although it is impractical to involve all staff to this extent your objective should be to ensure that they all view the survey in a positive light. Encourage them to see it as an exercise which will help the company and help them and certainly not as something which might threaten them. Portray the exercise as a leading edge technique which will make the company more competitive. This can be strongly reinforced by the action you take after the survey (see Chapter 16).

INVITATION TO CUSTOMERS

In business markets customers should be informed and invited to participate by letter. If you are using a self-completion survey the letter will accompany the questionnaire. If you are undertaking personal or telephone interviews the letter should precede any attempt to make an appointment. Figure 13.1 summarizes the main points to include in your introductory letter.

The letter should cover three main areas. These are:

- objectives of the survey, including benefits for customers;
- how the survey will be carried out;
- what will happen after the survey, including benefits for customers.

Yes, the letter is a selling exercise, designed to obtain maximum customer participation (in terms of the numbers who agree to participate and the level of commitment given to the exercise). The letter should emphasize the benefits for customers, clearly and frequently.

Start with the survey objectives, which allows you to include at least two customer benefits in the first paragraph, the objectives of understanding what is important to customers and improving the service provided to customers.

The second paragraph explains how the survey will be conducted. If customers are to be

```
┌─────────────────────────────────────────┐
│        ┌──────────────────────┐          │
│        │   Customer Survey    │          │
│        └──────────────────────┘          │
│  Dear Customer                            │
│     ┌────────────────┐                    │
│     │ 1. Objectives  │                    │
│     └────────────────┘                    │
│        •  Improve our understanding of your needs │
│        •  Gather your feedback on our performance │
│        •  Improve the service we provide to you   │
│                                           │
│     ┌────────────────┐                    │
│     │ 2. Survey      │                    │
│     └────────────────┘                    │
│        •  Telephone interviews            │
│        •  No more than 10 minutes         │
│        •  Make an appointment convenient for you  │
│                                           │
│     ┌────────────────┐                    │
│     │ 3. Afterwards  │                    │
│     └────────────────┘                    │
│        •  Summary of survey findings      │
│        •  Key issues and proposed action  │
│        •  Even better service to you      │
│                                           │
│     Thank you in anticipation of co-operation │
└─────────────────────────────────────────┘
```

Figure 13.1   Introductory letter to customers

interviewed, the duration of the interview should be specified. Make it clear that customers will be contacted to make an appointment which is convenient to them, even for a telephone interview. In this paragraph, too, customers can be given advance notice of the topics to be covered in the survey, but under no circumstances should they be given a copy or a preview of the questionnaire for personal or telephone interviews. The reason for this is to ensure interview consistency – all questions asked in the same way at each interview. If respondents are given a copy of the questionnaire prior to the interview some will consider it carefully whilst others will totally disregard it until the interview resulting in a lack of consistency between respondents' positions. If nobody has previewed the questionnaire, all respondents will base their answers on their perceptions – the same perceptions on which they are making judgements and expressing opinions on suppliers most of the time.

The third paragraph is very important for two reasons. Firstly, it provides the customer with tangible evidence of the value of the exercise and, secondly, it commits your organisation to action after the survey. Incredibly, some organisations do invest significant sums of money in customer surveys and do not take appropriate action subsequently. In addition to wasting money, such behaviour can generate negative PR. Many customers will remember that there was a survey, that they received no feedback and that nothing has changed since!

You should therefore make a commitment to customers at this stage that you will provide feedback after the survey, outlining its results and key conclusions. Moreover, you should tell them that you will inform them of any action you propose to take as a result of the survey plus the timescales within which those actions will be taken.

Sometimes the sales force will wish to inform some customers personally about the survey in order to protect their close relationship with them. This should be viewed in a positive light, but the sales force must be briefed on what they should say, and this should closely mirror the contents of the letter. The role of the sales force should be to encourage participation, not to provide detailed information about the content of the survey. If the sales force wish to inform customers personally it must be scheduled and a clear date specified when the letter will be sent. To ensure consistency, the letter should be sent to all respondents in the sample, including any briefed personally by the sales force.

Surveys in consumer markets should follow the same procedure if a self-completion questionnaire, telephone interviews or personal interviews in the home are to take place. In consumer markets letters are frequently required to accompany postal questionnaires. The emphasis of a consumer letter should be no different from the example outlined in Figure 13.1. Just because it is going to consumers it does not mean that it has to degenerate into a timeshare mailshot with a prize draw leaping out from every corner of the page and at least three postscripts. It is true that an incentive may increase the response rate and this option should be tested (as outlined in Chapter 9), but many postal surveys achieve a very high response rate without incentives. This is achieved by concentrating on the purpose of the survey, how useful the respondent's information is, and how results will benefit all customers.

In consumer markets it is important to remove any element of suspicion in respondents' minds by emphasizing that the survey is for research purposes only, by outlining to them why they have been selected to participate and explaining the role of any agency involved. It will be useful if the letter is from a very senior person, preferably the chief executive, and it can help to include a photograph of him or her on the letter if four-colour print is being used. It is also helpful to strongly personalize the letter if your database is sufficiently sophisticated.

As well as addressing the letters to named individuals you may refer to their relationship with your organisation with phrases such as: 'As a member of XXXX for six years, we would particularly like your views on ...'. Or, 'As the buyer of a new Mondeo 2.0i within the last three months both we at Ford and the staff of the local dealership, XXXX, would very much welcome your views.'

However, if quota sampling is used it will not be practical to invite respondents to participate in this way, whether interviews are carried out in the street, in the home, or by telephone. For personal interviews a standard letter can be provided for the interviewer to hand out at the time of the interview. All respondents should be offered feedback on the survey results and their names and addresses recorded for this purpose.

It is also customary to follow up a small sample of respondents to verify that interviews were properly conducted.

Feedback to Customers

Immediately following the survey it is advisable to send out a brief letter to all respondents thanking them for their help and reminding them that they will receive feedback as soon as you have analysed the information and considered the results.

INITIAL FEEDBACK

This interim letter is a useful PR step; firstly, because it thanks the respondents fairly soon after their interview and, secondly, because it may be some time before you are in a position to provide the feedback report. The letter can be accompanied by a small thank you gift (say, a quality pen), particularly for those companies in business markets with a small customer base. You will be returning to many of the same customers in future years when updating your survey, so retaining their goodwill for the exercise is particularly important.

Whilst most surveys are anonymous, respondents sometimes voice a complaint during an interview which they wish to be forwarded to the supplier. Any direct complaints of this nature should obviously receive an immediate and personal response from the supplier with the matter resolved in the same way that you would handle any other customer complaint. If your own staff carry out the interviewing, a respondent making a negative comment probably expects a swift response so review each questionnaire to determine whether an individual response is required.

If an open comments box is included as part of an attributed self-completion questionnaire, you must be organized to respond individually to customers. Respondents will view the survey as a communication with the company (even if it is being sent back to an agency) and some will use the comments box for all kinds of purpose, often totally unconnected with the survey. Always respond to such queries and handle complaints, taking whatever action is required, in a timely manner.

FEEDBACK REPORT

Once the survey results have been analysed, you have reached agreement on PFIs and determined the action that will be taken by your organisation, you are in a position to provide feedback to respondents. This should be a short report, preferably no more than four sheets of A4 paper. Anything longer is likely to be lodged in a pending tray to be read later, when the recipient has time, which usually means never. For the tiny minority who may feel the report is too brief, a covering letter can invite them to contact you if they would like more information.

Following surveys in mass markets you still need to provide feedback but there may be less costly ways than posting an individual report to each respondent: you could publish the results in, say, a company newsletter, an in-flight magazine or the local newspaper. But do ensure the respondents are informed on the questionnaire when and where feedback will be presented. An increasingly attractive option in consumer markets is to create a customer survey feedback page on your website with results updated as required.

Your feedback report should include the following sections.

Introduction

This is very brief and includes the dates of the survey, the sample size and its representative nature.

Results

This concentrates on customers' priorities and your own company's performance. These two core questions can be conveyed in one simple bar chart, listing the customer satisfaction criteria in order of importance to the customer, then showing the results for importance to the customer and for your own organisation's performance, as shown in Figure 13.2.

Using this format it should be possible to fit the introduction and the results onto one page of your report even for lengthy questionnaires, such as the ABC Ltd personal interview example. A more concise alternative is to show only the satisfaction scores on the chart (Figure 13.2) since the importance results are less relevant to customers.

Some companies are reluctant to provide respondents with a complete set of results, particularly if their own performance scores are rather unimpressive. They are tempted to provide a general summary such as the example shown in Figure 13.3. Our view is that in customer satisfaction measurement feedback, as in many other aspects of relationships with customers, there is more to be gained than lost through openness. If you don't report the scores but provide a short written report on the results there is a danger that it will be bland and meaningless and customers will view it as a worthless exercise. Moreover, performance scores which are less than brilliant will be obvious to customers, especially as they have only just commented on your performance and provided the scores for the survey. They will soon spot an attempt at a cover up. Customers are not dim and shouldn't be treated as such!

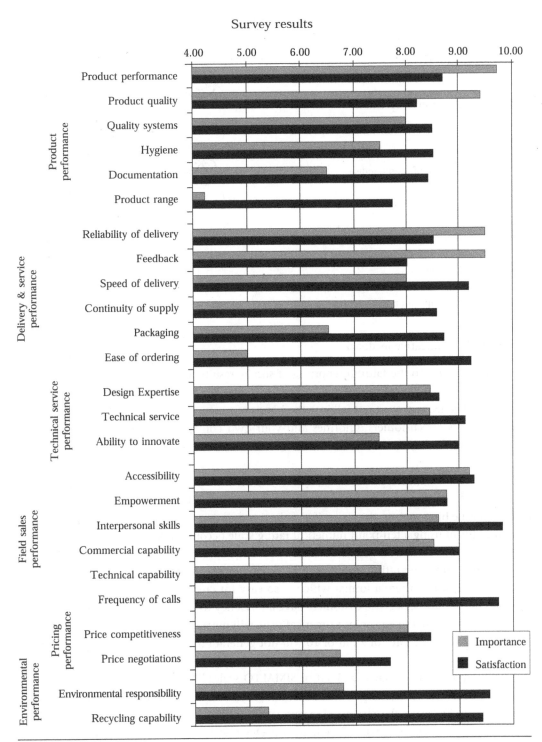

Figure 13.2 Customer feedback on the ABC Ltd Survey

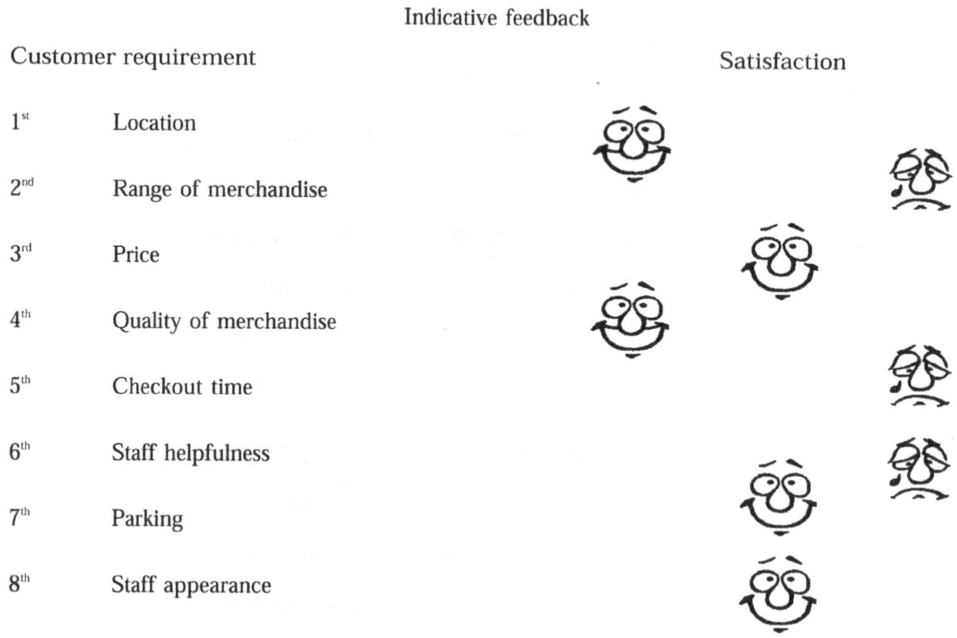

Indicative feedback

Customer requirement   Satisfaction

1st   Location

2nd   Range of merchandise

3rd   Price

4th   Quality of merchandise

5th   Checkout time

6th   Staff helpfulness

7th   Parking

8th   Staff appearance

Figure 13.3   Indicative feedback

The only exception to the faithful reporting of survey results will be the scores for the relative performance of competing suppliers generated by a market standing survey. This is valuable market intelligence and must not fall into the hands of a competitor. We would therefore report back the scores for customers' priorities and your own company's performance as suggested earlier and simply make no reference to the scores of other suppliers.

If your questionnaire involved other questions, such as questions 3–5 in the ABC Ltd questionnaire, you should report very briefly on the findings. This may provide an opportunity to inject a little humour into the report if a projective question is involved. At the feedback stage more benefits of using a ten-point numerical rating scale become apparent.

Firstly, there is no other rating scale which could be reported at concisely as the results shown in Figure 13.2, nor is there a format which is so easy for customers to understand. Secondly, and more importantly, because customers have a tendency to give marks ranging from 5–6 out of 10 to 10 out of 10, the ten-point numerical scale will portray your performance in a positive light. Even mediocre scores of 7 out of 10 will not generate negative PR.

Faithfully reporting the results of Likert or SIMALTO scales blatantly demonstrates that some customers have rated you very poorly; even when only a small number of customers rate you in this way it can be very embarrassing. One very large multinational computer company's survey used a five-point Likert scale with 'Excellent' and 'Diabolical' as the extremes. Predictably, some customers rated the company as diabolical on some performance attributes. When the chief executive insisted on giving customers accurate feedback on the results the sales force had sleepless nights over their company's dented image, particularly if competitors' sales people got hold of the information!

PFIs

This section should outline your conclusions. By focusing on 'Priorities for Improvement' and using it as the title for this section of your feedback report you can present a positive image to customers, both about the attitude of your organisation and the value of the survey. It is most effective simply to list the PFIs as bullet points.

Action

This is the section that will make the greatest impression on your readers. Subdivide it into two parts – measures already actioned and measures agreed for future action.

If a customer satisfaction measurement exercise is taken seriously by senior management, they will want to have the results hot off the press, and meetings will have been scheduled in advance to agree PFIs and action to be taken. Companies as committed and as organized as this almost certainly will have implemented some measures to improve areas of poor performance before the customer feedback report is prepared. For example, a company was criticized for its project management by respondents to its customer survey. When respondents received feedback, the company was able to report that it had formed a project management department and now provided training in project management skills for relevant staff. Such a response is impressive and the supplier will show a significant net gain in customer loyalty as a result.

The only organisations that have fears about reporting survey results to customers are those doubting their ability to address PFIs. It is almost always true that organisations who acknowledge the fact that they are experiencing problems with customers and take positive steps to remedy matters, end up with a net gain in customer loyalty.

No matter how swiftly you identify PFIs and take appropriate action, you will almost certainly have some measures which are not completed if only because much of the action that arises out of a customer survey will inevitably take time to implement. For example, if you have been rated poorly on delivery reliability, an immediate step may be to introduce a monitoring system, but resolving the problem will take longer and certainly will not happen until you have discovered the exact causes of late deliveries. For any future action it is vital that as well as outlining the measures to be taken you also include timescales for completion or for reaching decision points.

One final point about action concerns any areas where there is evidence that you have been incorrectly rated poorly by customers. It is not unusual for customers' perceptions of an organisation's service to lag behind the reality, particularly in cases where significant improvements have taken place in recent times. To take the previous example, you may know that your delivery reliability has improved and you may even have records which demonstrate virtually no late deliveries in the last three months. The two golden rules in this situation are, firstly, don't ever tell customers they are wrong and, secondly, don't attempt to justify your record.

It is far more effective to report back that you have introduced a daily monitoring system, will be investigating and recording the causes of any late deliveries in future, and will take any appropriate action to overcome the problem. Customers will view this as a very positive move. Also, it provides an opportunity to double check on all aspects of delivery to make sure there really isn't a problem. For example, are shipments leaving your factory on time but some customers receiving late deliveries due to transport problems? Once you have fully assured yourself that your delivery reliability is excellent you can implement measures to educate customers and modify their perceptions.

Future feedback

Inform customers that you will provide further feedback on the results of your action to address PFIs. If you publish a customer newsletter it can provide an appropriate channel of communication. If not, write to respondents after three months and six months to report on progress. Finally you should inform respondents when you plan to update the survey.

Modifying Perceptions

Customer surveys measure customers' perceptions of an organisation's performance. The perceptions of some customers will be more accurate than those of others. But, always remember Tom Peters' comment, 'Customer perception is the only reality'. On these perceptions, whether accurate or inaccurate, millions of purchasing decisions are made every day – in business as well as in consumer markets. As discussed in Chapter 6, most purchase decisions are made on less than perfect knowledge. Time constraints place a limit on informed decision making, typically resulting in our memory providing a level of information with which we are comfortable when making a purchase decision.

But our memory is not always accurate and often not up to date. Most people form attitudes quickly but change them only slowly. This works to the advantage of good suppliers who are 'allowed' a few minor lapses but if suppliers perform poorly in a given area customers will remember it for a long time. Suppliers have to perform very well and work extremely hard to overcome negative perceptions.

Consequently, it is possible that a poor performance rating in a given area such as delivery reliability may not mean that your deliveries are very unreliable, but simply that customers perceive you as a company which tends not to deliver on time. Perhaps they have been frequently let down in the past and still retain that perception. The first step is to determine the truth of the matter. Don't ever assume customers are wrong! Chapter 16 outlines how complementary techniques – such as benchmarking and mystery shopping – can be used to validate customer perceptions about your organisation, particularly where they are negative.

Let's assume that you have accumulated all the objective evidence necessary to demonstrate that your delivery reliability has improved to the point where late deliveries have been virtually eliminated. You now know the implication of your poor score on delivery reliability. You do not need to implement measures to improve delivery performance but you do have a communication task. You need to make customers realize how much your performance has improved and change their perceptions. This is not an easy task. Customers tend to notice problems but take good service – and improved service – for granted. Never underestimate how hard you have to work to change perceptions. The golden rules are to:

- emphasize your intentions;
- clarify your systems;
- highlight your successes.

The initial feedback report to customers on the results of the survey provides the obvious opportunity to highlight your intentions, but this should be reinforced where possible, for example, by sales staff through verbal communications. Having told customers what you are trying to achieve, impact will be increased if you also explain to them how you will go about achieving it. If you clarify your systems they will understand the efforts you are making and that in itself will probably improve their perception of your performance in the area concerned. So tell them you are carrying out internal benchmarking, tell them you have formed a continuous improvement team to examine the issue, tell them precisely how you are going to address the problem and that you will report back on progress.

We would introduce formal customer briefing, which works in exactly the same way as internal team briefing except that it systematically uses the sales force to communicate consistent messages to customers. They may not realize they are being briefed but they will get the message!

Reporting on progress provides another opportunity to highlight your successes. To change perceptions, successes must be promoted frequently and strongly. If a customer newsletter is your communications medium for this exercise, make sure that the information is reported very prominently, preferably on the front page, or at least clearly signposted on the front page. A customer newsletter will, of course, be distributed to all customers and it is important to note that if you have identified a perception problem your efforts to overcome it need to be directed at all customers and not just respondents to the survey.

There is no guarantee that customers will read a newsletter. Therefore, if you really need to modify perceptions you should try to introduce some tangible measures which will be difficult for customers to ignore. For example, to address the perceived problem of delivery reliability you could introduce a 'Priority Fax-bak' form (Figure 13.4). This is very tangible, will be noticed, can be delivered and reinforced in person by the sales force or posted and explained over the telephone. It is important to deliver a specific number of forms to each customer (say, five) so that follow-up can be made at planned intervals to replenish the customer's stock. If no forms have been used it will demonstrate how reliable deliveries really are, and if forms do have to be used it will at least demonstrate how seriously you are treating the problem, as well as highlighting to everyone in your company that there really is a problem.

We also know companies with perception problems on delivery reliability who have faxed every customer every month with a statement of their delivery record both overall and for that particular customer. A year later their delivery reliability was no better (it was good previously) but the customer satisfaction score for delivery reliability had increased significantly.

Conclusions

- Always make a point of fully briefing your own staff about the survey before introducing it to customers.

PRIORITY FAX-BAK

FAX NO: 01234 567899

Delivery
problem **?**

FOR THE <u>IMMEDIATE</u> ATTENTION OF
Mr J Bloggs MD ABC Ltd

From _____
Date _____
Time _____
Problem _____
_____

Figure 13.4   Tangible measures to modify percecptions

- Make sure that the introductory letter to customers emphasizes the benefits for them and covers:
    - the objectives of the survey;
    - the practical details of the survey;
    - the feedback to be provided after the survey.
- Send a brief thank you letter and, maybe, a gift to respondents after the survey and, when feasible, send a feedback report covering:
    - the results of the survey;
    - the PFIs;
    - action already implemented and action planned;
    - future feedback and date of the next survey.
- If you have identified that poor ratings have been caused by a perception problem you will have to work very hard to modify customers' perceptions in the area concerned. To do so you should follow three rules:
    - emphasize your intentions;
    - clarify your systems;
    - highlight your successes.

14 MEASURING LOYALTY

AIMS

By the end of this chapter you will:

- Know how to ask a range of questions to accurately understand the loyalty of your customers.
- Be able to distinguish varying levels of commitment amongst customers.
- Understand how to build a loyalty profile summarizing loyalty levels across your customer base.
- Be able to undertake loyalty segmentation to understand customers' differing needs and to develop appropriate strategies for defending your own customer base and for targeting competitors' customers where appropriate.

As we said in Chapter 3, there are many different types of loyalty – from habitual loyalty, where the apparently loyal customer may have little real commitment to the supplier, right through to totally committed customers. Since loyalty is such an imprecise word, it is much more useful to think in terms of customer commitment and to measure loyalty in terms of varying degrees of commitment. The following sections will explore ascending levels of commitment, will suggest questions that can be used to measure each level and will indicate how the results should be displayed.

Customer Retention

Customer retention is the lowest form of loyalty and is simply a measure of whether customers are remaining customers. This is still as far as many organisations go in terms of measuring and monitoring loyalty and it is often measured historically. Figure 14.1 shows a straightforward customer retention indicator, developed initially by Rank Xerox, which displays an answer to the simple question, 'How many of our customers that we had one year ago do we still have today?'. Records can be progressively built up showing new customers each year and their subsequent retention, as well as demonstrating an overall retention indicator. The chart shows

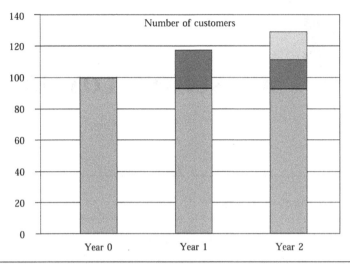

Figure 14.1 Historical customer retention indicator

that in year 1 the retention rate is 96 per cent (96 customers retained from 100 serviced in Year 0). In Year 2 the retention rate has improved to 96.67 per cent (116 customers retained from 120 serviced in Year 1).

Of course, management decisions are better made on information that predicts the future rather than data which shows what has already happened. Historical customer retention indicators should therefore be supplemented by information on anticipated future customer retention, and this is best obtained by asking the customers a basic question such as, 'Do you think you will still be a customer of ABC in one year's time?'.

Clearly, you need to adjust the time scale to one which is relevant for your organisation – shorter where there is much more customer churn and possibly (but unusually) longer in markets characterized by very stable customer–supplier relationships. In some situations, e.g. a restaurant, the intended loyalty question can be more appropriately, 'Do you think you will re-visit the ABC restaurant?'.

Both questions are best asked as an open question, closed response with five-point verbal scales from 'definitely' to 'definitely not'. You can then analyse the results as a frequency distribution and display the answer in a simple bar chart like the one shown in Figure 14.2.

Share of Wallet

More committed customers allocate a greater proportion of their category spend to their favoured supplier. If your customers are becoming more committed you would therefore expect

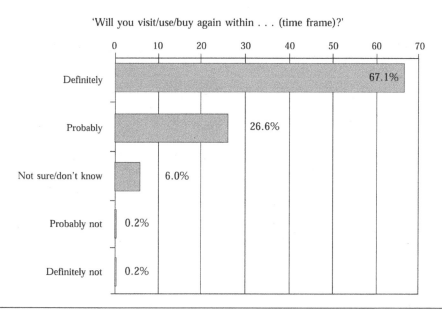

'Will you visit/use/buy again within . . . (time frame)?'

Figure 14.2 Anticipated customer retention

to see average customer spend or average account value figures rising. Like customer retention, this can be monitored retrospectively from accounts figures.

Figure 14.3 shows average account size or average customer spend. This can be very useful in a competitive environment where customers may use a number of suppliers to meet their needs in a particular product/service area. An increase in average customer spend will suggest that the supplier is attracting a larger proportion of consumers' expenditure in that product area, thus indicating an increase in loyalty. This indicator is also a useful measure in areas such as retailing where the more conventional customer retention indicator may be impossible to track because individual customers are not known.

However, it is possible that the average spend per customer could be increasing even though you have only a small percentage of customers' category spend, and it is the share of the customer's wallet that indicates the extent of their commitment. This should be ascertained by asking the customers. In some markets it may be feasible to ask a very precise question: 'What percentage of your credit card spend is on your XXX card?' (see Figure 14.4).

Often customers do not have a precise recollection or even awareness of the proportion of their spend allocated to competing suppliers. In those circumstances a more general question must be asked, such as: 'When shopping for food, how often do you use XXX compared with other supermarkets?' (see Figure 14.5).

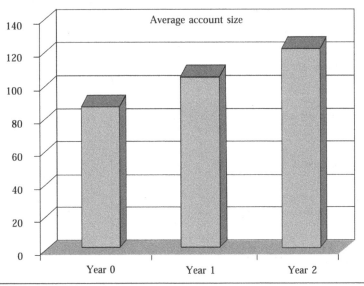

Figure 14.3 Average account size/customer spend

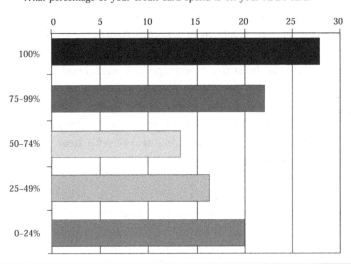

Figure 14.4 Share of wallet (precise)

Recommendation

Recommendation is another good indicator of customer commitment. Questions about recommendation have often been included on customer survey questionnaires over many years, but the results have tended to be viewed in isolation rather than as part of a more meaningful loyalty/commitment measure. There are many ways of asking questions about recommendation; probably the most common is on willingness to recommend. This is a rather

'When shopping for food, how often do you use XXX compared with other supermarkets?'

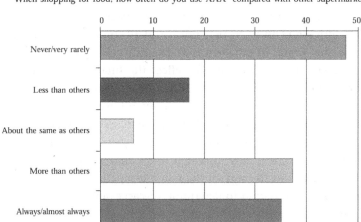

Figure 14.5   Share of wallet (general)

'Have you ever recommended XXX to anyone else?'

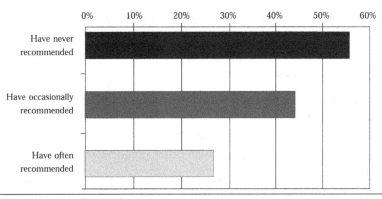

Figure 14.6   Recommending behaviour

weak question since it is far too easy to give a positive answer, perhaps without ever having recommended the supplier in the past or even being likely to recommend it in the future. A better question is therefore to ask respondents how likely it is that they will recommend the supplier in future, but the most meaningful is to ask about what they have actually done: (see Figure 14.6). 'Have you ever recommended XXX to anyone else?'

Accessibility of Alternatives

The questions outlined so far will start to give a good indication about how committed, how emotionally attached, customers feel towards the supplier or brand, but other more practical matters will have a strong influence on customers' actual loyalty in the real world. Whatever your level of commitment to a supplier, it is far easier to switch suppliers in some markets than in others. In extreme cases there is a monopoly. Customer retention is guaranteed whilst the monopoly persists, although customers may not feel at all committed to the supplier – if there were an alternative they would be attracted to it. Even in free markets there are often barriers to change in customers' minds. These might reflect the financial cost of change or simply the perceived effort and hassle factor involved in changing suppliers. In these situations our research shows that customers will often tolerate a much lower level of supplier performance (i.e. a higher level of dissatisfaction) before they will change to an alternative supplier. At the other extreme, if customers' perception of the value package offered by their supermarket, pub or petrol station deteriorates, it is easy to switch to an alternative supplier. In that situation they will tolerate much less in the way of poor supplier performance before switching. It is therefore advisable to ask a question to determine the accessibility of alternatives and Figure 14.7 shows the type of contrasting results that can be generated.

Attraction of Alternatives

However easy or difficult it is to change suppliers, you need to understand how attracted your customers are to those other alternatives. Before asking a question on this subject, it is useful to encourage customers to think about the range of alternatives that they perceive. You might therefore ask questions such as:

- 'When going out for an occasion where you would visit the XXX, which other venues would you consider?'
- 'When doing your weekly food shop, which other stores would you consider using?'
- 'When buying (product or service), which other suppliers would you consider?'

Having made the respondent think about the full range of suppliers, it is then a simple matter

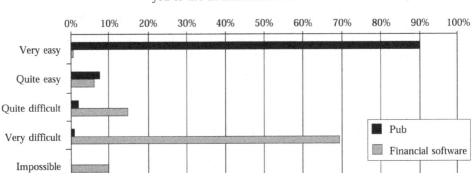

Figure 14.7 Accessibility of alternatives

Compared with other suppliers that you use, how would you rate . . .?

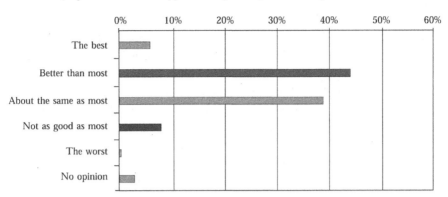

Figure 14.8 Attraction of alternatives

If you were starting from scratch, would you choose XXX as your supplier?

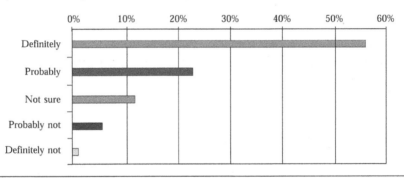

Figure 14.9 Commitment to current supplier

to ask how your organisation compares with those alternatives. The truly committed customers will reply that you are 'the best'. Figure 14.8 shows how the results can be displayed.

Sometimes customers have little awareness of, or familiarity with, the range of alternative suppliers. In a monopoly situation there are none, and even in a free market situation customers may feel that there are no alternatives for them (e.g. inner-city housing estate tenants of a local authority, housing association or private landlord). In that case, a question focusing on comparisons with alternative suppliers loses much of its meaning, so a better measure of commitment is to ask whether they would choose that supplier again if they could turn the clock back to when they first made the decision. Possible questions are:

- 'If you were starting from scratch with a blank piece of paper, would you choose XXX as your supplier?'
- 'If you could turn the clock back to the time when you first (chose the supplier/bought the product/signed the contract), would you choose XXX again?'

The outcome is shown in Figure 14.9.

Loyalty Profiles

As we have seen, loyalty is a complex issue which cannot be adequately measured by one simple loyalty question. From the range of possibilities outlined in this chapter, you need to select several questions (at least two and preferably three or four) to cover different aspects of loyalty. Together, the answers to those questions will establish the degree of commitment that customers feel towards your organisation and this can be displayed in the form of a 'loyalty profile' (see Figure 14.10).

To produce the profile you need to allocate points to the scores from your loyalty questions and establish the number of points required for each commitment level. You should make it difficult rather than easy to achieve high levels of commitment on your loyalty profile. For example, imagine a company had asked just two loyalty questions, the anticipated customer retention question and the attraction of alternatives question, the development of the loyalty profile is summarized in Tables 14.1 and 14.2

If you have several companies in your group, brands or outlets in your company, it is interesting to compare their respective loyalty profiles. This comparison is best made using the type of chart shown in Figure 14.11.

Loyalty Segmentation

Once you have established a loyalty profile you can compare the attitudes of customers at different commitment levels. It can be very enlightening to contrast your most and least

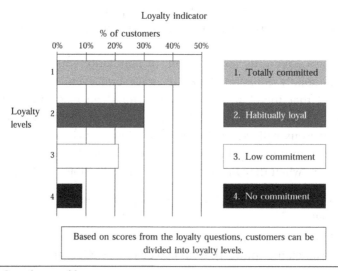

Figure 14.10 Loyalty profile

Table 14.1   Allocating points to loyalty questions

Loyalty points		
Response category		Points scored
Definitely	The best	5
Probably	Better than most	4
Not sure	About the same as most	3
Probably not	Not as good as most	2
Definitely not	The worst	1

Table 14.2   Establishing commitment levels

Loyalty profile	
Commitment level	Points required
Totally committed	10
Habitually loyal	8
Low committment	6
No committment	5 and below

committed customers to identify what is making your most committed customers highly satisfied and why your least committed customers are much less satisfied. By comparing the satisfaction scores given by your most and least committed customers a sample outcome is achieved (see Figure 14.12).

You can use this information both to defend your most loyal customers and to combat the customer decay caused by the defection of the least satisfied. In Figure 14.12 the loyalty of the most committed customers could be enhanced by improving the company's performance regarding 'on time delivery', the area where the most committed customers are least satisfied. To understand the causes of customer decay, you should ask yourself the question: 'Which factors are causing some of our customers to be much less satisfied than others?'. To find the answer, you must identify the biggest gaps between the satisfaction scores of the most and the least committed customers. It is very clear in Figure 14.12 that committed customers are extremely satisfied with 'problem resolution' but uncommitted customers are far less satisfied. Similar large gaps can be found on 'helpfulness of staff' and, to a lesser extent, on keeping 'promises and commitments'. It is in these areas that some customers are receiving, or perceiving, much

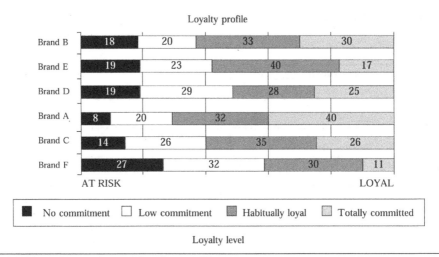

Figure 14.11   Comparison of loyalty profiles

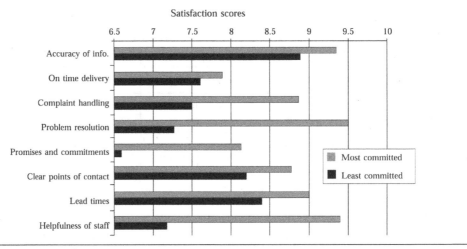

Figure 14.12   Loyalty segmentation

lower levels of service. Addressing them would help to combat customer decay.

If you have carried out a market standing survey you can also segment your competitors' customers according to their loyalty levels. Having done this, you can highlight your own vulnerable segments and introduce strategies to defend them and pinpoint your competitors' vulnerable segments and set goals to attack them. This approach is most suited to markets with large numbers of customers since you need a large sample if analysis of subgroups is to be based on valid sample sizes.

Extending the principles discussed earlier in this section to the results of a market standing survey enables you to identify loyalty segments for your own and your competitors' customers.

Table 14.3   Loyalty segments from a market standing survey

	Our customers	Competitors' customers
FAITHFUL	Strongly loyal, rate our performance highly, little interest in competitors	Strongly loyal, rate competitor highly, little interest in us
VULNERABLE	Apparently loyal customers but high level of inertia or some interest in competitors	Repeat buyers with competitors but little positive loyalty and some interest in us
FLIRTATIOUS	Little positive loyalty, actively interested in alternatives	Little loyalty to competitors, may be receptive to our advances
AVAILABLE	Customers showing a strong preference for alternative suppliers	Competitors' customers who already rate us as superior to their existing supplier

When disseminating the results internally it can be helpful to assign descriptive names to the commitment levels, as shown in Table 14.3.

The basic principle of using customer satisfaction measurement data to build customer loyalty is covered in more detail in the next chapter. In essence it involves 'doing best what matters most to customers' which means focusing on customers' top priorities, especially those where your own performance is rated poorly. Using loyalty segmentation does not change the basic principle, but enables you to target it more accurately and consequently to implement it more effectively. Loyalty segmentation will often suggest different strategies for each segment and, in particular, differing communications strategies. Your less loyal customers may be 'flirtatious' because they have an unclear or erroneous perception of the benefits offered by your organisation. Equally you must not ignore retention strategies to further strengthen the relationship with the 'faithful' segment, since these are probably your most profitable customers.

Clearly the success of such strategies is dependent on the sophistication of your system for managing customer relationships. If you have to rely on mass marketing techniques such as advertising you will not be able to benefit as much from loyalty segmentation. Ideally you need a well developed customer database which enables you to target and to communicate with different customer groups in different ways.

Loyalty segmentation based on data from a market standing survey can be very useful for predicting shifts in market share. As well as identifying and quantifying where you are most at risk of losing customers, loyalty segmentation will also help you to predict and target likely gains (see Table 14.4). Once more, a well developed in-house database is helpful, although in consumer markets the ability to segment and target through external databases is improving all the time.

Table 14.4   Strategies based on loyalty segmentation

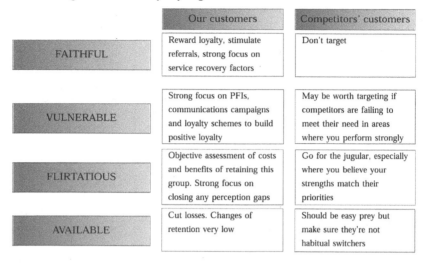

	Our customers	Competitors' customers
FAITHFUL	Reward loyalty, stimulate referrals, strong focus on service recovery factors	Don't target
VULNERABLE	Strong focus on PFIs, communications campaigns and loyalty schemes to build positive loyalty	May be worth targeting if competitors are failing to meet their need in areas where you perform strongly
FLIRTATIOUS	Objective assessment of costs and benefits of retaining this group. Strong focus on closing any perception gaps	Go for the jugular, especially where you believe your strengths match their priorities
AVAILABLE	Cut losses. Changes of retention very low	Should be easy prey but make sure they're not habitual switchers

Loyalty segmentation can also provide a very firm basis for making management decisions on resource allocation. Most organisations do not have the resources to focus on everything at once. They usually have to make choices. It may be better, for example, to place little emphasis on retaining your own 'available' customers if their top priority is low price, but put effort into targeting defined competitor segments with an unfulfilled need for superior service. The insight you can gain from loyalty segmentation will considerably improve the effectiveness of any attempts to win competitors' 'flirtations' and 'available' customers since you will know exactly where they are least satisfied with the performance of their current supplier. All in all, this adds up to a strong reason for becoming better than your competitors at customer satisfaction measurement and loyalty segmentation.

Conclusions

- Loyalty is not a simple concept but a complex one involving varying levels of customer commitment to your organisation.
- To understand customer loyalty it is therefore necessary to ask a number of questions which address the full range of customer commitment.
- Results from loyalty questions should be combined to produce a loyalty profile which can be monitored in the future and compared across group companies, brands or outlets.
- By comparing the satisfaction scores of the different loyalty segments, appropriate strategies can be developed to protect your own customers and, provided a market standing survey has been undertaken, attack vulnerable segments of your competitors' customers.

15 MODELLING AND FORECASTING

AIMS

By the end of this chapter you will:

- Understand how relationships in the customer satisfaction chain can be measured, analysed and modelled.
- Be able to assess the potential for increasing profitability in your organisation by improving customer satisfaction.

Introduction to Forecasting

There are only two ways of forecasting – trend extrapolation or scenario modelling. Trend extrapolation involves gathering historical data, such as the mature height of people in a population, and after concluding that on average they are getting taller at a regular rate, estimating future average height. This is a fairly primitive form of forecasting and it is much better to build a model. Models involve the measurement of relationships and assume that if a change in one or more related factors resulted in a change in other factors, then it will happen again in similar circumstances. In crop experimentation, for example, it is normal to take several sets of seeds and subject them to different influences. One might be planted in a new compost, one might receive more light, another may be sprayed daily with a chemical and so on. One set will be allowed to grow without new methods and in due course it will be possible to measure the effect of each of the treatments in comparison to the normal group. In this way the increased yield from investing in a new treatment can be estimated and the most successful and cost effective adopted for the full crop. If the analogy needs to be taken further, consider what will happen to a seed that is planted (the first sale) and then left alone – it will probably wither and die.

In the researcher's perfect world you could split your customers into three identical groups, work hard and invest resources to create high satisfaction in group A, ignore group B (the control group) and actively create low satisfaction in group C. You could conduct this experiment for five years and assess the result with a high degree of statistical reliability. Doing this would ensure that all other factors which may influence customer loyalty such as new competition, national marketing campaigns, the state of the economy, fashion, the weather and anything else which changes over time, would not affect one group more than any other. So the resulting change in customer base would be almost certainly due to the differing levels of customer satisfaction in the three groups over the period.

Ask the CEO of your organisation if such an experiment can be conducted and the likelihood is that you will be seeking new employment fairly quickly. Plain common sense tells us that if we treat customers badly they will go elsewhere, so the proposed treatment for group C will gain little support. Most CEOs accept the premise that ignoring customers is unlikely to generate any affinity, and in recent research it was shown that two-thirds of defecting customers move supplier simply because no one had kept in touch. Yet many companies operate exactly in this way. If it is natural to assume that group A will be the most loyal, and therefore most profitable, why not adopt for all customers the approach that should create that result? As we have shown throughout this book it is not that simple. You first have to understand what your customers want (and many organisations do not) and then make serious efforts to ensure that your company is fully focused and organized to provide it. The remainder of this chapter examines the techniques for producing evidence of the return on this investment.

Statistical Modelling

To conduct the experiment described above may not be as impossible as it seems. Most consumer markets and many business markets serve their customers through a network of local distribution points and some of them will be achieving higher levels of customer satisfaction than others. Even in industrial markets some accounts may be managed differently from others. Grouping outlets or customers in terms of their satisfaction score will allow you to isolate the factors which seem to make the difference, but it also allows you to calculate the potential return on investment.

The normal management performance indicators, such as sales volume, market share, turnover, profit, staff retention etc., are probably already collected, and if customer and employee satisfaction research is carried out at branch level the results can be analysed using correlation techniques.

Correlation techniques are used to measure the extent to which two or more variables are related. This is the basis of statistical modelling or 'what if' scenario building and is a step beyond the more straightforward forecasting methods of time-series and seasonality analysis which are used for projecting trends. The objective is to establish the long-term direction in a historical series (such as the use of dishwashers or a stock market index) and then explain the variations around the trend by identifying factors which may have influence, such as

Table 15.1   Example data for forecasting

Outlet	Profit %	CSI	Very likely to reselect %	Quite likely to reselect %
1	13	84	73	17
2	22	92	84	10
3	1	73	28	32
4	14	80	62	25
5	-2	70	18	32
6	15	86	80	15
7	-22	55	1	24
8	-6	65	10	30
9	5	75	38	33
10	11	83	68	20
11	-13	60	2	28
12	19	90	83	12
13	7	78	50	30
14	To	53	0	18
15	be	76	40	30
16	predicted	85	70	22
17		56	0	15
18		95	95	3
19	↓	45	0	12

inflation, interest rates, unemployment or other factors of the economic cycle. The idea is that if explanatory variables can be identified, and predicted more easily than the series you are really trying to predict, you have created a useful predictive model.

Whilst he was responsible for planning and forecasting in the motor industry, one of the authors, Jim Alexander, developed models for the car, van and truck markets in the UK which proved to be remarkably accurate. By taking historical sales data and a range of economic variables, including GDP, consumer expenditure, house prices, interest rates and others, he was able to identify how the market would react to changes in the other variables (which are more easily predictable over the long term). In earlier years he constructed a model which isolated the effect of weather on daily sales of cider to produce an estimate of the return on advertising investment. We will now explain how these techniques are applied to customer satisfaction.

Forecasting

Keeping it simple for illustrative purposes, taking the results of a satisfaction survey and client or outlet profitability the data in Table 15.1 might be extracted.

We have survey results for 19 outlets and profit results for 13. Using the relationships which exist between satisfaction, loyalty and profit for the 13 we can predict profits for the other 6 or for a theoretical outlet achieving a set of targeted results.

The mathematics involved in multiple correlation would take a chapter to explain and are not the subject matter of this book. Suffice it to say that they involve manipulating the data by multiplying, squaring, averaging and dividing to produce a set of simultaneous equations which, when solved, produce constants which form an overall equation for the relationships. In this instance the equation looks like this:

Profit = –86.7971+(1.108081*CSI)+(0.046173*V.Likely)+(0.216522*Q.Likely)

Using the formula we can calculate a predicted value for all 19 outlets and check the degree of accuracy for the 13 where actual results are known. If the fit is good then confidence in the prediction will be high. Figure 15.1 shows the predicted and actual values along with the forecast ones.

This is a somewhat idealized example to illustrate the principles and it is likely that other factors may influence profitability and distort the picture a little. If these other factors can be adjusted for or included in the calculations it should be possible to do this with your own results.

The more actual data points you can put into the process the better. Results for 200 car dealers showed that the more satisfied customers were with their communications with the dealer the more likely they were to recommend them to others and remain loyal themselves. Dealers who achieved closer relationships were more successful than the others. This finding resulted in a major review of national and dealership marketing with an increased emphasis on individual

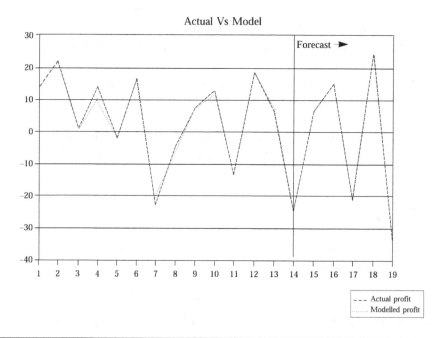

Figure 15.1   Predicted, actual and forecast values

Table 15.2 Return on investment by customer

Annual spend	Lifespend (10 years)	Overall satisfaction	Total annual spend	10-year total lifespend	Share of spend or clean sheet loyalty	New sat. (up one level)	New share of spend/ loyalty	New annual spend	New lifespend	Increase	Profit increase @ 20%	Lifetime cost of improving sat.	Return
200000	2000000	8	230000	2300000	87.0%	9	92%	211600	2116000	116000	23200	7000	231%
100000	1000000	7	140000	1400000	71.4%	8	86%	120400	1204000	204000	40800	10000	308%
50000	500000	9	55000	550000	90.9%	10	96%	52800	528000	28000	5600	5000	12%
25000	250000	5	90000	900000	27.8%	6	48%	43200	432000	182000	36400	21000	73%
72000	720000	4	360000	3600000	20.0%	5	28%	100800	1008000	288000	57600	30000	92%
15000	150000	6	30000	300000	50.0%	7	72%	21600	216000	66000	13200	15000	-12%
15000	150000	2	300000	3000000	5.0%	3	7%	21000	210000	60000	12000	60000	-80%
60000	600000	4	300000	3000000	20.0%	5	28%	84000	840000	240000	48000	30000	60%
120000	1200000	8	140000	1400000	85.7%	9	92%	128800	1288000	88000	17600	7000	151%
90000	900000	6	190000	1900000	47.4%	7	72%	136800	1368000	468000	93600	15000	524%
10000	100000	6	22000	220000	45.5%	7	72%	15840	158400	58400	11680	15000	-22%

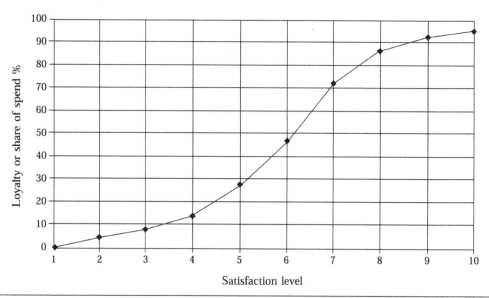

Figure 15.2 Customer commitment curve

relationship marketing for the company in question. The pioneering work done in the UK was soon adopted around the world.

In the same way, the relationships between employee satisfaction, staff turnover, customer satisfaction, customer commitment and customer retention can be established to prove the points that have been made earlier in this book.

To fully assess the potential benefit of investing in customer satisfaction it would be necessary to examine the data at individual customer level because the size of the return depends on the value of the customer and their initial level of satisfaction. In a business market with relatively few customers this can be done and Table 15.2 shows some example data. In consumer markets it would be necessary to cluster customers according to size of spend and satisfaction level before conducting this analysis.

Actual expenditure with a specific supplier is shown in the first column and assuming a lifetime of ten years produces the second column. Initial satisfaction has been gathered from a research programme. The customer's total spend on similar products or services is shown next and from this we calculate the share the supplier has captured. If this data cannot be obtained we can substitute the results of loyalty questioning and infer what total spend might be. Now, if we assume that by means of staff training, new communication methods, refocused employee activity etc. we can raise each customer's satisfaction by one level (perhaps over three years), our share of business will move one step up the customer commitment curve (see Figure 15.2). The curve is first created from as much actual data as possible and then used as a predictive tool.

We can then calculate the new level of expenditure and the associated increase in profits. As an example, the amount of investment required to move a customer from a satisfaction level of 8 to 9 will generally be less than to move one from 5 to 6. Since it is usually very difficult to recover from very low levels of satisfaction, to move a customer from 2 to 3 will often exceed the cost of attracting a new customer. It is unlikely that you will have many customers who score you less than 4 overall – at that level of satisfaction they are more likely to be using another supplier.

Individual decisions may therefore need to be made about whether to retain some customers. Establishing the level of investment needed is highly dependent on what is wrong and the nature of your organisation. If the PFIs are mainly related to human factors then recruitment, training, working practices, communication (both with customers and inside the organisation) and reward systems will need to be reviewed, whilst if it is a quality, capacity or competitive pricing problem, other solutions will be needed. In the example we have assumed that in total 3 per cent of annual turnover is spent each year and in reality the way this was spent would change over the years. Given that many companies spend as much as 10 per cent of turnover on customer acquisition with far less certainty of success this does not seem excessive. In many cases the funding is not additional but substitutional because in reality the mass marketing budget is reduced and relationship marketing increases. Even at this level the return on investment is significant, but you should now substitute your own data and assumptions into this template to see what could be achieved. New business practices will have an effect on all customers so the amount spent need not relate to customer value, but the return certainty will.

In addition to the revenue and profit which would result from satisfying current customers more fully, we should add the amount which would result from additional referrals (from those extra 9s and 10s) and take account of the benefit of reducing the number of 'terrorists'. Remember that increased satisfaction leads to greater customer retention, so the base of (increasingly profitable) customers will expand. Further increases in profitability are likely to result from lower staff turnover, less absenteeism, and increased productivity as they become more expert and get to know the customers better.

A 1999 benchmarking report from the UK Department of Trade and Industry based on data from 1500 companies has shown that the top 25 per cent achieve profit margins five times greater than the bottom 25 per cent. They also achieve 98 per cent delivery reliability (vs 85 per cent), spend 10 times as much on training and have staff absenteeism rates up to 75 per cent lower than the bottom quartile. These results did not differ greatly by sector, which confirms the findings of our own *Satisfaction Benchmark* database that high achieving companies perform well across a range of factors independently of industry. The Confederation of British Industry has estimated that if companies across all sectors increased their competitiveness to that of the best performers, it would generate £300 billion of additional revenue in the UK alone.

Conclusions

- The relationship in the customer satisfaction chain can be measured, analysed and modelled.
- The potential for increasing profitability in several ways is demonstrably clear.
- The most successful companies in terms of customer and employee satisfaction are often the most profitable.

16 MAXIMIZING THE BENEFITS

AIMS
_____

By the end of this chapter you will:
- Be able to decide on the optimum time interval required between customer surveys.
- Understand the distinct roles of continuous, tactical measures and periodic strategic surveys.
- Be able to combine customer satisfaction measurement with other complementary techniques to provide additional management information and improve decision making.

How Often to Survey?

Many organisations assume that measuring customer satisfaction on an annual basis is the logical thing to do, but there is no reason why 365 days should be the most appropriate interval.

With a fixed budget there is more to be gained from a thorough survey carried out less often. For example, it is better to undertake a telephone survey or personal interviews with a carefully drawn representative sample and a comprehensive questionnaire once every two years rather than sending out a brief annual self-completion questionnaire with measurements and conclusions based on the sample of customers who had the time or a reason to send it back. However, within the overall advice of carrying out a more thorough survey less often, there are additional factors which should influence your frequency of survey.

In markets where customer satisfaction and customer loyalty are likely to be more volatile you should survey more often. In areas where customer satisfaction is likely to remain more stable you can survey less often (see Figure 16.1).

Instability of customer satisfaction is linked with factors such as high levels of competition,

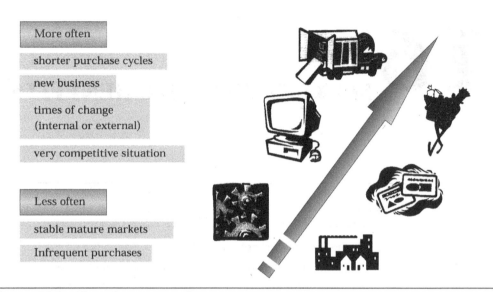

Figure 16.1 How often to survey?

short purchase cycles and times of change. Several factors could initiate change in your relationship with customers, including change within your organisation, such as moving premises or replacing a product range, changes in technology, new legislation, or competitor initiatives. If any of these factors apply you should be measuring customer satisfaction at least annually and possibly more frequently. Federal Express conduct daily customer surveys by telephone with recent purchasers using a 101 point scale (0–100) to 'measure microshifts in customer opinion'.

In stable markets, customers will be less volatile and you can survey less frequently. These will include mature industrial markets, products or services with longer purchase intervals and markets which are less competitive. Some organisations may therefore need to survey more frequently for some parts of their business than for others. A local authority, for example, may need to survey more frequently for its leisure services if there is significant private sector competition in the locality and for recently contracted out services and less frequently in areas such as the library service or housing. Companies (such as capital equipment manufacturers or estate agents) with a high involvement but very infrequent relationship with their customers will need to carry out post-transaction research. This will take the form of a thorough survey (not a brief self-completion form) because there are likely to be many complex components of customer satisfaction. The research should be administered shortly after final completion of the transaction and for many suppliers in this situation it will be feasible to carry out a census survey. Due to the depth of the relationship it will usually not be anonymous, so line managers can deal quickly with any immediate problems. Results should be aggregated on a periodic basis for more strategic analysis. The period will depend on the number of transactions, since 50 responses should be seen as the absolute minimum sample size for analysis purposes.

Tactical and Strategic Surveys

Some organisations with very frequent customer contact, such as hotels, will want to monitor customer satisfaction on a continuous basis. Typically, this is implemented through self-completion questionnaires made available to customers at the point-of-service consumption (the hotel bedroom), or simple electronic touchpad surveys (e.g. on checkout).

There are three problems with this type of survey. Firstly, questionnaires have to be very short; even then, they tend to be filled in very quickly and often with very little thought. Secondly, and more seriously, such brief and rapidly completed questionnaires can only cover customers' immediate satisfaction with the service offered and virtually never include the equally important section on customers' priorities. Without that information you can never answer the most critical question – 'Are you doing best what matters most to customers?'. The third, and most serious, problem is of course the sampling – or lack of it. The only organisations which will achieve a representative sample from this type of survey will be those who can ensure a census – training companies are well placed in this respect as they can ask delegates to complete an evaluation form at the end of each course.

Most organisations using continuous self-completion surveys will derive responses only from customers who have a reason to respond. Such respondents will include prize draw hunters and dissatisfied customers making a complaint, and it will even be a low proportion of dissatisfied customers who will complete the questionnaire. All the research evidence points to the fact that for every customer who complains several do not make the effort, particularly for minor niggles and sometimes for major ones. As additional complaints channels, and as early warnings for significant service problems, the questionnaires serve a very useful purpose, but they do not provide a valid measure of customer satisfaction.

To provide reliable data on customer satisfaction from which you can identify PFIs it is necessary to undertake a much more comprehensive survey on a periodic basis, annually in the case of a hotel. This should include some exploratory research (a hotel is in an ideal position to mount focus groups) which would establish the criteria of most importance to customers when selecting and evaluating a hotel as well as providing useful qualitative information.

The exploratory research will facilitate the design of a customer-focused questionnaire which will objectively uncover customers' perceptions of the hotel's performance against their own priorities. It can also indicate customers' perceptions of competitors' performance. It will be possible to draw a random sample accurately reflecting different customer groupings such as corporate clients (for conferences) and different types of hotel guest (frequent, occasional and once only stayers).

Although a hotel is in an ideal position to undertake personal interviews of guests, the survey should be based on telephone interviews, with respondents in their own home or workplace environment. Surveys on site (including point-of-consumption questionnaires) generate perceptions which are heavily influenced by recent experience during the respondents' stay at the hotel in question. The results given by respondents at point of consumption may therefore differ significantly from the more considered view they will provide once removed from the hotel both in distance and in time. This is the only way of generating reliable comparisons with competitors and it also more accurately reflects the customer's state of mind when selecting a hotel for his or her next booking.

In brief, you must distinguish between tactical and strategic customer surveys.

Tactical surveys are helpful for line management to manage customer service on an ongoing basis. They are typically carried out through simple continuous tracking methods, such as point-of-consumption questionnaires with the results aggregated weekly or, at most, monthly. Along with other indicators such as mystery shopping, they enable line managers to judge whether or not performance is broadly on course and also serve as an early warning of any repetitive problems. Tactical surveys need to be based on factors under the control of the line managers concerned. There is no point including questions on issues outside their control.

Strategic surveys help senior management to review the performance and direction of the company and should therefore cover everything of importance to customers. Sometimes referred to as 'baseline surveys' they are used to redefine issues that line managers must focus on and monitor through their customer tracking surveys and other measures.

Other Customer Satisfaction Indicators

Although customers must be the ultimate arbiters of your organisation's ability to produce customer satisfaction, it is helpful to supplement customer survey data with other relevant indicators of your organisation's performance. Many books and articles on customer service have been published, full of ideas for this type of internally driven indicator. Here we consider the use of four indicators: internal benchmarking; mystery shopping; complaints; customer retention indicators.

INTERNAL BENCHMARKING

Benchmarking is a huge subject in its own right and is well documented in books and articles. This book does not purport to provide any new information on benchmarking or how to carry it out, but simply to suggest ways in which you might use benchmarking techniques (see Figure 16.2) to add value to your customer satisfaction measurement.

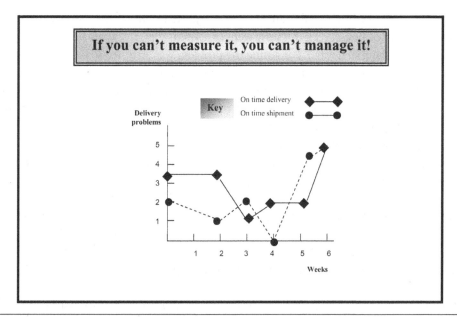

Figure 16.2   Internal benchmarking

Customer surveys identify customers' perceptions of your organisation's performance. They do not necessarily reflect the reality of that performance in any given area, for example, delivery reliability. As was suggested in Chapter 13 customers often take time to notice improvements in service and when they do their attitudes tend to change slowly. It is therefore not uncommon for suppliers to feel aggrieved that they are rated unreasonably poorly by customers, particularly in an area where significant improvements have been made in recent times.

Thus, if your organisation is rated poorly in a specific area such as delivery reliability, it could be that you have a real problem caused by an unacceptable proportion of late deliveries or that your delivery reliability is fine but you have a customer perception problem – your customers' attitudes have not kept up with reality, they still believe your deliveries are unreliable. Your survey will tell you only that there is a problem, not whether it is a real problem of delivery reliability or a perception problem.

Therefore, before you can address the problem you need reliable information on your actual delivery performance and this can be provided through internal benchmarking. Benchmarking parameters should be designed from the customer's perspective. In Figure 16.2 the two performance indicators are monitored to clarify a customer perception of poor delivery reliability. Using only the traditional indicator of on-time delivery (ex works dispatch) may fail to identify that the customer is receiving late delivery due to unreliable transport. Figure 16.2 shows that in weeks 3 and 5 the problem was entirely caused by the supplier's failure to have some of its orders ready for dispatch on time. In weeks 1, 2 and 4 however most of the problem was occurring after dispatching the orders, maybe due to the poor performance of a sub-contract carrier.

This has been reinforced by Royal Mail who have reported that customers' perceptions of the next-day reliability of first-class letter post were consistently poorer than the Royal Mail's own internal benchmarking suggested. For a time the problem was assumed to be a communications gap but when customers' perceptions failed to improve the matter was investigated more deeply. The Royal Mail carried out objective 'end-to-end' research using a panel of customers to send letters to each other, recording all their posting and receipt times. The results showed next-day delivery reliability to be 65 per cent, a score quite close to that recorded by customer perception surveys. The Royal Mail's quality of service measures had showed that 94 per cent of first-class letters were 'ready for delivery' the next day! Having pinpointed the problem it was easier to deal with.

The Royal Mail's experience is not unusual. Many companies have found that the service levels perceived by customers do not match up to the performance portrayed by internal benchmarking. Before you assume that the customer is wrong, you should try to resolve the issue through a different approach, such as mystery shopping.

You should also use customer satisfaction measurement results to influence your benchmarking programme. If success is achieved through 'doing best what matters most to customers', you should examine any areas of performance that are currently benchmarked and consider whether they are the most appropriate. In reality you should 'benchmark what matters most to customers'.

MYSTERY SHOPPING

Most commonly used in retail markets, mystery shopping involves a researcher posing as an ordinary customer, doing all the things that customers do from making an enquiry to buying the product or service and perhaps consuming it, for example, a meal in a restaurant. Experienced researchers trained in observational skills will make a mental note of the supplier's performance across a range of criteria prior to completing a rating sheet (Table 16.1) at the earliest opportunity.

In busy retail environments, where internal benchmarking may prove impossible, data from mystery shopping can be used to interpret customer survey results. Unlike benchmarking, mystery shopping can also be used to provide a regular measure of subjective criteria such as friendliness of staff. Although it is more prevalent in retail markets mystery shopping can also be used in business-to-business markets. More accurately called 'mystery customer research', the technique can be used very effectively to assess supplier behaviour in business markets and to carry out comparisons with competitors. Performance criteria such as responding to enquiries, providing quotations, dealing with customers on the telephone, problem solving and general customer care skills can all be included in this exercise.

It is not essential to use an outside agency for mystery customer research, but the exercise has to be handled very carefully if results are to be reliable. Researchers must be well trained, the exercise must be carried out authentically (for example, if couples typically make an enquiry

Table 16.1   Mystery shopping rating sheet for a restaurant

Attribute	Score	Remarks
Exterior signage		
General appearance		
Car park		
Reception area		
Welcome		
Waiting time		
Cleanliness of dining area		
Quality of starter		
Quality of main course		
Quality of dessert		
Friendliness of service		
Efficiency of service		
Promotion of offers		
Cleanliness of toilets		
Accuracy of billing		
Value for money		

for a mortgage, couples should carry out the mystery shopping) and the methodology should always be piloted before results are utilized.

A good example of customer perception surveys and mystery shopping working together would be the Royal Mail's monitoring of its 65 customer service centres. The centres' role is to respond to customer enquiries and handle complaints. Each month a sample of service centre users is contacted to research customers' perceptions of matters such as ease of contact, speed of response, and staff knowledgeability, courtesy and helpfulness. Sampling and analysis ensure the performance of each individual service centre, as well as national averages, is monitored. The perception survey is supplemented by a mystery shopping exercise which provides objective and consistent feedback on the centres' success in meeting service standards in the areas covered by the perception survey.

COMPLAINTS

Customer complaints can act as an indicator that the level of customer satisfaction is falling. It is very inadvisable to rely solely on complaints for this purpose since research has consistently demonstrated that much customer dissatisfaction is never reported back to the supplier – although it is usually voiced to colleagues, family, and friends.

This suggests that organisations should take steps to make it as easy as possible for customers to complain. Virgin Airways' policy on this is to maximize communications from customers, using a variety of methods to stimulate feedback. The methods include in-flight forms, airport forms, visitors' books, letters, and the full reporting of all verbal comments made to Virgin staff. As a result, in 1993 alone, the company generated 18,000 communications from customers. Like Dell Computers, Virgin involves senior management in communicating with customers, a proportion of complaints being handled by senior staff. In the earlier years of both companies, Richard Branson and Michael Dell used to take part in this exercise.

As far as customer satisfaction measurement is concerned it is very useful to maximize customer communications (positive or negative) as they provide valuable pointers to topics which should be covered in your customer survey and should certainly be incorporated into exploratory research. It is therefore a good idea to retain records, or preferably, summary analyses, of complaints to aid the familiarization process of the customer satisfaction measurement team.

CUSTOMER RETENTION INDICATORS

Customer retention indicators are very useful for showing how you are performing in practice in the marketplace. When your customer satisfaction scores, as shown by customer surveys, are steady or improving but your customer retention indicators are declining the indications are that you have a competitive problem or a market problem. Your service has not deteriorated but competitors have improved at a faster rate, gaining market share at your expense. Alternatively, you may be doing nothing wrong on a day-to-day basis but if you are operating in a declining market (customer demand is falling) you will probably be losing customers – not to competitors but because they are dropping out of your marketplace.

Clearly, customer satisfaction measurement cannot be used to solve all strategic problems and must be supplemented by other performance indicators as necessary. However, do not be tempted into thinking that customer retention indicators could replace customer satisfaction measurement because, although these indicators tell you how successful you have been at retaining customers' loyalty, they cannot tell you why you are keeping or losing them.

Conclusions

- It is far better to do a more thorough survey less often than to carry out frequent but more superficial surveys.
- The frequency of surveys varies between business sectors with more volatile (times of

change, intense competition and frequent purchases) sectors needing to measure customer satisfaction more often than stable sectors.

- For organisations with very frequent customer contact, it is valid to monitor customer satisfaction continuously, using typically brief paper or electronic questionnaires at the point-of-sale or consumption. These tactical tracking surveys need to be re-benchmarked periodically through a detailed strategic survey based on a representative sample.
- Internal benchmarking can be used to help interpret survey results, especially to determine whether poor ratings are due to real problems or misperceptions. However, steps must also be taken to validate the results of internal benchmarking.
- Mystery shopping can be used for the same purpose, particularly in busy retail environments and mystery customer research can also be useful in business markets.
- As well as providing an ongoing barometer of customer opinion, complaints can be useful to help focus exploratory research and records should be kept for this purpose.
- Customer retention indicators provide a definitive check that customer survey scores are being translated into acceptable performance in the marketplace, but they are not a substitute for customer satisfaction measurement because they can indicate only whether, but not why, you are keeping or losing customers.

Overall Conclusions

During our involvement in CSM over the last two decades we have seen a huge growth in the number and variety of organisations that measure customer satisfaction. This brief section outlines the reasons why they are doing so and summarizes the benefits of customer satisfaction and loyalty measurement.

1. Doing best what matters most to customers is the surest way to competitive advantage in commercial markets and to organisational success in public service environments. Thorough customer satisfaction measurement, as outlined in this book, is the only way to measure performance in this respect, and if you can't measure it you can't manage it.
2. It is more profitable to build your business by plugging the hole in the bottom of the bucket than by pouring more new customers in at the top. The higher your customer retention indicators the more profitable your company is likely to be. This has long been recognized by companies such as Rank Xerox who operate customer satisfaction-related pay. The company produces a customer satisfaction index based on its customer retention indicators and on the results of its customer surveys. Managers' pay awards can be increased or reduced by up to 50 per cent according to their success or otherwise in raising the customer satisfaction index.
3. Customer surveys provide a powerful vehicle for concentrating the attention of all staff on the merits of delivering customer satisfaction. Correctly managed, this becomes a virtuous circle as staff strive to improve customer satisfaction and take pride in their success at doing so. However, for customer surveys to be truly effective in this respect staff

must be convinced of the reliability of the results. In addition to keeping staff properly informed, this is achieved only through a professional research methodology, especially the use of a representative sample.

4. Customer satisfaction measurement, using the approach outlined in this book, allows you to accurately identify PFIs and thus focus your resources on those areas where improved performance will have the greatest impact on customer satisfaction.

5. A closer understanding of customers' needs and priorities provides the basis for most management decisions. Companies which meet customers' needs more closely are able to charge higher prices than their competitors (by an average of 9 per cent according to the PIMS database in the USA), because most customers will pay more for a product or service which precisely matches their needs.

6. Of course, satisfaction is only a means to an end not an end in itself. Customer retention is the real goal. When measuring their success and monitoring progress in this area, it is more productive to focus on the concept of commitment rather than loyalty.

7. Leading edge companies are starting to use customer satisfaction and commitment measures to build service-profit chain models, giving them a powerful new strategic management tool.

8. Profits in many organisations can be traced back to a satisfaction–profit chain. Keeping customers longer boosts profits and customer retention is usually driven by customers' level of commitment to the organisation. This very accurate measure of customer loyalty can be derived from CSM surveys and correlated with customer satisfaction, producing a precise satisfaction–loyalty relationship. Customer satisfaction is based on 'doing best what matters most to customers', providing them with a customer value package that, they feel, meets their needs more closely than any alternative packages available from other suppliers. 'Doing best what matters most' is often dependent on an employee force which is motivated to meet customers' needs. A customer-focused organisational culture is important here, but there is growing evidence of a positive correlation between employee satisfaction and customer satisfaction in many companies. It seems that happy staff do indeed produce happy customers. As with all chains, the satisfaction–profit chain is only as strong as its weakest link. To be more profitable, organisations need to measure the strength of each link, establish the precise relationship between the links and use that information to set PFIs (for customer and/or employee satisfaction) that will most effectively translate into business success for the organisation.

APPENDIX 1

Examples of Customer Satisfaction Questionnaires

The questionnaires in this appendix are designed to illustrate the overall concepts of questionnaire design, such as how to word the introduction and other instructions and the differences between questionnaires for different methods of data collection such as telephone and self-completion. They are not meant to suggest specific wording that applies to all organisations, especially for the list of customer requirements that are scored for importance and satisfaction. As you know from reading Chapter 7, these questions are company-specific, based on what's important to your own customers and are generated by exploratory research.

Questionnaire A therefore illustrates typical wording for a B2B company using personal interviews for its CSM. Questionnaires B and C take this hypothetical example and show how that same questionnaire would be worded if the customers were surveyed by telephone or post respectively. This illustrates the different approaches to the way the questions are asked depending on the method of data collection and shows how some methods, especially face-to-face interviews enable a longer questionnaire and the collection of more qualitative data.

Questionnaire D is once more the same CSM questionnaire, but this time it is worded for an internal survey, where the organisation is measuring the extent to which its own staff understand customers.

To conclude therefore, please don't copy these questionnaires, but do feel free to use them to get the structure and format of your questionnaire, with the customer requirements that you score for importance and satisfaction being determined by your own exploratory research.

Questionnaire A

Personal interview

ABC Ltd

Date: _____ Interviewer: _____

Respondent name: _____

Company: _____

Position: _____

Segment: _____

Location: _____

Company's business:

_____
_____
_____

Respondent's role:

_____
_____
_____

1. What is important to the customer?

We've just been speaking about products your company uses and how you source them. I'd like you to imagine that you had to undertake a complete review of suppliers of .... (product in question), starting with a completely blank piece of paper and no preconceptions.

1.2 Which companies would be on a list of potential suppliers?

Unprompted	**Prompted**
1. _____	1. _____
2. _____	2. _____
3. _____	3. _____
4. _____	4. _____
5. _____	5. _____

1.1 Having drawn up your list, you would have to decide how to rate these potential suppliers against each other. To do this you would have to specify your requirements and judge each supplier against its ability to meet those requirements. What would those requirements be?

1. _____	4. _____
2. _____	5. _____
3. _____	6. _____

Which of those is the most important single requirement for you?

1. _____

1.3 I'm now going to suggest a more detailed list of requirements and I'd like you to indicate how important or unimportant each one is to you by giving it a score out of 10, where 10 out of 10 would mean extremely important and 1 out of 10 would mean of no importance at all. When deciding your score, you may find it helpful to compare the importance of the requirement in question with your Number One requirement of ....(repeat it)

		IMPORTANCE	
		Customer requirement	**Score**
a)		**Product performance**	
	1.	Consistency of product quality	
	2.	Technical performance of product	
	3.	Comprehensiveness of product range	
	4.	Supplier's quality systems	
	5.	Supplier's standards of hygiene	
	6.	Other documentation e.g. health & safety	
b)		**Delivery and service performance**	
	1.	Reliability of delivery (delivery promises kept)	
	2.	Speed of delivery (lead times)	
	3.	Packaging of deliveries	
	4.	Ease of ordering	
	5.	Feedback, especially on problems	
	6.	Confidence of continuity of supply	
c)		**Technical service performance**	
	1.	Ability to innovate (R&D expertise)	
	2.	Design expertise	
	3.	Responsiveness on technical service	
d)		**Field sales performance**	
	1.	Frequency of visits	
	2.	Technical capability of representative	
	3.	Commercial capability of representative	
	4.	Interpersonal skills of representative	
	5.	Empowerment of representative	
	6.	Accessibility of representative (available when needed)	
e)		**Pricing performance**	
	1.	Competitiveness of price	
	2.	Handling of price negotiations	
f)		**Environmental performance**	
	1.	Environmental responsibility	
	2.	Recycling capability	

2. Performance

I'd now like to ask how ABC performs against the same requirements and how their performance compares with other suppliers. Please answer by giving a score out of 10 as before, where 10 represents excellent performance and 1 represents extremely poor performance

SUPPLIERS' PERFORMANCE				
Requirement	**ABC**	Competitor 1	Competitor 2	Competitor 3
a) Product performance				
1. Consistency of product quality				
2. Technical performance of product				
3. Comprehensiveness of product range				
4. Supplier's quality systems				
5. Supplier's standards of hygiene				
6. Other documentation e.g. health & safety				
b) Delivery and service performance				
1. Reliability of delivery (delivery promises kept)				
2. Speed of delivery (lead times)				
3. Packaging of deliveries				
4. Ease of ordering				
5. Feedback, especially on problems				
6. Confidence of continuity of supply				
c) Technical service performance				
1. Ability to innovate (R&D expertise)				
2. Design expertise				
3. Responsiveness on technical service				
d) Field sales performance				
1. Frequency of visits				
2. Technical capability of representative				
3. Commercial capability of representative				
4. Interpersonal skills of representative				
5. Empowerment of representative				
6. Accessibility of representative (available when needed)				
e) Pricing performance				
1. Competitiveness of price				
2. Handling of price negotiations				
f) Environmental performance				
1. Environmental responsibility				
2. Recycling capability				

If any item is scored 5 or lower, probe reasons	
Item no:	

3. Supplier's image

You mentioned a number of suppliers at the beginning of the interview. I'd like you to think for a moment about the different images that those suppliers create in your mind and what distinguishes them as companies. Let me give you some examples.

BMW, Jaguar and Volvo are not dissimilar. They all have an image of high quality, engineering excellence and success. But they have differences.

BMW is often perceived as more aggressive, more ostentatious, more dynamic.

Jaguar is still a symbol of success that should be noticed, but less flamboyant, maybe older and less impetuous.

Volvo could be seen as very solid and reliable but maybe less ostentatious, more cautious and safe.

🚗 **Which car comes closest to your image of ABC?**

_____

🚗 **Why do you say that?**

_____
_____
_____
_____

🚗 **And what about ....(other suppliers), which cars would they be?**

_____
_____
_____

🚗 **Why is that?**

_____
_____
_____

4. Industry trends

What would you say are the main trends in your industry at the moment and how do you think they will affect a supplier like ABC?

Prompts:

1. Environmental management / recycling / waste recovery
2. E-commerce
3. Partnership sourcing
4. JIT deliveries / consignment stocks
5. New products / new technologies

_____

_____

_____

5. Priorities for change

Finally, I'd like you to imagine you were the Chief Executive of ABC. What would be your top priorities for the company over the short term (urgent priorities) and over the longer term?

Short term:

_____

_____

Long term:

_____

_____

Do you have any other comments about anything we've discussed?

_____

_____

_____

Thank you very much for taking part in the survey.

Your answers have been most helpful.

Questionnaire B

Telephone interview

ABC Ltd

Date: _____ Interviewer: _____

Respondent name: _____

Company: _____

Position: _____

Segment: _____

Location: _____

Introduction:

Good morning / afternoon Mr / Mrs ....

My name is Jim Alexander from The Leadership Factor and I'm calling on behalf of ABC. I understand that Mr Smith has written to you explaining that we have been asked to carry out a customer satisfaction survey on ABC's behalf. Did you receive the letter?............

Would it be convenient to spend 10 minutes answering a few questions now or would you prefer me to make an appointment for a more convenient time?

I'd like to assure you that in accordance with the Market Research Society code of conduct the information you provide will not be linked with your name unless you want it to be, but will be combined with other responses to provide information which will help ABC to fully understand and meet customers' needs.

I'd like to start by exploring the factors that are important to you when dealing with ABC

1. What is important to the customer?

I'm going to start with some questions about what is important to you as a customer. I'd like you to imagine that you had to undertake a complete review of suppliers of …………….. (product in question), starting with a completely blank piece of paper and no preconceptions.

1.1 Which companies would be on a list of potential suppliers?

Unprompted	Prompted
1. _____	1. _____
2. _____	2. _____
3. _____	3. _____
4. _____	4. _____
5. _____	5. _____

1.2 Having drawn up your list, you would have to decide how to rate these potential suppliers against each other. To do this you would have to specify your requirements and judge each supplier against its ability to meet those requirements. What would those requirements be?

1. _____	4. _____
2. _____	5. _____
3. _____	6. _____

Which of those is the most important single requirement for you?

1. _____

1.3 I'm now going to suggest a more detailed list of requirements and I'd like you to indicate how important or unimportant each one is to you by giving it a score out of 10, where 10 out of 10 would mean extremely important and 1 out of 10 would mean of no importance at all. When deciding your score, you may find it helpful to compare the importance of the requirement in question with your Number One requirement of ....(repeat it)

		IMPORTANCE	
		Customer requirement	**Score**
a)		**Product performance**	
	1.	Consistency of product quality	
	2.	Technical performance of product	
	3.	Supplier's quality systems	
	4.	Supplier's standards of hygiene	
b)		**Delivery and service performance**	
	1.	Reliability of delivery (delivery promises kept)	
	2.	Speed of delivery (lead times)	
	3.	Feedback, especially on problems	
	4.	Confidence of continuity of supply	
c)		**Technical service performance**	
	1.	Ability to innovate (R&D expertise)	
	2.	Design expertise	
	3.	Responsiveness on technical service	
d)		**Field sales performance**	
	1.	Technical capability of representative	
	2.	Commercial capability of representative	
	3.	Interpersonal skills of representative	
	4.	Empowerment of representative	
	5.	Accessibility of representative (available when needed)	
e)		**Pricing performance**	
	1.	Competitiveness of price	
f)		**Environmental performance**	
	1.	Environmental responsibility	

2. Performance

I'd now like to ask how ABC performs against the same requirements and how their performance compares with other suppliers. Please answer by giving a score out of 10 as before, where 10 represents excellent performance and 1 represents extremely poor performance

SUPPLIERS' PERFORMANCE

	Requirement	ABC	Competitor 1	Competitor 2	Competitor 3
a)	**Product performance**				
1.	Consistency of product quality				
2.	Technical performance of product				
3.	Supplier's quality systems				
4.	Supplier's standards of hygiene				
b)	**Delivery and service performance**				
1.	Reliability of delivery (delivery promises kept)				
2.	Speed of delivery (lead times)				
3.	Feedback, especially on problems				
4.	Confidence of continuity of supply				
c)	**Technical service performance**				
1.	Ability to innovate (R&D expertise)				
2.	Design expertise				
3.	Responsiveness on technical service				
d)	**Field sales performance**				
1.	Technical capability of representative				
2.	Commercial capability of representative				
3.	Interpersonal skills of representative				
4.	Empowerment of representative				
5.	Accessibility of representative (available when needed)				
e)	**Pricing performance**				
1.	Competitiveness of price				
f)	**Environmental performance**				
1.	Environmental responsibility				

If any item is scored 5 or lower, probe reasons

Item no:	

3. Industry trends

What would you say are the main trends in your industry at the moment and how do you think they will affect a supplier like ABC?

Prompts:

1. Environmental management / recycling / waste recovery
2. E-commerce
3. Partnership sourcing
4. JIT deliveries / consignment stocks
5. New products / new technologies

_____

_____

_____

_____

_____

Do you have any other comments, about anything we've discussed?

_____

_____

_____

Thank you very much for taking part in the survey.

Your answers have been most helpful.

Questionnaire C

Self-completion questionnaire

ABC Ltd

Introduction & Guidance

The purpose of this survey is to find out what you expect from ABC Ltd as a supplier and how satisfied or dissatisfied you are with the service you receive. We need everyone to answer the questionnaire very honestly, and to encourage this, the survey is being conducted by an independent, professional agency, The Leadership Factor, and in accordance with the Market Research Society Code of Conduct they will guarantee the anonymity of everyone who completes it,.

The questionnaire is divided into two main sections, (A and B). Both sections cover the same topics, but in section A we want to know how **important or unimportant** each item is to you, and in section B, **how satisfied or dissatisfied** you are with ABC's performance on each item. Please complete the questionnaire and return it in the pre-paid envelope to The Leadership Factor by ....(date)

How to complete section A
In this section, we would like you to score **how important or unimportant** various issues are to you.

Some issues may be more important than others, and we want to get a good idea of your priorities. So, first of all, read through all the questions before deciding which is the most important one. Then score the level of importance out of ten using the following scale.

| 1 | 2 | 3 | 4 | 5 | 6 | 7 | 8 | 9 | 10 |

Of no importance at all — Extremely important

Score your most important issue first, then score the rest in that section.

For example, look at Question 1 'Consistency of product quality'. If 'Consistency of product quality' is your most important requirement you should circle box number 10 as shown.

1. 'Consistency of product quality' | N/A | 1 | 2 | 3 | 4 | 5 | 6 | 7 | 8 | 9 | (10)

Then score the remaining items in the list using the same scale. You can circle any number between 1 and 10. It does not matter if you circle the same score for two or more questions. If you feel that an item is not relevant to you or you have no direct experience of what is being asked, you should circle the box marked 'N/A' (not applicable).

Section A: Importance

How **important or unimportant** are the following items to you as a customer of ABC

N/A	1	2	3	4	5	6	7	8	9	10

Of no importance at all — Extremely important

1.	Consistency of product quality	N/A 1 2 3 4 5 6 7 8 9 10
2.	Technical performance of product	N/A 1 2 3 4 5 6 7 8 9 10
3.	Supplier's quality systems	N/A 1 2 3 4 5 6 7 8 9 10
4.	Supplier's standards of hygiene	N/A 1 2 3 4 5 6 7 8 9 10
5.	Reliability of delivery (on time)	N/A 1 2 3 4 5 6 7 8 9 10
6.	Speed of delivery (lead times)	N/A 1 2 3 4 5 6 7 8 9 10
7.	Feedback, especially on problems	N/A 1 2 3 4 5 6 7 8 9 10
8.	Confidence of continuity of supply	N/A 1 2 3 4 5 6 7 8 9 10
9.	Ability to innovate (R&D expertise)	N/A 1 2 3 4 5 6 7 8 9 10
10.	Design expertise	N/A 1 2 3 4 5 6 7 8 9 10
11.	Responsiveness on technical service	N/A 1 2 3 4 5 6 7 8 9 10
12.	Technical capability of representative	N/A 1 2 3 4 5 6 7 8 9 10
13.	Commercial capability of representative	N/A 1 2 3 4 5 6 7 8 9 10
14.	Interpersonal skills of representative	N/A 1 2 3 4 5 6 7 8 9 10
15.	Empowerment of representative	N/A 1 2 3 4 5 6 7 8 9 10
16.	Accessibility of representative	N/A 1 2 3 4 5 6 7 8 9 10
17.	Competitiveness of price	N/A 1 2 3 4 5 6 7 8 9 10
18.	Environmental responsibility	N/A 1 2 3 4 5 6 7 8 9 10

Additional comments

Section B: Satisfaction

We'd now like to know how **satisfied or dissatisfied** you are with the performance of ABC. Again circle the number which best reflects your views. This time show your level of **satisfaction or dissatisfaction** using the following scale as a guide. Circle any number between 1 and 10 or circle the N/A box if you have no experience of the item listed.

N/A	1	2	3	4	5	6	7	8	9	10

Completely dissatisfied — Completely satisfied

#	Item	N/A	1	2	3	4	5	6	7	8	9	10
1.	Consistency of product quality	N/A	1	2	3	4	5	6	7	8	9	10
2.	Technical performance of product	N/A	1	2	3	4	5	6	7	8	9	10
3.	Supplier's quality systems	N/A	1	2	3	4	5	6	7	8	9	10
4.	Supplier's standards of hygiene	N/A	1	2	3	4	5	6	7	8	9	10
5.	Reliability of delivery (on time)	N/A	1	2	3	4	5	6	7	8	9	10
6.	Speed of delivery (lead times)	N/A	1	2	3	4	5	6	7	8	9	10
7.	Feedback, especially on problems	N/A	1	2	3	4	5	6	7	8	9	10
8.	Confidence of continuity of supply	N/A	1	2	3	4	5	6	7	8	9	10
9.	Ability to innovate (R&D expertise)	N/A	1	2	3	4	5	6	7	8	9	10
10.	Design expertise	N/A	1	2	3	4	5	6	7	8	9	10
11.	Responsiveness on technical service	N/A	1	2	3	4	5	6	7	8	9	10
12.	Technical capability of representative	N/A	1	2	3	4	5	6	7	8	9	10
13.	Commercial capability of representative	N/A	1	2	3	4	5	6	7	8	9	10
14.	Interpersonal skills of representative	N/A	1	2	3	4	5	6	7	8	9	10
15.	Empowerment of representative	N/A	1	2	3	4	5	6	7	8	9	10
16.	Accessibility of representative	N/A	1	2	3	4	5	6	7	8	9	10
17.	Competitiveness of price	N/A	1	2	3	4	5	6	7	8	9	10
18.	Environmental responsibility	N/A	1	2	3	4	5	6	7	8	9	10

Additional comments

3. Priorities for change

Finally, if you were the Chief Executive of ABC what would be your top priorities for the company over the short term (urgent priorities) and over the longer term?

Short term:

_____

_____

_____

Long term:

_____

_____

_____

Any other comments?

_____

_____

_____

_____

Please leave personal details blank if you prefer to remain anonymous

Name: _____

Position: _____

Company: _____

Thank you very much for your help in completing this questionnaire. Please return it in the freepost envelope provide no <u>later than</u> ....date........ If you have mislaid the reply envelope please return it in any envelope to The Leadership Factor, Taylor Hill Mill, Huddersfield HD4 6JA.

Questionnaire D

Internal survey questionnaire

ABC Ltd

Introduction & Guidance

As an employee of 'ABC', we would like to know what your perceptions are of customers' requirements and their satisfaction with ABC. We need everyone to answer the questionnaire very honestly, and to encourage this, The Leadership Factor, our research agency, guarantees to protect the identity of everyone who completes it. The questionnaire is entirely confidential. When you have completed the questionnaire please seal it in the envelope provided and return it directly to The Leadership Factor.

The questionnaire is divided into two main sections, (A and B). Both sections cover the same topics, but in Section A we want to know how **important or unimportant** you believe each factor is to customers and in Section B how **satisfied or dissatisfied** you feel customers are with ABC's performance on each factor.

How to complete section A

In this section, we would like you to score **how important or unimportant** you believe various items are to ABC's customers.

Some issues may be more important to customers than others, and we want to get a good idea of your views about customers' priorities. So, first of all, read through all the questions before deciding which factor you believe is the most important one for customers. Then score the level of importance out of ten using the following scale.

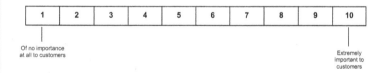

| 1 | 2 | 3 | 4 | 5 | 6 | 7 | 8 | 9 | 10 |

Of no importance
at all to customers

Extremely
important to
customers

For example, look at Question 1 'Consistency of product quality'. If you believe 'Consistency of product quality' would be the most important requirement for ABC's customers, you should circle box number 10 as shown.

1. 'Consistency of product quality' | N/A | 1 | 2 | 3 | 4 | 5 | 6 | 7 | 8 | 9 | (10)

Then score the remaining items in the list according to how **important or unimportant** you think they are to customers. You can circle any number between 1 and 10. It does not matter if you circle the same score for two or more questions. If you feel that an item is not relevant to you or you have no direct experience of what is being asked, you should circle the box marked 'N/A' (not applicable).

Section A: Importance

How **important or unimportant** do you think the following items are to customers of ABC?

N/A	1	2	3	4	5	6	7	8	9	10

Of no importance at all to customers — Extremely important to customers

		N/A	1	2	3	4	5	6	7	8	9	10
1.	Consistency of product quality											
2.	Technical performance of product											
3.	Supplier's quality systems											
4.	Supplier's standards of hygiene											
5.	Reliability of delivery (on time)											
6.	Speed of delivery (lead times)											
7.	Feedback, especially on problems											
8.	Confidence of continuity of supply											
9.	Ability to innovate (R&D expertise)											
10.	Design expertise											
11.	Responsiveness on technical service											
12.	Technical capability of representative											
13.	Commercial capability of representative											
14.	Interpersonal skills of representative											
15.	Empowerment of representative											
16.	Accessibility of representative											
17.	Competitiveness of price											
18.	Environmental responsibility											

Additional comments

Section B: Satisfaction

We'd now like to know how **satisfied or dissatisfied** you think customers are with the performance of ABC. Again circle the number which best reflects your views about customers' level of **satisfaction or dissatisfaction** using the following scale as a guide. Circle any number between 1 and 10 or circle the N/A box if you have no experience of the item listed.

N/A	1	2	3	4	5	6	7	8	9	10

Customers are completely dissatisfied — Customers are completely satisfied

		N/A	1	2	3	4	5	6	7	8	9	10
1.	Consistency of product quality	N/A	1	2	3	4	5	6	7	8	9	10
2.	Technical performance of product	N/A	1	2	3	4	5	6	7	8	9	10
3.	Supplier's quality systems	N/A	1	2	3	4	5	6	7	8	9	10
4.	Supplier's standards of hygiene	N/A	1	2	3	4	5	6	7	8	9	10
5.	Reliability of delivery (on time)	N/A	1	2	3	4	5	6	7	8	9	10
6.	Speed of delivery (lead times)	N/A	1	2	3	4	5	6	7	8	9	10
7.	Feedback, especially on problems	N/A	1	2	3	4	5	6	7	8	9	10
8.	Confidence of continuity of supply	N/A	1	2	3	4	5	6	7	8	9	10
9.	Ability to innovate (R&D expertise)	N/A	1	2	3	4	5	6	7	8	9	10
10.	Design expertise	N/A	1	2	3	4	5	6	7	8	9	10
11.	Responsiveness on technical service	N/A	1	2	3	4	5	6	7	8	9	10
12.	Technical capability of representative	N/A	1	2	3	4	5	6	7	8	9	10
13.	Commercial capability of representative	N/A	1	2	3	4	5	6	7	8	9	10
14.	Interpersonal skills of representative	N/A	1	2	3	4	5	6	7	8	9	10
15.	Empowerment of representative	N/A	1	2	3	4	5	6	7	8	9	10
16.	Accessibility of representative	N/A	1	2	3	4	5	6	7	8	9	10
17.	Competitiveness of price	N/A	1	2	3	4	5	6	7	8	9	10
18.	Environmental responsibility	N/A	1	2	3	4	5	6	7	8	9	10

Additional comments

3. Priorities for change

Finally, if you were the Chief Executive of ABC what actions would you implement for improving customer satisfaction over the short term (urgent priorities) and over the longer term?

Short term:

_____

_____

_____

Long term:

_____

_____

_____

Any other comments?

_____

_____

_____

_____

Please leave personal details blank if you prefer to remain anonymous

Name: _____

Department:_____

Thank you very much for your help in completing this questionnaire. Please return it in the freepost envelope provided no later than ....date........ If you have mislaid the reply envelope please return it in any envelope to The Leadership Factor, Taylor Hill Mill, Huddersfield HD4 6JA.

APPENDIX 2

SERVQUAL

A model designed to measure customers' perceptions of service quality, SERVQUAL was developed in the 1980s by three American academics, Parasuraman, Zeithaml and Berry. Based on twelve focus groups they developed a questionnaire comprising the 22 criteria most commonly used by the focus group participants to assess service quality.

Following further research, Parasuraman *et al.* grouped the 22 criteria into five service quality dimensions which, they claim, will determine customers' perception of any service business. The dimensions are:

Tangibles—The physical facilities, equipment and appearance of personnel.
Reliability—The ability to perform the promised service dependably and accurately.
Responsiveness—Willingness to help customers and provide prompt service.
Assurance—Knowledge and courtesy of employees and their ability to inspire trust and confidence.
Empathy—Caring, individualized attention that the firm provides its customers.

In 1988, another academic, Gronroos, added a significant sixth dimension to these five – 'recovery' – which concerns the organisation's ability to rectify problems.

More recently other academics have suggested additional criteria, some as many as 15 dimensions, but most practitioners are happy with the five SERVQUAL dimensions plus the important addition of recovery.

Parasuraman *et al.* also used their research as the basis for the service quality gap model. They defined service quality as a function of the gap between customers' expectations of a service and their perceptions of the actual service delivered. As described in Chapter 2, the overall service quality gap can be formed by one or more of several specific gaps. The 'gap' research emphasizes the requirement to explore customers' expectations as well as their experience when measuring customer satisfaction.

Some market research agencies have adopted SERVQUAL as their methodology for customer satisfaction measurement, but the approach does have its critics. Some academics, for example Cronin and Taylor (1992), claim that it is adequate to measure only perceptions in service quality research and unnecessary to measure expectations. Cronin, Taylor and Teas (1993) suggest that SERVQUAL is more appropriate for measuring post-transaction satisfaction than for measuring customers' underlying satisfaction with a service or an organisation. Teas (1993) highlights the distinction between 'transaction specific quality' and 'relationship quality'. In this book the terms 'continuous tracking' and 'baseline survey' are used to make this distinction.

Our view is that the fundamental problem with SERVQUAL is that it only encompasses service provision and is not suitable for any business providing tangible products of any kind, whether as a manufacturer or distributor. Parasuraman *et al.* take the view that 'goods quality can be measured objectively by such indicators as durability and number of defects' but that such objective yardsticks cannot be applied to services. Therefore, they say, 'In the absence of objective measures an appropriate approach for assessing the quality of a firm's service is to measure consumers' perceptions of quality'. It is our contention, however, that customers' assessments of product quality are frequently based on subjective perceptions rather than objective measures.

We also maintain that the SERVQUAL approach with its 22 questions grouped into five dimensions is a far too rigid approach. Even amongst service providers, the criteria used to measure customer satisfaction cannot be standardized to the same 22 factors which are equally applicable to customers of a bank and customers of a hairdresser, or to customers of a dentist and customers of a training provider.

The approach advocated in this book is to let the customers set the agenda. Chapter 7 explains the exploratory research techniques recommended for identifying what matters most to your customers. It is important that your questionnaire incorporates these factors and that questions reflect the wording used by customers. However, despite the above criticisms, the SERVQUAL model should be studied by anyone planning to carry out a customer survey and especially by those in the service sector. It will provide useful guidance for the areas that should be covered by your exploratory research.

A SERVQUAL questionnaire is shown on pages 269 to 273. Note that the first section covers customers' expectations, followed by a section designed to measure the relative importance of the five service dimensions which is essential for anyone wishing to calculate importance weightings. The third section covers customers' perceptions of the service they have received from a particular supplier. You would tailor this questionnaire to your own company simply by entering your own business sector in the blank spaces. For example, the opening sentence of the first directions would become, 'Based on your experience as a consumer of insurance services, please think about the kind of insurance company that would deliver excellent quality of service.'

Before reading through the SERVQUAL questionnaire remember that, as mentioned earlier, the 22 factors are divided into five dimensions:

Tangibles	1–4
Reliability	5–9
Responsiveness	10–13
Assurance	14–17
Empathy	18–22

The SERVQUAL questionnaire occupies the next five pages.

EXAMPLE OF A SERVQUAL QUESTIONNAIRE

Directions

Based on your experiences as a consumer of ————— services, please think about the kind of ————— company that would deliver excellent quality of service. Think about the kind of ————— company with which you would be pleased to do business. Please show the extent to which you think such a ————— company would possess the features described by each statement. If you feel a feature is *not at all essential* for excellent ————— companies such as the one you have in mind, circle the number 1. If you feel a feature is *absolutely essential* for excellent ————— companies, circle 7. If your feelings are less strong, circle one of the numbers in the middle. There are no right or wrong answers – all we are interested in is a number that truly reflects your feelings regarding companies that would deliver excellent quality of service.

		Strongly disagree					Strongly agree	
1.	Excellent ————— companies will have modern-looking equipment.	1	2	3	4	5	6	7
2.	The physical facilities at excellent ————— companies will be visually appealing.	1	2	3	4	5	6	7
3.	Employees at excellent ————— companies will be neat-appearing.	1	2	3	4	5	6	7
4.	Materials associated with the service (such as pamphlets or statements) will be visually appealing in the excellent ————— company.	1	2	3	4	5	6	7
5.	When excellent ————— companies promise to do something by a certain time, they do so.	1	2	3	4	5	6	7
6.	When a customer has a problem, excellent ————— companies will show a sincere interest in solving it.	1	2	3	4	5	6	7
7.	Excellent ————— companies will perform the service right the first time.	1	2	3	4	5	6	7
8.	Excellent ————— companies will provide their services at the time they promise to do so.	1	2	3	4	5	6	7

9. Excellent ———— companies will insist on error-free records.   1 2 3 4 5 6 7

10. Employees in excellent ———— companies will tell customers exactly when services will be performed.   1 2 3 4 5 6 7

11. Employees in excellent ———— companies will give prompt service to customers.   1 2 3 4 5 6 7

12. Employees in excellent ———— companies will always be willing to help customers.   1 2 3 4 5 6 7

13. Employees in excellent ———— companies will never be too busy to respond to customers' requests.   1 2 3 4 5 6 7

14. The behaviour of employees in excellent ———— companies will instil confidence in customers.   1 2 3 4 5 6 7

15. Customers of excellent ———— companies will feel safe in their transactions.   1 2 3 4 5 6 7

16. Employees in excellent ———— companies will be consistently courteous with customers.   1 2 3 4 5 6 7

17. Employees in excellent ———— companies will have knowledge to answer customers' questions.   1 2 3 4 5 6 7

18. Excellent ———— companies will give customers individual attention.   1 2 3 4 5 6 7

19. Excellent ———— companies will have operating hours convenient to all their customers.   1 2 3 4 5 6 7

20. Excellent ———— companies will have employees who give customers personal attention.   1 2 3 4 5 6 7

21. Excellent ———— companies will have the customers' best interests at heart.   1 2 3 4 5 6 7

22. Employees of excellent ———— companies will understand the specific needs of their customers.

       1   2   3   4   5   6   7

Directions

Listed below are five features pertaining to ———— companies and the services they offer. We would like to know how important each of these features is to you when you evaluate a ———— company's quality of service. Please allocate a total of 100 points among the five features *according to how important each feature is to you* – the more important a feature is to you, the more points you should allocate to it. Please ensure that the points you allocate to the five features add up to 100.

1. The appearance of the ———— company's physical facilities, equipment, personnel and communication materials.

   ———— points

2. The ———— company's ability to perform the promised service dependably and accurately.

   ———— points

3. The ———— company's willingness to help customers and provide prompt service.
   ———— points

4. The knowledge and courtesy of the ———— company's employees and their ability to convey trust and confidence.

   ———— points

5. The caring, individualized attention the ———— company provides its customers.
   ———— points

Total points allocated   100 points

Directions

The following set of statements relate to your feelings about XYZ Company. For each statement, please show the extent to which you believe XYZ Company has the feature described by the statement. Once again, circling a 1 means you strongly disagree that XYZ Company has that feature, and circling a 7 means that you strongly agree. You may circle any of the numbers in the middle that show how strong your feelings are. There are no right or wrong answers – all we are interested in is a number that best shows your perceptions about XYZ Company.

The statements in the final section, covering customers' perceptions of the service received, use the same seven-point Likert scale as shown in the first section. Here the statements alone are reproduced.

1. The ————— company has modern looking equipment.

2. The ————— company's physical facilities are visually appealing.

3. The ————— company's employees are neat-appearing.

4. Materials associated with the service (such as pamphlets or statements) are visually appealing at the ————— company.

5. When the ————— company promises to do something by a certain time, it does so.

6. When you have a problem, the ————— company shows a sincere interest in solving it.

7. The ————— company performs the service right the first time.

8. The ————— company provides its services at the time it promises to do so.

9. The ————— company insists on error-free records.

10. Employees in the ————— company tell you exactly when services will be performed.

11. Employees in the ————— company give you prompt service.

12. Employees in the ————— company are always willing to help you.

13. Employees in the ————— company are never too busy to respond to your requests.

14. The behaviour of employees in the ————— company instils confidence in you.

15. You feel safe in your transactions with the ————— company.

16. Employees in the ————— company are consistently courteous with you.

17. Employees in the ————— company have the knowledge to answer your questions.

18. The ————— company gives you individual attention.

19. The ————— company has operating hours convenient to customers.

20. The ————— company has employees who give you personal attention.

21. The ————— company has your best interests at heart.

22. Employees of the ————— company understand your specific needs.

FURTHER READING ON SERVQUAL

For those readers who are interested in pursuing the original academic articles on SERVQUAL and also the work published by its critics the following references will be useful.

Cronin, J. J. and Taylor, S. A. (1992) 'Measuring service quality: a re-examination and extension', *Journal of Marketing*, vol. 56, July, pp. 55–68.

Cronin, J. J. and Taylor, S. A. (1994) 'SERVPERF versus SERVQUAL: reconciling performance-based and perceptions-minus-expectations measurement of service quality', *Journal of Marketing*, vol. 58, January, pp. 125–31.

Parasuraman, A., Zeithaml, V. A. and Berry, L. L. (1985) 'A conceptual model of service quality and its implications for future research', *Journal of Marketing*, vol. 49, Fall, pp. 41–50.

Parasuraman, A., Zeithaml, V. A. and Berry, L. L. (1988) 'SERVQUAL: a multiple item scale for measuring consumer perceptions of service quality', *Journal of Retailing*, vol. 64, no. 1, Spring, pp. 14–40.

Parasuraman, A., Zeithaml, V. A. and Berry, L. L. (1991) 'Refinement and reassessment of the SERVQUAL scale', *Journal of Retailing*, vol. 67, no. 4, Winter, pp. 420–50.

Parasuraman, A., Zeithaml, V. A. and Berry, L. L. (1994) 'Reassessment of expectations as a comparison standard in measuring service quality: implications for further research', *Journal of Marketing*, vol. 58, January, pp. 111–24.

Teas, R. K. (1993) 'Expectations, performance evaluation and consumers' perceptions of quality', *Journal of Marketing*, vol. 57, October, pp. 18–34.

APPENDIX 3

Glossary of Terms

Arithmetic mean

The sum of the observed values of a statistic divided by the number of observations. The responses 'Not stated' and 'Don't know' are usually excluded from this calculation when survey data are used and constitute a possible source of bias.

Average

Correctly termed the arithmetic mean.

Baseline survey

Comprehensive customer survey carried out periodically to establish or update key benchmarks such as customers' priorities and organisational performance.

Census

Survey where the whole of the target population is questioned.

Closed question

A question with a limited number of pre-coded logical answers.

Clustered sampling

Method of sampling employed to reduce costs and widely used in commercial face-to-face interviewing. In a simple random sample respondents would be spread over a wide area geographically with the consequence of costly travelling expenses to visit each respondent. Instead respondents within a close geographical proximity are interviewed. This method implies greater sampling error so for a given sample size many small clusters are preferable to a few large clusters.

Coding

Process whereby open-ended responses are categorized, usually in the exploratory stages of interviewing, feeding directly into questionnaire design. When open questions are included in the main interview these responses are coded at the data processing stage to facilitate analysis.

Cognitive dissonance

Doubt felt by a consumer when it is realized that unchosen alternatives may have desirable attributes.

Consumer markets

Markets where the purchase is made by an individual for his or her own consumption or for the consumption of family, friends etc.

Contact sheet

Record of the contacts and attempted contacts made by an interviewer.

Convenience sample

Sample selected merely because it is convenient; such samples are liable to bias.

CSI (customer satisfaction index)

A single value, usually expressed as a percentage, representing customers' level of overall satisfaction. The accuracy of the index is improved by using importance weightings to modify performance scores before calculating the average of the weighted performance scores.

Customer perception survey

Survey of existing customers to measure their satisfaction with the total product provided by a company/organisation.

Customer pyramid

Hierarchy of customer types depicting different shades/degrees of loyalty.

Customer retention indicator

A measure of customer loyalty based on an organisation's success in retaining the business of its existing customers.

Customer satisfaction

A measure of how a company or organisation's total product performs in relation to a set of customer expectations.

Disproportionate sample

Sample drawn with a variable sampling fraction across different strata.

DMU (decision-making unit)

A group (formal or informal) of individuals involved in a purchase decision.

Focus group

Method used in qualitative research where groups of between six and eight individuals led by a facilitator engage in depth discussions with the aim of exploring attitudes and feelings about a particular subject.

Gap analysis

Using the gap between two sets of related measures (for example, importance and satisfaction) as an indicator of a third characteristic; in this example, the organisation's success in meeting its customer's requirements.

Internal benchmarking

Data gathered internally and used to quantify and monitor aspects of service performance such as delivery reliability.

Judgement sample

Also called a 'purposive sample'. Any non-random sample but typically one in which individuals have been deliberately selected because of their perceived contribution to the problem in hand.

Likert scale

Type of verbal rating scale in which respondents are asked to indicate the extent of their agreement or disagreement with a series of statements. Also called 'agree/disagree' scale.

Loyalty

Positive level of commitment by the customer to the supplier.

Market standing survey

Survey of all buyers of a given product or service to ascertain how a company's performance compares with that of other suppliers of the same product or service.

Median

Middle of a set of numbers, one half of the numbers being larger and one half smaller.

Mode

Most frequently occurring value in a set of data.

Mystery shopping

Also called 'mystery customer research' in business-to-business markets. Involves the collection of information by researchers posing as ordinary customers.

Non-random sample

Types of sample other than random (probability) sample.

Numerical rating scale

Any scale represented by numbers as distinguished from diagrammatic and from verbal scales.

Open question

Where there are many possible answers and the response has not been pre-coded. The answer is recorded verbatim and coded at a later stage.

Ordinal scale

Produces a ranking in terms of precedence (first, second, third, etc.) where the distances between the points on the scale have no meaning.

Organisational markets

Markets where the customer is an organisation, usually a business but sometimes a public sector organisation such as a hospital or a not-for-profit organisation such as a charity. Individuals place orders on behalf of the organisation.

Performance profile

Method of displaying results from verbal rating scales such as Likert and semantic differential scales. A grid is created showing the performance criteria down the side with the number of points on the scale displayed across the top. Customers' responses must then be given numerical values (say, 5 for 'Strongly agree' or 1 for 'Strongly disagree' and so on). The average scores are then plotted against the scale resulting in 'profiles' or 'maps' (see Figure 12.2).

Personal interview

Face-to-face communication between interviewer and respondent.

PFIs (priorities for improvement)

Those areas where improvements in performance would make the greatest contribution to increasing customer satisfaction.

Piloting

A pilot survey is a small-scale replica of the main survey, carried out beforehand in order to reveal any problems likely to be encountered, or to help in the design of the main survey.

Population

Individuals or organisations from which a sample for survey purposes may be drawn. Also known as the 'survey population' or 'target population'.

Probing

Stimulus used by an interviewer to obtain an answer from a respondent, to encourage elucidation of the original answer, to seek additional detail. Probing is used extensively in qualitative research, and also in conjunction with open-ended questions contained in otherwise structured questionnaires. Instructions to probe must be clearly given to the interviewer.

Product

What is sold. It encompasses intangible services as well as tangible goods.

Projective techniques

Interview method used in qualitative research to facilitate respondents' articulation of their beliefs and attitudes.

Prompting

Interview technique where the interviewer suggests possible answers to questions. Instructions on prompting must be clearly given.

Proportionate sample

Sample drawn with a uniform sampling fraction across different strata.

Qualitative research

Research techniques distinguishable from quantitative methods because they do not attempt to make measurements. Instead, information is obtained through more flexible, less structured methods such as group discussions and depth interviews. Often used in the exploratory stages of research.

Quantitative research

Research which involves measurements.

Questionnaire

List of carefully structured and researched questions, usually including instructions for its completion, and provision for the recording of answers.

Quota sample

Form of non-random, or purposive sampling, widely used in consumer markets, where quotas are set for particular kinds of people, to ensure that they are represented in the sample in the same proportions as they are represented in the target population.

Random survey

Also called a 'probability sample'. A sample in which each individual in the target population has a known (and non-zero) chance of inclusion.

Range

Difference between the highest and the lowest of a set of values.

Rating scale

Scale used by a respondent when answering a question. The term is not usually applied when there are less than three choices.

Respondent

Officially labelled 'informants' by the Market Research Society, a respondent is any individual who provides information contributing to the results of a survey. Respondents are normally individuals but could include groups or organisations.

Response rate

Number of adequately completed interviews, questionnaires obtained from a survey, expressed as a percentage of the number of eligible individuals in the survey. Response rates cannot be calculated for quota samples, although it is sometimes possible to estimate refusal rates.

Sampling

Process of selecting a part, or subset, of a target population to investigate the characteristics of that population at reduced cost in terms of time, effort and money. A sample must therefore be representative of the whole.

Sampling fraction

Size of the sample (n) divided by the size of the target population (N) gives (k), known as the sampling fraction. Where the same (uniform) sampling fraction is used throughout all strata of the sample, the sample is a proportionate sample. Sometimes, especially in business surveys, different (variable) sampling fractions may be used in the different strata giving a disproportionate sample.

Sampling frame

Means of identifying sampling units which comprise the target population from which a sample is drawn, typically a list of qualifying individuals or organisations.

Sampling interval

In systematic sampling from a randomly ordered sampling frame the sampling fraction is used to determine the intervals at which to draw respondents to the survey.

Segment

Part of a market or population which has identifiable characteristics of actual or potential economic interest; for example, product usage, amount of product used, type of product used.

Self-completion questionnaire

No interviewer involvement. Carefully worded instructions guide the respondent logically through all stages of the questionnaire. Non-response can be a major problem leading to serious bias in survey findings.

Semantic differential scale

Type of attitude scaling technique where extreme ends of a continuum are described by an opposing set of adjectives, the odd number of points between being degrees along this scale. The respondent chooses a point on the scale to express where his/her opinion lies between these two extremes.

SIMALTO scales

Sometimes termed 'fully descriptive verbal scales', SIMALTO stands for 'simultaneous multi-attribute level trade off'. The scales use precise verbal definitions which can be used to specify customers' expectations and their perception of the level of service provided.

Standard deviation

Statistical measure of spread or dispersion, applicable to any frequency distribution.

Stratification

Means of dividing the target population into identifiable and mutually exclusive subgroups (strata); for example, by size in industrial markets to ensure all these strata are represented in the survey. A random sample can then be taken in each stratum using a sampling fraction.

Telephone interview

Communication between respondent and interviewer by telephone.

Total product

Encompassing the entire range of benefits that a company/organisation provides when customers make a particular purchase. In addition to the core product it may include added value benefits such as guarantees, fast delivery, free on-site maintenance.

Tracking

Repeated surveys using the same basic questionnaire either continuously or at regular intervals to identify changes in respondents' perceptions.

Variance

Statistical measurement of the variability of dispersion of a set of numbers. The standard deviation is the square root of the variance.

Weighting

Process which assigns numerical coefficients (weights or weighting factors) to each of the elements in a set, in order to provide them with a desired degree of importance relative to one another.

APPENDIX 4

Additional Information

SPECIALIST SOFTWARE

Keypoint from Cambridge Software
Publishing
124 Cambridge Science Park
Milton Road
Cambridge CB4 0ZS

Tel: 01223 425558
www.camsp.com/keypoint

SNAP from
Snap Surveys
Greener House
66-68 Haymarket
London SW1Y 4RF

Tel: 020 7747 8900
www.snapsurveys.com

SPSS from SPSS (UK) Ltd
1st Floor
St. Andrew's House
West Street
Woking
Surrey GU21 1EB

Tel: 0845 345 0936
www.spss.co.uk

FOCUS GROUP STUDIOS

Provincial

Bristol Focus
165 Luckwell road
Ashton
Bristol BS3 3HB
www.bristolfocus.co.uk

4 Discussion
Crown House
Manchester Road
Wilmslow
Cheshire SK9 1BE
Tel: 01260 299634

Chatterbox – Nottingham
Van Gaver House
48–50 Bridgford Road
West Bridgford Road
Nottingham NG2 6AP

Tel: 0115 981 6445

Manor Research Studios
143 Bower Street
Oldham OL1 3PN
Tel: 0161 665 0965

Profile in View
5 St Andrew's Court
Wellington Street
Thame
Oxfordshire OX9 3WT
Tel: 01844 215672

Quota View
93-95 Terenure Road East
Dublin
Ireland IE6
Tel: +353 (0) 1492 5540

Roundhay Research
452 Street Lane
Moortown
Leeds
West Yorkshire LS17 6RB

Tel: 01132 665 440

The Scottish View
Citywall House
32 Eastwood Avenue
Glasgow G41 3NS

Tel: 0141 533 3306

Seen & Sound (Newcastle)
28 Osbourne Road
Jesmond
Newcastle-upon-Tyne
Tyne and Wear NE2 2AJ

Tel: 0191 270 6920

Seen & Sound (Reading)
Reading RG1 1HG

Tel: 0118 958 8552

The View on Scotland
21 Murrayfield Avenue
Edinburgh EH12 6AU

Tel: 0131 332 7809

West Midlands Viewing Facility
86 Aldridge Road
Perry Bar
Birmingham B42 2TP

Tel: 0121 344 4848

London & Suburbs

2CV Viewing
34 Rose Street
Covent Garden
London WC2 9EB

Tel: 020 7655 9900

Esprit Studios Ltd
Supreme House
Regent Office Park
Finchley Central
London N3 2TL

Tel: 020 8346 4499

Marketlink Studios
37 Warple Way
London W3 0RX

Tel: 020 8740 5550

The Research House Ltd
124 Wigmore Street
London W1U 3RY

Tel: 020 7935 4979

Spectrum
23 The Green
Southgate
London N14 6EN

Tel: 020 8882 2448

Summit Studios
2-4 Spring Bridge Mews
Off Spring Bridge Road
Ealing
London W5 2AB

Tel: 020 8840 2200

Surrey Research Centre
Hillcrest House
51 Woodcote Road
Wallington
Surrey SM6 0LT

Tel: 020 8647 9151

The White Rooms
1st Floor Hart House
6 London Road
St. Albans AL1 1NG

Tel: 01727 798399

The Treehouse
Olympia Mews
Queensway
London W2 3SA

Tel: 020 7243 2229

DATABASE PROVIDERS

Dudley Jenkins   Tel: 020 7871 9000; www.djb.co.uk

TLS Data   Tel: 01892 544400; www.tlsdata.co.uk

Eagle Direct Marketing   Tel: 0117 902 0073; www.eagledirectmarketing.co.uk

Electric Marketing   Tel: 020 7419 7999; www.electricmarketing.co.uk

Data HQ   Tel: 01277 355015; www.datahq.co.uk

APPENDIX 5

Bibliography

Christopher, M. (1992) *The Customer Service Planner*, Butterworth-Heinemann: CIM Marketing Practitioner Series.

Cochran, W. G. *Sampling Techniques*, John Wiley.

ESOMAR (1993) 'The ideal product, the ideal customer, the ideal company. New perspectives in customer satisfaction research', ESOMAR conference papers, ISBN 92-831-1193-1.

Fornell, Claes *et al* (2005) *The American Customer Satisfaction Index at Ten Years: implications for the economy, stock returns and management*, Stephen M Ross School of Business, University of Michigan.

Gale, Bradley T. (February 1994) 'Customer satisfaction – relative to competitors – is where it's at', *Marketing and Research Today*.

Gordon, Wendy and Langmaid, Roy (1998) *Qualitative Market Research*, Gower.

Gould, Graham (1995) 'Why it is customer loyalty that counts (and how to measure it)', *Managing Service Quality*, vol. 5, no. 1.

Green, J.L. (1997) '*SIMALTO – a technique for improved product design and marketing*', ESOMAR, Oslo.

Gruca, Thomas S. and Rego, Lopo L. (2003) *Customer Satisfaction, Cash Flow and Shareholder Value*, Marketing Science Institute.

Hague, Paul (1993) *Interviewing*, Kogan Page.

Hague, Paul (1993) *Questionnaire Design*, Kogan Page.

Hague, Paul and Harris, Paul (1993) *Sampling and Statistics*, Kogan Page.

Hallowell, Roger (1996) 'The relationships of customer satisfaction, customer loyalty and profitability: an empirical study', *International Journal of Service Industry Management*, vol. 7, no. 4.

Heskett, James L., Jones, Thomas O., Loveman, Gary W., Sasser Jr., Earl and Schlesinger, Leonard A. (1994) 'Putting the service-profit chain to work', *Harvard Business Review*, March–April.

Heskett, James L., Sasser Jr., Earl and Schlesinger, Leonard A. (1997) *The Service-Profit Chain*, The Free Press, New York.

Heskett, James L., Sasser Jr., Earl, Schlesinger, Leonard A. (2003) *The Value-Profit Chain*, The Free Press, New York.

Hill, Brierley and MacDougall (2003) *How to Measure Customer Satisfaction*, Gower, Aldershot

Jones, Thomas O. and Sasser Jr., Earl (1995) 'Why satisfied customers defect', *Harvard Business Review*, November–December.

Kish, L. *Survey Sampling*, John Wiley.

Kreuger, Richard A. (1989) *Focus Groups: a practical guide for small businesses*, Sage Publications.

Market Research Society, *Guide to Sources of Samples for Telephone Research*.

Oliver, R. (1997) *Satisfaction: a behavioural perspective on the consumer*, McGraw-Hill, New York.

Oppenheim, A. N. (1970) *Questionnaire Design and Attitude Measurement*, Heinemann.

Parasuraman, A., Zeithaml, V. and Berry, L. (1986) 'SERVQUAL: a multiple item scale for measuring customer perceptions of service quality research', Marketing Sciences Institute.

Parasuraman, A., Zeithaml, V. and Berry, L. (1990) *Achieving Service Quality: Balancing perceptions and expectations*, The Free Press.

Peters, T. (1985) *A Passion for Excellence*, Wm. Collins.

Reichheld, Frederick F. (1996) 'Learning from customer defections', *Harvard Business Review*, March–April.

Reichheld, Frederick F. and Sasser Jr., W. Earl (1990) 'Zero defections: quality comes to services', *Harvard Business Review*, September–October.

Rucci, Anthony J., Kirn, Steven P. and Quinn, Richard T. (1998) 'The employee customer profit chain at Sears', *Harvard Business Review*, January–February.

Rust, Roland T. and Zahorik, Anthony J. (1993) 'Customer satisfaction, customer retention and market share', *Journal of Retailing*, vol. 69, no. 2, Summer.

Schneider & White (2004) *Service Quality: Research Perspectives*, Sage Publications.

Stone, Claire Louise and Banks, J. Maria (1997) 'The use of customer and employee-based performance measures in The Times Top 500 companies', *The TQM Magazine*, vol. 9, no. 2.

Taylor, Christopher (ed.) *Managing Service Quality: an academic journal on customer service*, MCB. Details from the editor (Tel: 01522 79422).

Taylor, Christopher (1995) 'The case for customer satisfaction measurement', *Managing Service Quality*, vol. 5, no. 1.

White & Schneider (2000) Climbing the Advocacy Ladder: the impact of disconfirmation of service expectations on customer behavioural intentions, *Journal of Services Research* 2(3).

Wolfe, A. (ed.) (1984) *Standardised Questions: a review for market research executives*, Market Research Society, 15 Northburgh Street, London EC1V 0AH (Tel: 0171 490 4911).

Zeithaml & Bitner (2000) *Services Marketing: integrating customer focus across the firm*, McGraw-Hill, Boston.

INDEX